Rail
Facts and Feats

The Canadian Pacific Railway transcontinental freight crossing the Rockies in winter. (Canadian Pacific Rail.)

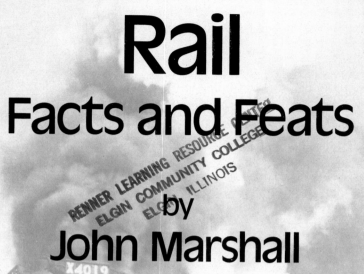

Rail
Facts and Feats

by
John Marshall

**THE TWO CONTINENTS
PUBLISHING GROUP**
30 EAST 42 STREET, NEW YORK

© GUINNESS SUPERLATIVES LIMITED 1973

THE TWO CONTINENTS PUBLISHING GROUP LTD
NEW YORK 1974

Library of Congress No. 73-86961

ISBN 0-8467-0005-0

Printed and bound in Great Britain by
Jarrold and Sons Limited, Norwich

Contents

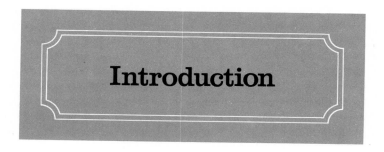

Introduction

I n compiling this book I have used sources which I consider to be reliable, and I have carefully checked anything doubtful. Source references, however, are omitted because to name them for each statement would almost double the size of the book without adding to its value. Principal sources were various issues of the *Railway Directory & Year Book* and its forerunners the *Universal Directory of Railway Officials* and the *Railway Year Book*; *World Railways* (Sampson Low); Bradshaw's *Railway Manual*; Minutes of Proceedings of the Institution of Civil Engineers; *The Dictionary of National Biography*; *Modern English Biography* (Boase); files of *The Railway Magazine, The Engineer, Engineering*; *The Railway Gazette* and *Modern Railways*, and numerous railway and locomotive books, British and foreign, biographies, atlases and maps.

Although I accept full responsibility for accuracy, I realise that in such a collection of assorted statements as this from so many sources there may be mistakes, and I shall be grateful for notification of any of these. It is also possible that statements such as the most powerful locomotives or the fastest speeds may be out of date when the book is published or soon afterwards. The selection of illustrations from all those available has not been easy and in a subsequent edition there may be many changes in the illustrations, and records will be brought up to date.

The book has not been compiled without the help of other persons. Chief among these is Mr. A. Barlow of New York. To state simply that he "helped" would be a superlative among understatements. Besides sending many American photographs he has ferreted out numerous obscure pieces of information.

Others to whom I am grateful for material or information are Colonel Rixon Bucknall, Messrs. A. F. Cook, A. G. Ellis, Brian Fawcett, R.H.N. Hardy, G. Harrop, W. Hennigan, T. E. Rounthwaite, John Thomas; Messrs. C. W. Cook (York), J. Edgington (Euston) and N. Sprinks (Paddington) of British Rail Public Relations Department; Canadian National Railways; Canadian Pacific Railway; French Railways Ltd. (S.N.C.F.); Messrs. C. Makepeace and H. Milligan, Manchester Museum of Science and Technology; and the staff of the Social Sciences Library, Manchester Public Libraries.

No attempt has been made to compile a bibliography. For books on British railway subjects the reader should consult *A Bibliography of British Railway History* compiled by George Otley (Allen & Unwin 1965), though numerous important books have appeared since this was published. American railway books are equally legion. Unfortunately not all railway books are of reliable authenticity and some discrimination is needed in their use.

J.M., Bolton, Lancashire, 1972

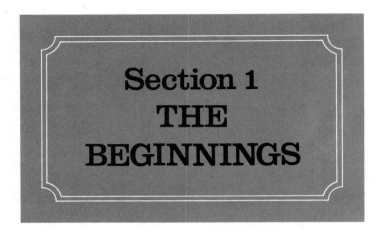

Section 1
THE
BEGINNINGS

T he oldest known illustration of anything resembling a railway is a window high in Freibourg
Cathedral, Switzerland, dating from about 1350. A Flemish painting, dated 1544, entitled
Les Travaux de la Mine, on a wood panel 42 × 22 in, was discovered about 1940. It shows a miner
pushing a four-wheeled truck along a railway out of a mine. It is probable that the painter obtained
his information from a mining book *Der Ursprung gemeynner*, published about 1520.

The earliest record of a railway in the generally accepted sense is an illustration of a narrow-gauge
mine railway at Leberthal in Alsace in *Cosmographae Universalis* by
Sebastian Münster, dated 1550.

In 1556 rail wagons were described and illustrated by Georg Bauer
(in English George Farmer) who called himself Georgius Agricola in
De Re Metallica, first published in 1556.

*Mine truck as illustrated
by Georg Bauer, 1556.
(The Science Museum,
London.)*

The oldest surviving relic of this period is a sixteenth-century mine wagon with flanged wooden
wheels, some track and a switch or point, as used in gold-mines at Sieben-

bürgen in Transylvania. It can be seen in the Verkehrs und Bau Museum, Berlin. It establishes that railways were in general use in central Europe in the late Middle Ages.

The first recorded "railway" in Britain was a line made of baulks of timber from coal-pits at Wollaton and Strelley near Nottingham to the River Trent. It was built by Huntingdon Beaumont in the late sixteenth century.

The most famous of the early British wagonways was the Tanfield Wagonway in County Durham. The first section was built certainly by 1671 and possibly as early as 1632. It was extended in 1726. The Tanfield, or Causey, Arch, built in 1727 by master-mason Ralph Wood, has a span of 103 ft and is probably **the world's oldest major railway bridge.** The Tanfield line, but not the arch, remained in use until 18th May 1964. The arch still carries a footpath across the gorge.

Tanfield Arch, built in 1727 for the Tanfield Wagonway—the oldest railway bridge in the world —designed by Ralph Wood. (John Marshall.)

The first railway in Scotland was the Tranent–Cockenzie Wagonway, about 10 miles east of Edinburgh, laid down with wooden rails in 1722. Part of the line was used on 21st September 1745 in the course of a battle with the Young Pretender, Prince Charles Edward. Iron rails were used from 1815. It continued in use as a horse tramway until after 1880 when part of it was converted into a steam colliery railway.

A wooden wagonway was constructed at Prior Park, Bath, England, in 1750 to convey stone from quarries to the town. A well-known engraving by Anthony Walker, published in 1752, was the first illustration of an English railway.

The first recorded use of iron in wheels was in 1731 when a cast-iron rim was placed round a wooden centre. The use of flanged wheels hastened the disappearance of the L-shaped plate-rails.

The first railway authorised by Parliament in Britain was the line from the colliery at Middleton into Leeds, Yorkshire, on 9th June 1758. **It was the first railway on which steam locomotives were commercially used.** The first two engines built by Matthew Murray of Leeds (see *The Pioneers*) to an order by John Blenkinsop first ran on 12th August 1812. Because Blenkinsop believed that smooth wheels would not grip the rails, it was propelled by a toothed wheel engaging on a rack on one of the rails. Two more similar engines were built in 1813. The rack-engines continued in service until 1835. The wheels of one are preserved on a section of the original track in York Railway Museum.

A portion of the Middleton Railway is still active, preserved by the Middleton Railway Trust, founded in 1959 with the co-operation of the National Trust. Steam locomotives are still at work after 160 years, a world record.

John Blenkinsop's locomotive, built by Matthew Murray in 1812 for the Middleton Colliery Railway, Leeds. (The Science Museum, London.)

The earliest recorded use of iron rails in Britain was at Coalbrookdale in Shropshire in 1767 and at Sheffield in 1776.

The oldest surviving railway wagon in Britain is a quarry truck of 1797 from the Peak Forest Canal Company, Derbyshire. It can be seen at York Railway Museum. It has flat-rimmed wheels for running on L-shaped tramway plates.

The first malleable iron edge-rails were used at Walbottle Colliery near Newcastle upon Tyne in England in 1805. They were faulty, however, and were replaced by cast iron.

The oldest wagon with flanged wheels in Britain, also at York Railway Museum, is from the Belvoir Castle Railway in Leicestershire. This was a 4 ft 4·5 in gauge railway with "fish-bellied" cast-iron rails 3 ft long, laid in 1815 by the Butterley Company, to carry supplies from the Grantham Canal up to Belvoir Castle. Horses were used until the line closed in 1918. It was dismantled in 1940, but parts near Belvoir Castle remain *in situ*.

A wagon of the Stratford & Moreton Railway on the original rails at Stratford-on-Avon which were constructed in 1826 and used until 1881. (John Marshall.)

The first public goods railway in the world to be sanctioned by Parliament was the Surrey Iron Railway on 21st May 1801. It was 4 ft gauge and opened from Wandsworth to Croydon on 26th July 1803 and was extended by the Croydon, Merstham & Godstone Railway, incorporated by Act of Parliament on 17th May 1803, and opened from Croydon to Merstham on 24th July 1805.

The first railway to convey fare-paying passengers was the Oystermouth Railway, also known as the "Swansea & Mumbles Railway", incorporated by Act of Parliament on 29th June 1804. It was opened about April 1806 and carried passengers from 25th March 1807. Horse-traction was used at first, and even sail-power was tried.

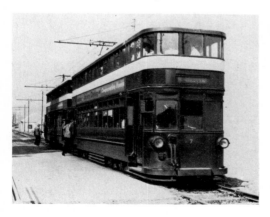

Cars of the Swansea & Mumbles Railway at Mumbles. (John Marshall.)

From about 1826 horse buses began plying along a turnpike-road beside the railway and completely stole the passenger traffic, probably the first instance in the world of a railway succumbing to road competition! Passenger traffic was resumed in 1860 after the track was relaid. Steam-power was introduced on 16th August 1877 and lasted for fifty-two years until, on 2nd March 1929, electric double-decked cars were put in service. They were the largest electric tramway cars in Britain, seating 106 passengers.

For goods traffic a petrol locomotive was obtained in 1929 and a diesel in 1936, making in all seven forms of motive power on one short railway.

For the second time, on 5th January 1960, the railway succumbed to a bus service. This time, however, it was dismantled.

It was the first railway in the world to celebrate 150 years of passenger services.

The first proper railway in Scotland was the Kilmarnock & Troon Railway, incorporated on 27th May 1808 and opened for horse traffic on 6th July 1812. Steam-traction was introduced in 1817.

The oldest portion of the former Midland Railway, England, and one which still survives, was the Mansfield–Pinxton Railway, incorporated on 16th June 1817 and opened on 13th April 1819. It was taken over by the M.R. in 1848, completely rebuilt, and reopened for steam-traction on 9th October 1849.

The first rolled-iron rails were made at Bedlington, Northumberland, under a patent granted to John Birkenshaw on 23rd October 1820. They had a swelled upper edge and were in 18 ft lengths. The patent even included welding the rail-ends. Until this time iron rails were cast, either L-shaped tramway plates or "fish-bellied" edge-rails.

The first public railway to use steam from the beginning was the Stockton & Darlington Railway, opened on 27th September 1825. Steam locomotives were used at first only for goods trains.

The steam locomotive first established itself as a reliable form of motive power at the Rainhill Trials on the Liverpool & Manchester Railway from 6th to 14th October 1829. The locomotives entered included *Rocket* (George and Robert Stephenson), *Sanspareil* (Timothy Hackworth) and *Novelty* (Braithwaite and Ericsson). The £500 prize was awarded to the *Rocket* on the last day.

Site of the eastern end of the measured 1·75 miles of the Rainhill Trials held from the 6th to 14th October 1829. (British Rail.)

Full-size replica of Stephenson's Rocket *in its 1829 original form. (British Rail.)*

The Canterbury & Whitstable Railway was opened on 3rd May 1830. Stephenson's locomotive *Invicta* was driven by Edward Fletcher, later to be Locomotive Engineer of the North Eastern Railway.

The Liverpool & Manchester Railway, opened on 15th September 1830, was the first public railway to be operated entirely by steam locomotives, except for a winding engine at Edge Hill, Liverpool, for working traffic to and from the docks, Crown Street, and later Lime Street Station.

Ackermann print of the Liverpool & Manchester Railway at Edge Hill, Liverpool. The two outer tunnels, about 200 yd long, led to Crown Street Terminus. The 1 mile 351 yd central tunnel leads down to the docks at Wapping. (Drawing by T. T. Bury; British Rail.)

The first railway amalgamation to be authorised by Act of Parliament was the formation of the North Union Railway on 22nd May 1834, uniting the Wigan Branch Railway with the Wigan & Preston Railway.

EARLY AMERICAN RAILROADS

The first railroad was built in 1795 when a short length of wooden track was laid on Beacon Hill, Massachusetts, to carry building material for the State House. A railway was laid on the same hill in 1807 to carry bricks.

In 1811 a railway was built at Falling Creek near Richmond, Virginia, to serve a powder-mill.

In 1818 another was built at Bear Creek Furnace, near Pittsburgh, Pennsylvania.

The first steam locomotive in America was built by John Stevens in 1825 and was tested on a circular track at his home at Hoboken, New Jersey. It had four flat-tyred wheels guided by four vertical rollers running against the insides of the rails, and it was propelled by a central toothed rack.

One of the first American Railroad Charters was granted to John Stevens on 21st March 1823 for a steam-powered railroad from Philadelphia to Columbia, Pennsylvania. The company was incorporated under the title of the "Pennsylvania Railroad" which established that name as the oldest among the numerous railroad companies of the U.S.A. It was 1829, however, before any part of the railroad was opened and the whole line was not opened until 16th April 1834.

The first American railroad tunnel was the Staple Bend Tunnel, 300 yd long, 4 miles east of Johnstown, Pennsylvania, on the Allegheny Portage Railroad opened in 1834. This section of the Pennsylvania Railroad, linking canals between Johnstown and Hollidaysburg, formed part of the route between Philadelphia and Pittsburgh. It was abandoned about 1858.

Charles Dickens travelled over this route in 1842 and described the journey in his *American Notes*.

Another of the first American Railroad Charters was issued to the Delaware & Hudson Canal Company on 23rd April 1823, for a line from Carbondale to the canal at Honesdale in the Lackawanna Valley. The railroad was built by John Bloomfield Jervis (1795–1885) and was opened on 9th October 1829.

Drawing of the Stourbridge Lion *built by Foster, Rastrick & Company in 1829.* (The Engineer, *9th January 1925.)*

For this railroad a steam locomotive named *Stourbridge Lion* was obtained from Foster, Rastrick & Company, Shropshire, England, and it was tried on the line on 8th October 1829. But it was too heavy for the wooden rails covered with iron strips and for many years afterwards the line was worked as a gravity railroad. The gauge was 4 ft 3 in. It later became part of the present Delaware & Hudson system.

The *Stourbridge Lion* weighed 8 tons and measured 15 ft high and 7 ft 7 in wide. It ran only a few trial trips. About 1845 the boiler and one cylinder were sold to a foundry for use as a stationary engine and the boiler worked until 1871. This and a few other parts are preserved in the Smithsonian Institution, Washington, D.C. A full-size operating replica built by the Delaware & Hudson Railroad in 1932 is exhibited at Honesdale, Pennsylvania.

The first American railroad to offer a regular service as a public carrier was the Baltimore & Ohio Railroad. This was chartered on 28th February 1827. Work began on 4th July 1828 and the first 13 miles between Baltimore and Ellicott's Mills, Maryland, were opened for passenger and freight traffic on 24th May 1830. Horse-traction was used until July 1834.

The first steam locomotive on the B. & O., *Tom Thumb*, was built in 1829 by Peter Cooper (1791–1883) and first run on 28th August 1830. It developed only 1·43 hp which, however, was more than three times that of Stephenson's *Rocket*. It had a vertical boiler.

The first B. & O. rails were 6 in wood baulks topped by iron straps. Mount Clare Station, Baltimore was completed on 24th May 1830 and is America's oldest surviving railroad station.

On 30th June 1831 the B. & O. became the first railroad in America to carry troops.

The first U.S. President to travel by train was Andrew Jackson, on the B. & O. in 1833.

The first train into Washington was run by the B. & O. on 24th August 1835, and in 1842, shortly after Charles Dickens had travelled on it, it was extended to Cumberland.

The first regular steam railroad in America was the South Carolina Railroad, opened on 15th January 1831.

The first successful steam locomotive to be built in America, *Best Friend of Charleston*, was built for the South Carolina Railroad in 1830 and was first tested with passengers on 14th December. It entered service on Christmas Day. It had a vertical boiler, weighed under 4 tons and developed about 6 hp.

The Best Friend of Charleston *built in the U.S.A. for the South Carolina Railroad. (The Science Museum, London.)*

The first steam train in New York State was pulled by the *De Witt Clinton* on the Mohawk & Hudson Railroad from Albany to Schenectady on 13th August 1831. The engine was built at West Point Foundry. It was a 0–4–0 with cylinders 5·5 × 16 in, 54 in wheels, and weighed 4 tons.

The original drawing of the inside-cylinder 0–4–0 De Witt Clinton, *the third steam locomotive in the U.S.A. and the one which pulled the first train in New York State on the Mohawk & Hudson Railroad from Albany to Schenectady on 13th August 1831. (The Science Museum, London.)*

U.S. mail was first carried by rail in 1831.

The first passenger train accident in U.S. railroad history occurred on 9th November 1833 on the Camden & Amboy Railroad main line between Spotswood and Hightstown, New Jersey. One carriage overturned and twelve of its twenty-four passengers were seriously injured, including Captain Vanderbilt, formerly of the steamboat *New Brunswick*.

The oldest eight-wheeled passenger car in existence, built about 1836 for the C. & A., is preserved in the Smithsonian Institution, Washington, D.C.

EARLY RAILWAYS IN CANADA

The first railways in Canada were coal railways in Nova Scotia, at Pictou in 1827 and North Sydney in 1828. Both used horses. They were 4 ft 8·5 in gauge and were probably the first in America to use iron rails, cast in 5 ft lengths.

Canada's first steam railway was the Champlain & St. Lawrence Railway, 16 miles long, chartered in 1832 and opened from La Prairie on the St. Lawrence to St. John on the Richelieu on 21st July 1836, with a 5 ft 6 in gauge. The first locomotive, delivered in 1837, was by Robert Stephenson & Company, Newcastle upon Tyne, and named *Dorchester*.

A 6 mile railway was built in 1839 to carry coal from the Albion Mines to Pictou Harbour, Nova Scotia. The three steam locomotives, *Samson*, *Hercules* and *John Buddle* were **the first coal-burning locomotives in Canada.** *Samson* is still preserved in Halifax Station.

The Erie & Ontario Railway, built in 1839, was the first railway in Upper Canada. It ran round Niagara Falls from Queenston to Chippawa. The original gradients were too steep for locomotives and horses were used. It was later rebuilt with easier grades for locomotives.

The Lachine Railway from Montreal to Lachine was opened in 1847, using 18 ton American locomotives which took twenty-one minutes to cover the 8 mile journey.

The first locomotive from Great Britain to be imported into Lower Canada was the *James Ferrier*, built at Dundee, Scotland. It made its first trip on the Lachine Railway on 24th July 1848. This was one of the only lines to use the British-type compartment carriage, for three classes of passengers.

Railway mileage in Canada grew from 22 in 1846, to 66 in 1850, and to 2,065 by 1860.

The gauge war in Canada developed fairly soon. In 1851 the gauge of the St. Lawrence & Atlantic Railway, required by Charter to be 4 ft 8·5 in, was changed to 5 ft 6 in to match the Champlain & St. Lawrence Railway. It was opened in 1853. Neighbouring American lines were 4 ft 8·5 in.

The Great Western Railway of Canada, begun at London in 1847, was forced to adopt a third rail. It was opened from Niagara to London in 1853. The Grand Trunk Railway, chartered in 1852, was also built to the 5 ft 6 in gauge.

The broad gauge held out until 1871 by which time most Canadian and American railways had adopted standard gauge. Conversion of the Grand Trunk system took until September 1874. The Intercolonial Railway between Halifax and St. John, New Brunswick, was converted to standard gauge by 1875, and the connection from Halifax to Rivière du Loupe was opened on 1st July 1876, bringing the mileage of the Intercolonial to 700.

The first locomotive to be built in Canada was named *Toronto*. It was built at the Toronto Locomotive Works and made its first run on the Northern Railway on 16th May 1853.

Canada's first major railway crash occurred on the Great Western Railway west of Chatham in 1854, when a train of ballast for the line collided with a passenger train, killing forty-seven people.

Through trains were inaugurated between Montreal and Toronto on 27th October 1856 by the Grand Trunk Railway, later part of the Canadian National Railways.

Early Grand Trunk Railway train, Canada. (Canadian National.)

Crests of various British Railway companies photographed at the Museum of British Transport, Clapham, London.

FURTHER RAILWAY DEVELOPMENTS

In Austria-Hungary the first railway opened on 7th September 1827, from Budweis (Budejovice, Czechoslovakia) to Trojanov, with horse-traction. It was the first section of the Linz-Budweis Railway. Locomotives were not used until 1872.

The first railway wholly in modern Austria was from Vienna to Florisdor and Deutsch Wagrum, opened on 6th January 1838.

The first railway in France was from Saint-Étienne to Andrézieux, formally opened on 1st October 1828. The Concession had been granted on 26th February 1823 and it was used unofficially from May 1827. Passenger traffic began on 1st March 1832, but horse-traction was used until 1st August 1844.

On 7th June 1826 a Concession was granted for the Saint-Étienne–Lyon Railway and the section from Givors to Rive-de-Gier was opened on 25th June 1830.

It was on this line that Marc Seguin (see *The Pioneers*) tried out his locomotive on 7th November 1829. This was the first locomotive with a multi-tubular boiler. The remainder of the railway was opened from Lyon to Givors on 3rd April 1832 and from Rive-de-Gier to Saint-Étienne for goods on 18th October 1832 and passengers on 25th February 1833.

The first railway in Ireland was the Dublin & Kingstown (now Dun Laoghaire) Railway opened on 17th December 1834. It was to standard 4 ft 8·5 in gauge but was converted to the Irish standard of 5 ft 3 in. in 1857. The first locomotive, the 2–2–0 *Hibernia*, was built by Sharp, Roberts & Company, Manchester.

The Dublin & Kingstown Railway 2–2–0 Hibernia *built by Sharp Roberts & Company of Manchester in 1834. (The Science Museum, London.)*

The first locomotive to be built in Ireland was *Princess*, a 2–2–2 with outside cylinders, built in Dublin in April 1841 for the Dublin & Kingstown Railway.

Tomb Thumb, the first steam locomotive on the Baltimore & Ohio Railroad, built in 1829. (Smithsonian Institution, Washington, D.C.)

The oldest eight-wheeled passenger car in existence, built about 1836 for the Camden & Amboy Railroad. (Smithsonian Institution, Washington, D.C.)

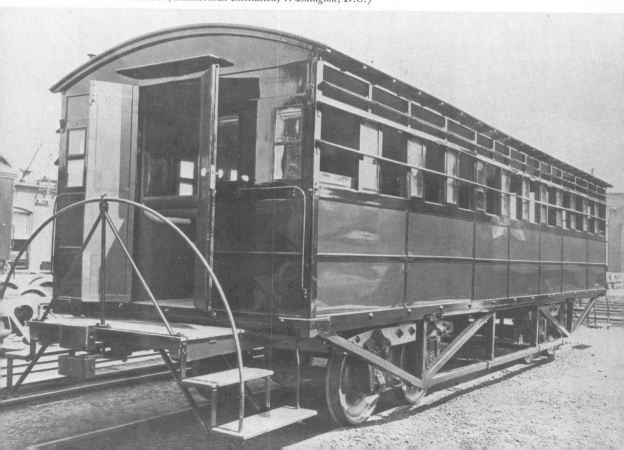

An old Bury 2–2–2 No. 36
on the 5 ft 3 in gauge
Great Southern & Western
Railway. It is now
preserved at Kent Station,
Cork, Ireland.
(K. B. Smith.)

The Great Western
Railway 4–4–0 No. 3217
on the Bluebell Railway,
Sussex. (N. Fields.)

The Great North of
Scotland Railway 4–4–0
No. 49 Gordon
Highlander at Midcalder,
Midlothian. (N. Fields.)

The Caledonian Railway
4–2–2 No. 123 at
Auchentray between
Edinburgh and Carstairs.
(N. Fields.)

The first section of the Ulster Railway, from Belfast to Lisburn, was opened on 12th August 1839 and was extended to Armagh on 1st March 1848. The gauge was originally 6 ft 2 in.

A story, possibly apocryphal, relates how an Army officer was asked to settle the Irish gauge question. He simply rounded off the gauges to 6 ft and 4 ft 6 in, added them together and divided by 2. His answer came to 5 ft 3 in which was thenceforth adopted as the Irish standard gauge. The Ulster Railway was converted to 5 ft 3 in gauge in 1847.

The Northern Counties Railway from Belfast to Ballymena, 33·5 miles, was opened on 11th April 1848.

'In Belgium the first railway, from Brussels to Malines, was opened on 5th May 1835. It was built and worked, as part of a planned national system, by the Belgian Government and was thus the first nationalised railway. The first locomotives, inside-cylinder 2–2–2s, *La Flèche* and *Stephenson*, were built by Robert Stephenson & Company, Newcastle upon Tyne.

In Germany the first railway, the Ludwigsbahn from Nuremberg to Fürth, was opened on 7th December 1835. Robert Stephenson & Company again built the first locomotive *Der Adler*, similar to the Belgian locomotives.

In Tasmania in 1836 a wooden railway was laid across a peninsula. Passengers paid a shilling to ride in trucks pushed by convicts to avoid a stormy sea crossing.

The first railway in Russia was the St. Petersburg & Pavlovsk Railway, built to a gauge of 6 ft. The first portion, Pavlovsk to Tsarskoe Selo, was opened for horse-traction on 9th October 1836. The entire railway was opened on 30th October 1837. Robert Stephenson & Company built the first locomotive in 1836.

The first railway in London was the London & Greenwich Railway incorporated on 17th May 1833 and opened on 8th February 1836 from Spa Road to Deptford, extended to London Bridge on 14th December 1836 and to Greenwich on 24th December 1838. The railway, 3·75 miles long, was almost entirely on a brick viaduct of 878 arches.

The first British "trunk railway" was the Grand Junction Railway from Birmingham to Warrington engineered by Joseph Locke and opened on 4th July 1837. It became part of the London & North Western Railway on the formation of that company on 16th July 1846. It had already absorbed the Liverpool & Manchester Railway. With the opening, on 17th December 1846, of the Lancaster & Carlisle Railway it formed a section of the main line from London (Euston) to Carlisle.

The opening of the Caledonian Railway from Carlisle to Glasgow and Edinburgh on 15th February 1848 completed the West Coast route from London to Scotland.

The first railway across Britain was the Newcastle & Carlisle Railway, opened on 18th June 1838. It became part of the North Eastern Railway on 17th July 1862.

The oldest main line into London, the London & Birmingham Railway, was opened from London (Euston) to Birmingham on 17th September 1838. With the Grand Junction and the Manchester & Birmingham railways it became a part of the L.N.W.R. on 16th July 1846.

Birmingham was by-passed by the opening of the 39·75 mile Trent Valley line from Rugby to Stafford on 15th September 1847.

The London & Birmingham Railway—the Euston Arch under construction in 1838. (British Rail.)

The Euston Arch in 1838. (Lithograph by J. C. Bourne; British Rail.)

The Euston Arch being demolished to make way for the new station on 3rd January 1962. (British Rail.)

The first main line to London south of the Thames was the London & Southampton Railway. It was opened from Nine Elms, London, to Woking on 21st May 1838 and was completed to Southampton on 11th May 1840. With the Act of Parliament authorising the branch to Gosport opposite Portsmouth on 4th June 1839 the name was changed to the "London & South Western Railway". The Gosport Branch opened on 7th February 1842. The L.S.W.R. was extended from Nine Elms to Waterloo on 11th July 1848.

The first section of the Great Western Railway engineered by I. K. Brunel, with a gauge of 7 ft, was opened from London (Paddington) to Maidenhead on 4th June 1838. It was extended to Twyford on 1st June 1839, to Reading on 30th March 1840 and was completed to Bristol on 30th June 1841. Brunel was then only thirty-five years old. The present Paddington Station was designed by Brunel and opened on 16th January 1854.

In the Netherlands the first railway was opened from Amsterdam to Haarlem on 24th September 1839.

The first railway in Italy was from Naples to Portici, opened on 4th October 1839.

The oldest principal section of the East Coast route, the Great North of England Railway from York to Darlington, was opened on 4th January 1841 for goods trains and on 30th March for passengers.

The first trans-Pennine railway, the Manchester & Leeds Railway, was opened throughout on 1st March 1841. On 9th July 1847 it became the Lancashire & Yorkshire Railway.

The Manchester & Leeds Railway Summit Tunnel— 1 mile 1,125 yd in length. (Lithograph by A. F. Tait.)

The first conference of railway managers was held in Birmingham, England, on 19th January 1841, to draw up a code of rules, signalling, etc.

The Railway Clearing House to settle rates for through traffic over different British railway companies' systems began operating on 2nd January 1842. The Irish Railway Clearing House was established on 1st July 1848.

The Midland Railway was formed on 10th May 1844 by amalgamation of the North Midland (Derby–Leeds), Midland Counties (Derby–Rugby), and Birmingham & Derby Junction railways. Derby became and remained the Headquarters of the Midland Railway until it became part of the London, Midland & Scottish Railway on 1st January 1923.

The first railway to Oxford was the Great Western line from Didcot, opened on 12th June 1844.

Cambridge saw its first trains on 29th July 1845, with the Eastern Counties Railway. Cambridge Station still has only one main platform 1,250 ft long, even after remodelling in 1863.

In Switzerland the first railway, from Basle to St. Ludwig, opened on 15th June 1844. The Zürich–Baden Railway, 14·5 miles, opened on 9th August 1847.

The first railway from Manchester to Sheffield was opened throughout on 23rd December 1845. It passed through Woodhead Tunnel, 3 miles 13 yd long, then the longest railway tunnel in Britain.

The year when the greatest number of Railway Acts was passed was 1846, during the "Railway Mania", when 272 Bills received the Royal Assent in Britain.

The first steam railway in Hungary, 20·5 miles from Pest to Vacz, was opened on 15th July 1846. An early line from Pest to Köbanya, was opened in August 1827.

The London, Brighton & South Coast Railway was formed on 27th July 1846 by the amalgamation of the London & Croydon and London & Brighton Railways. The L. & C. was opened on 5th June 1839. It was opened through to Brighton on 21st September 1841. The Engineer was J. U. Rastrick (see *The Pioneers*).

The oldest railway in modern Denmark is the Copenhagen–Røskilde Railway, opened on 26th June 1847. (The Altona–Kiel Railway, opened in 1844, was afterwards annexed with its territory by Prussia.)

The first railway in Spain, 17 miles from Barcelona to Mataro, was opened on 28th October 1848.

A through railway between London and Aberdeen was completed with the opening of the Scottish North Eastern (later Caledonian) Railway between Perth and Aberdeen on 1st April 1850.

The first section of the Great Northern Railway (England) from Louth to Grimsby was opened on 1st March 1848.

The East Coast route from London (Euston) to Edinburgh via the Midlands was completed in 1848 with the opening, on 29th August, of a temporary bridge over the Tyne between Gateshead and Newcastle and, on 10th October, a temporary viaduct over the Tweed at Tweedmouth.

    The Tyne Bridge was replaced by Robert Stephenson's High Level Bridge, opened for rail traffic above on 15th August 1849 and for road traffic below on 4th February 1850.

    The Royal Border Bridge across the Tweed, also by Robert Stephenson, was opened on 29th August 1850.

    The Great Northern Railway was opened from Werrington Junction to Maiden Lane, London, 79 miles, on 7th August 1850. King's Cross became the terminus of the East Coast route when the G.N.R. was extended from Maiden Lane on 14th October 1852.

The High Level Bridge at Newcastle upon Tyne was designed by Robert Stephenson and built by Hawkes Crawshary & Company. The height of the rails above high water was 120 ft and the length 1,372 ft. It was opened in September 1849. (John Marshall.)

The Chester & Holyhead Railway was completed with the opening of Robert Stephenson's Tubular Bridge over the Menai Strait on 18th March 1850.

The first railway in India, part of the Great Indian Peninsula Railway, was opened on 18th April 1853 from Bombay to Thana with 5 ft 6 in gauge.

The first railway in Brazil was the 5 ft 6 in gauge line, running 10 miles from Maua at the end of the Bay of Rio to the foot of the Petropolis Serra. It was opened on 30th April 1854, and was later converted to metre gauge. On its extension to Petropolis it climbed the Serra de Estrella for 4 miles at 1 in 6·7 with a Riggenbach-type rack. In 1897 it became part of the Leopoldina Railway.

Australia's first steam-operated railway was the 2·5 mile long, 5 ft 3 in gauge Melbourne & Hobson's Bay Railway, opened from Flinders Street, Melbourne, to Sandridge on 12th September 1854.

The first passenger railway, however, was the 7 mile Port Elliot & Goolwa Railway in South Australia, also 5 ft 3 in gauge, opened with horse-traction on 18th May 1854.

In 1827 an inclined tramway of iron rails was laid from Newcastle down to the waterfront to carry coal from mines.

The first railway in New South Wales, Australia, was opened from Sydney to Parramatta on 26th September 1855. It was built by the Sydney Railway Company, but was taken over by the New South Wales Government before opening.

In South Australia the 5 ft 3 in gauge railway from Adelaide to Port Adelaide was opened on 21st April 1856. It was built and worked by the Government and is believed to be the first State-owned steam railway in the British Empire.

The first railways in Queensland (1865), Tasmania (1871) and Western Australia (1879) were built to 3 ft 6 in gauge.

On 14th June 1883 the railways of New South Wales and Victoria were joined at Albury after the completion of the bridge over the Murray River.

The North Eastern Railway was formed on 31st July 1854 by the amalgamation of the York, Newcastle & Berwick (which had absorbed the Great North of England in 1846), York & North Midland, Leeds Northern and Malton & Driffield Railways.

The Stockton & Darlington Railway was absorbed on 1st July 1863.

In Norway the first railway, from Christiania (later Oslo) to Eidsvoll, 42 miles, was opened on 1st September 1854.

In Portugal the first railway from Lisbon to Carregado, 23 miles, was opened on 28th October 1856.

The oldest portions of the Swedish State Railways, from Gothenburg to Jonsered and Malmö to Lund, were opened on 1st December 1856.

The first railway in Argentina, the line from Parque to Floresta, was opened on 30th August 1857. It was built to 5 ft 6 in gauge because its first locomotive, named *La Portena*, and built in 1856 by E. B. Wilson & Company, Leeds, was originally intended for India.

The Isle of Wight, off the south of England, measures only 20 miles east to west and 13 miles north to south, yet it had 45·25 miles of standard-gauge railway operated by seven separate companies.

The first railway in the Isle of Wight was the 4·5 mile long Cowes & Newport Railway, opened on 16th June 1862. The last steam trains ran on 31st December 1966.

All that is left on the island today is the short line from Ryde to Sandown operated with former London Underground electric trains.

W18 Ningwood *at Bembridge. (John Marshall.)*

The railway from London to Penzance was completed on 4th May 1859 following the opening of Brunel's Saltash Bridge on 11th April. The West Cornwall Railway, however, was standard gauge. It was rebuilt to 7 ft gauge and the first through passenger service between London and Penzance began on 1st March 1867.

The Royal Albert Bridge at Saltash, built by I. K. Brunel in 1859 and seen here on 25th April 1958 before the new suspension-bridge was erected alongside. (British Rail.)

The Great Eastern Railway was formed on 7th August 1862 by the amalgamation of the Eastern Counties Railway and other railways in East Anglia.

In South Africa the first railway was opened on 26th June 1860 from Durban to the Point, by the Natal Railway. It was acquired by the Natal Government on 1st January 1877.

    Cape Town's first railway was opened to Eerste River on 13th February 1862 and extended to Wellington in 1863.

The first railway in what is now Pakistan was the 105 mile line from Karachi to Kochi opened on 13th May 1861.

New Zealand opened its first steam railway from Christchurch to Ferrymead with 5 ft 3 in gauge on 1st December 1863.

The first Christchurch railway station, on the broad-gauge (5 ft 3 in) Christchurch–Ferrymead Railway, about 1865. Pilgrim, New Zealand's first locomotive, is seen on the train in the background. (High Commissioner for New Zealand.)

The first railway in Ceylon, from Colombo to Ambepussa, was opened on 2nd October 1865.

The first railway in Japan, from Yokohama to Shinagawa, was opened on 12th June 1872. It was completed to Tokyo on 14th October.

China had no railway until 1876 when a 2 ft 6 in gauge line was opened from Shanghai to Woosung, about 20 miles. It was operated by two tiny 0–4–0 saddle tanks built by Ransome & Rapier, England.

    The Chinese were hostile and suspicious and following a fatal accident, as soon as the redemption money was paid in October 1877 the railway was bought by the Government and torn up and the entire outfit was dumped on Formosa.

The first permanent railway in China was the 4 ft 8·5 in gauge Tongshan–Hsukuchuang line opened in 1880, extended to Lutai in 1886 and Tientsin in 1888. It now forms part of the Peking–Mukden Section of the Chinese People's Republic Railways. Steam-traction was introduced in 1883.

    After this Chinese railway mileage grew rapidly. By 1900 it was 1,458; in 1970 21,750.

Japanese railway mileage in the ten years from 1880 to 1890 grew from 98 to 1,459. By 1970 the total of 16,953 miles exceeded that in Great Britain of 13,261 miles. It is still increasing.

The first railway in Burma was the metre-gauge line between Rangoon and Prome, opened on 1st May 1877.

ATMOSPHERIC RAILWAYS

The first application of atmospheric power on a railway was in 1698. Sir Humphrey Mackworth had a car equipped with a sail and used it with success on an early mineral railway at Neath, South Wales.

Sail-power was also tried on the Swansea & Mumbles Railway, Wales, on 17th April 1807, covering the 4·5 mile line in forty-five minutes.

A sail-car was used for a time on the South Carolina Canal & Railroad in America after it was opened on 25th December 1830.

Sail-power was used as a matter of routine on the 2 mile railway to Spurn Head Lighthouse, Yorkshire, England.

The idea of running trains powered by a piston driven by atmospheric pressure along a pipe exhausted ahead of the train by a pumping engine was conceived by Samuel Clegg and Jacob and Joseph Samuda and was patented in 1839. It was first tried out at Wormwood Scrubs, London, in June 1840.

The first use on a public railway was in Ireland. It was installed on the Kingstown–Dalkey line which formed a 1·75 mile extension of the Dublin & Kingstown Railway. Experimental trains began running on 3rd October 1843 and passengers were carried, without charge, from December. It was officially opened on 29th March 1844. After a succession of troubles it closed on 12th April 1854 for conversion to a locomotive line.

The system was next tried on the London & Croydon Railway on which regular "atmospheric" trains ran from 19th January 1846, although passengers had been carried free since 27th October 1845. It was abandoned on 4th May 1847.

The great engineer I. K. Brunel was so bitten by the "atmospheric bug" that he decided to employ the system on the steeply graded South Devon Railway. It was introduced between Exeter and Teignmouth on 13th September 1847 and extended to Newton Abbot on 10th January 1848. After numerous exasperating failures, often caused by rats eating the leather flap which sealed the slot in the top of the tube, the system was abandoned on 10th September 1848.

In France atmospheric traction was tried on a 1 mile 646 yd section of the Paris–Saint-Germain Railway from Bois du Vésinet to Saint-Germain on 14th August 1847. It was abandoned in favour of steam on 2nd July 1860.

The last attempt at an atmospheric railway was in 1864 when an experimental line was built at the Crystal Palace, London. It consisted of a tubular tunnel in which the car fitted like a piston and was forced along by air pressure.

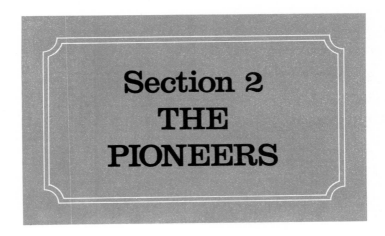

Section 2
THE
PIONEERS

William Jessop (1745–1814) was one of the leading early British civil engineers who, although mainly concerned with the construction of canals, was responsible for several important early railways. He was one of the founders of the Butterley Company in Derbyshire, close to the great tunnel on his Cromford Canal, a company which became responsible for many early iron railway bridges. After constructing several short lines of railway in connection with canals, Jessop engineered the Surrey Iron Railway, the first public railway in Britain to be sanctioned by Parliament (1801). It was followed by a line from Croydon to Merstham in 1805. In this he was assisted by his son Josias Jessop who later became Engineer of the Cromford & High Peak Railway in Derbyshire.

Matthew Murray (1765–1826) was one of the earliest steam-locomotive engineers. After training as a blacksmith he worked on flax-spinning machinery until 1795 when he entered into partnership with James Fenton and David Wood at Leeds. Murray took out a number of steam-engine patents from 1799. In 1812 he was engaged by Blenkinsop to build engines for the rack railway from Middleton Colliery to Leeds and built his *Salamanca* and *Prince Regent*. They had two double-acting cylinders and the piston-rods worked in vertical guides with connecting-rods to the spur-wheels which drove the 3 ft 2 in diameter cog driving-wheels. Murray can claim to have built the first commercially successful locomotive.

Edward Pease (1767–1858), a promoter of early railways, friend and supporter of George and Robert Stephenson. In 1818 he first projected the Stockton & Darlington Railway and in 1821 became acquainted with George Stephenson whom he appointed Engineer, also financing the construction of the first locomotive

on the railway, *Locomotion*. The first rail of the S. & D. was laid in 1823 and the railway was opened in 1825. Pease was a prominent Quaker and was active in efforts towards the abolition of slavery.

*Portrait of Edward Pease. (*Jubilee Memorial.*)*

Richard Trevithick (1771–1833) was the first to use high-pressure steam in an engine instead of atmospheric pressure as in the condensing steam-engines of Newcomen and Watt. He was born in Cornwall, but details of his early career and training are scanty; he taught himself about engines by observing them at the Cornish tin-mines. About 1797 he built a steam-engine for Herland Mine and in 1800 built a double-acting high-pressure engine for Coolis Kitchen Mine.

In 1796 he experimented with model steam locomotives and by the end of 1801 he had completed the first steam locomotive to pull a passenger carriage on a road. In 1803 a steam road carriage was tested in London, reaching speeds of 8 or 9 mile/h.

His first steam rail locomotive was constructed in 1803 to haul iron from Penydarran to the Glamorganshire Canal in Wales, and it was set to work in February 1804, but with a weight of 5 tons it was too much for the cast-iron tramway rails then in use. In 1808 he again attempted to popularise the steam locomotive, by running one on a circular track in London. The locomotive was a success but the public was not sufficiently interested and after this he abandoned work on locomotives.

In 1809 he began a tunnel under the Thames, but the project failed. A steam threshing-machine is recorded in 1811.

In this statue, at Camborne, in Cornwall, Richard Trevithick holds a model of his 1801 road locomotive. (Brian Fawcett, M.I.L.E.)

In 1816 he went to Peru to supervise the erection of his engines in mines, but in the insurrection in the 1820s he lost all his money. He was found, penniless, by Robert Stephenson who assisted his repatriation.

He took out his last patent, for the use of superheated steam in 1832 and the following year he died in poverty in Dartford, Kent.

The Trevithick Monument at Penydarren, Wales. Through the base are the original plate-rails of the first steam railway track. (Brian Fawcett, M.I.L.E.)

William Hedley (1779–1843) was closely associated with the early development of the steam loco-motive. From 1805 he was Colliery Viewer at Wylam, Northumberland and in 1811 with Jonathan Foster he helped Timothy Hackworth with the first locomotive to be built entirely at Wylam. He has been credited with the invention of the locomotive powered by smooth wheels, as opposed to the rack, and with the first use of the steam-blast, using exhaust-steam to draw the fire. These features, however, had been used by Trevithick in 1804.

John Urpeth Rastrick (1780–1856), like so many early British engineers, was a native of Northumber-land. After training with his father he joined Hazeldine at Bridgnorth, Shropshire. In 1814 he took out a patent for a steam-engine and was soon experimenting with steam-traction on railways.

His first major work was the cast-iron road bridge over the Wye at Chepstow in Monmouthshire (1815–16). In 1817 he became Managing Partner in the firm of Foster, Rastrick & Company of Stourbridge, Worcestershire, which built several early locomotives. In 1826–27 he constructed the tramway from Stratford on Avon to Moreton in Marsh which was the first line to use Birkenshaw's wrought-iron rails.

Rastrick was appointed one of the judges at the Rainhill Trials. His greatest work was the London & Brighton Railway of 1837–40, one of the most magnificently engineered railways in the world, including the Merstham, Balcombe and Clayton tunnels and the tremendous Ouse Viaduct.

George Stephenson (1781–1848), perhaps the most famous name in the history of railways. He was the second son of Robert Stephenson, Fireman at Wylam Colliery near Newcastle upon Tyne. He had almost no formal education, and gained his engineering experience working at various collieries, first as Fireman and later as Engineman, at the same time learning to read and write at a night school. In 1802 he married and the following year his only son Robert was born. His wife died of tuberculosis in 1806 and there followed a period of difficulty and hardship during which his father became incapable of further work and had to be supported as well as his mother. However, following his success in repairing a Newcomen pumping engine, he was appointed Enginewright at Killingworth Colliery in 1812 at a salary of £100 a year.

George Stephenson. (British Rail.)

His inventive genius was first applied to the production of a safety-lamp for miners. This was first tried on 21st October 1815. Unknown to each other, Sir Humphry Davy had been working on the same problem and he produced a lamp on the same principle at about the same time.

Following attempts by Blackett and Hedley in 1812 to produce steam locomotives for Wylam Colliery, Stephenson turned his attention to this problem and built his first steam locomotive in 1813–14. It could pull 30 tons up a gradient of 1 in 450 at 4 mile/h. This was the first recorded example of a locomotive in which the blast of the exhaust steam was used to create a draught for the fire.

Stephenson provided further locomotives for the 8 mile long Hetton Colliery Railway in County Durham, opened in 1822. Shortly after this he was appointed by Edward Pease to construct the Stockton & Darlington Railway for which he built the first locomotive, *Locomotion*, in 1825. This engine can still be seen on Darlington Station.

He was next appointed Engineer to the Liverpool & Manchester Railway. Despite its progress of nearly a quarter of a century, steam loco-motion was still held in doubt. It was only after the Rainhill Trials on the L. & M. in October 1829, at which the prize of £500 was won by the *Rocket*, specially constructed, mainly by his son Robert, that the proprietors became convinced of the advantage of steam locomotives.

Other railways to which George Stephenson was Chief Engineer were: the Grand Junction (Birmingham–Warrington), Manchester & Leeds, North Midland (Derby–Leeds), York & North Midland (Normanton–York) besides many shorter lines such as the Whitby & Pickering, and the Leicester & Swannington.

During the construction of the North Midland Railway, Stephenson opened up lime-works at Ambergate, and collieries at Clay Cross near Chesterfield. It was near here, at Tapton House, that he spent his last years, taking up his hobby of horticulture. He died there on 12th August 1848 and was buried at Trinity Church, Chesterfield.

John Blenkinsop (1783–1831) was born at Leeds, England. On 10th April 1811 he was granted a patent for a steam locomotive. The first engine to his order was built by Matthew Murray for the Middleton Colliery Railway, Leeds, in 1812. Its chief feature was a rack-wheel drive on to cogs cast into the side of one rail. At a test at Hunslet, Leeds, on 24th June 1812 it covered 1·5 miles in twenty-three minutes. Other Blenkinsop engines were used at Orrell Colliery near Wigan and at Willington, Kenton and Coxlodge collieries near Newcastle upon Tyne. A set of Blenkinsop wheels with rack rails is preserved at the York Railway Museum.

William Cubitt (1785–1861) was trained as a millwright in Norfolk, England, in 1807 taking out a patent for self-regulating windmill-sails. In 1817 he invented the treadmill for using the labour of convicts in prisons for grinding corn.

From 1826 to 1858 he practised as a civil engineer in London and was engaged in works on the Oxford and Liverpool Junction canals.

His principal work in railway engineering was the South Eastern Railway, which branched off from Rastrick's London & Brighton Railway at Redhill through the Weald of Kent to Folkestone. From here to Dover the line was carried through a succession of tunnels beneath the cliffs, and the work involved the blasting of Round Down Cliff with one 18,000 lb charge of gunpowder, exploded electrically on 26th January 1843.

In 1850–51 he superintended the erection of the Crystal Palace for the Great Exhibition in London, and in 1851 he was knighted at Windsor Castle. Other works included the floating landing-stages on the Mersey at Liverpool and the iron bridge over the Medway at Rochester.

Timothy Hackworth (1786–1850), one of the most important figures in the early development of the locomotive. He was the eldest son of John Hackworth, Foreman Smith at Wylam Colliery, Northumberland, and was trained in the same craft, first under his father who died in 1802, then under the supervision of Christopher Blackett, proprietor of the colliery. From 1816 to 1824 he was Foreman Smith at Walbottle Colliery near Newcastle upon Tyne and after a short period supervising the Forth Street Works of Robert Stephenson & Company while George Stephenson was away on the Liverpool & Manchester Railway and Robert in South America, he transferred to the Stockton & Darlington Railway and set up the Locomotive Works at New Shildon. Here he built the *Royal George* in 1827, the first six-coupled engine and the first in which the cylinders drove directly on to the wheels. In 1829 he built the *Sanspareil* which he entered in the Rainhill Trials and which narrowly missed success. In 1838 he introduced his successful 0–6–0

The Stockton & Darlington Railway 0–6–0 No. 25 Derwent, which was built in 1845 by W. & A. Kitching of the Hopetown Railway Foundry, Darlington, is a six-coupled mineral engine and weighs about 22 tons. (Museum of British Transport.)

type with inclined cylinders at the rear driving the front coupled wheels. One of these, the *Derwent*, is preserved on Darlington Station. His last locomotive, the 2–2–2 *Sanspareil No. 2*, was built in 1849.

Hackworth was also responsible for the first use of the following features on locomotives: the eight-wheeled bogie engine in 1813; side coupling-rods instead of chains (S. & D. *Locomotion* in 1825); spring-loaded safety-valve, instead of weights; self-lubricating bearings, with oil-reservoir; steam-dome on boiler to obtain dry steam; inside cylinders and crank-axle; valve gear reversed by single lever; "lap" in slide-valves to permit expansive working.

Marc Seguin (1786–1875), French engineer and scientist, the designer and builder of the first steam locomotive in France in 1829 for the Saint-Étienne–Lyon Railway. It was the first engine to incorporate a multi-tubular boiler which was patented by him in 1827. A forced draught was provided by two rotary fans on the tender, driven by the wheels. The engine weighed nearly 6 tons in working order and could haul 30 tons on a gradient of 1 in 167 at 4·5 mile/h.

Thomas Shaw Brandreth (1788–1873), mathematician, classical scholar and barrister-at-law, educated at Eton College and Cambridge University. His scientific bent resulted in a close friendship with George Stephenson and he was one of the original Directors of the Liverpool & Manchester Railway until the end of 1830. He was active in the survey of the line, especially with John Dixon, across Chat Moss.

When Parliament laid down a speed limit of 10 mile/h for steam locomotives Brandreth invented a carriage in which a horse walked on a moving platform, so turning the wheels. It was named *Cycloped* and was entered in the Rainhill Trials where it achieved a speed of 15 mile/h, but the success of the *Rocket* made it unnecessary. However, Brandreth's machine was used in Lombardy and in the U.S.A. in instances where the expense of a steam locomotive was not justified.

William Fairbairn (1789–1874), famous engineer, friend of George Stephenson, and builder of both bridges and locomotives for railways. He was born in Scotland, trained on Tyneside and in 1817 started a small engineering works in Manchester where he remained for the rest of his working life. His original partner, Lillie, was bought out and later he was joined by his two sons.

Fairbairn & Sons built about 400 locomotives from 1839 to 1862.

These included many bar-framed engines of Edward Bury's design. The most famous engines built by the firm were the "Large Bloomers", 2–2–2s of McConnell design, for the Southern Division of the London & North Western Railway, in 1852–54.

In 1845–49 Fairbairn devised the system of wrought-iron tubular girders used by Robert Stephenson at Conway and the Menai Strait in North Wales and at Montreal, Canada. Fairbairn built many other bridges using this type of girder, but of smaller section. In 1860 his firm rebuilt the timber viaducts at Mottram and Dinting on the Sheffield–Manchester Railway without interrupting the passage of some seventy trains daily.

The firm was wound up about the time of his death in 1874.

Benjamin Hick (1790–1842) was trained as an engineer under Matthew Murray in the firm of Fenton, Murray & Jackson, Leeds, the first locomotive works in the world. In 1810 he moved to Bolton, Lancashire, where he went into partnership with the Rothwells at the Union Foundry, builders of many early locomotives.

In 1833 he left to form the Soho Foundry, Bolton, which under his son John in partnership with William Hargreaves, became Hick, Hargreaves. This firm also built many locomotives from about 1848, including some of the Norris-type 4–2–0s used on the Lickey Incline on the Birmingham & Gloucester Railway.

Peter Rothwell (1792–1849) achieved distinction as a manufacturer of locomotives for many early railways. At an early age he joined his father at the Union Foundry, Bolton, of which he became Manager, for a time being joined by Benjamin Hick. The first locomotive was a 2–2–0, the *Union*, built for the Bolton & Leigh Railway in 1831. It had a vertical boiler and horizontal cylinders fixed to the framing instead of the boiler, an innovation at the time.

Perhaps the most famous engines built by Rothwells were the 7 ft gauge 4–2–4 tanks to Pearson's design for the Bristol & Exeter Railway in 1853–54, with 9 ft driving-wheels. Many other broad-gauge engines were built for the Great Western Railway.

Other railways for which Rothwells built engines included the London & Birmingham, Midland Counties, Grand Junction, Liverpool & Manchester, London & Southampton, London & North Western, London & South Western and Eastern Counties.

The last engines were built by the firm in 1860 making a total of 200 engines in thirty years. The firm later became the Bolton Iron & Steel Company and for a time was managed by F. W. Webb, later the famous Locomotive Superintendent of the L.N.W.R.

Thomas Edmondson (1792–1851) was the originator of the standard railway ticket. A native of Lancashire, he began in the cabinet-making trade, however in 1836 he became a clerk on the Newcastle & Carlisle Railway where he quickly grew dissatisfied with the system of making out individual tickets for passengers. In 1837 he invented a machine for printing railway tickets on cards of standard size, numbered consecutively, and a press for stamping dates on the tickets. Almost identical date-presses are still in use today. The N. & C. was not interested in his invention, so Edmondson applied to the Manchester & Leeds Railway where he was appointed at Manchester. His system was soon adopted for general use throughout Britain and in other parts of the world. He patented his invention, charging railways 10 shillings (50p) a mile per year for using it.

Thomas Rogers (1792–1856), American locomotive engineer and founder of the Rogers Locomotive Works in 1837. In 1849 he introduced the link motion (valve gear) in America, and was one of the first engineers to apply balance weights for rotating parts. In 1850 he introduced the "wagon-top", or tapered boiler to give a greater steam space over the firebox. This became a standard feature of early American locomotives.

His works continued until 1905, producing about 6,300 engines, before being absorbed by the American Locomotive Company (ALCO).

The 4–2–0 Sandusky *was the first engine built by Thomas Rogers in 1837. (The Science Museum, London.)*

Charles Blacker Vignoles (1793–1875) was one of the best known of the early railway civil engineers. He was born in Ireland and lost both his parents in infancy. The first part of his career was spent in the Army until 1816 when he began as a surveyor.

His first principal railway work was on the lines forming the North Union Railway (Parkside–Wigan–Preston), after which he laid out the Dublin–Kingstown line, the first railway in Ireland.

In 1837 he introduced the flat-bottomed rail section which bore his name and which is now standard throughout the world. During the "Railway Mania" of 1846–48 he was engaged on many lines in Britain and Ireland. In 1847 he made the first of many visits to Russia where he carried out many railway projects and in 1853–55 he was responsible for the first railway in western Switzerland. His last important line was from Warsaw to Terespol in 1865.

Edward Bury (1794–1858) was an early locomotive engineer and originator of the bar-frame, universally used in American steam-locomotive practice. He was born in Salford, Lancashire, and set up his works in Liverpool before 1829. Here his Works Manager was James Kennedy, who later became a partner in the firm of Bury, Curtis & Kennedy. His first locomotive, apart from an early unsuccessful attempt, was the 0–4–0 *Liverpool* in 1830, the first engine with inside cylinders and bar-frames. It had 6 ft diameter wheels, the largest up to that time. The upright cylindrical firebox with domed top became a standard feature of Bury's engines.

Portuguese metre-gauge train with the 0–4–4–0 articulated tank engine near Porto. (N. Fields.)

The metre-gauge Alcoy & Gandia Railway of Spain with a 2–6–2 tank built by Beyer Peacock & Company of Manchester. (N. Fields.)

A Bury 2–2–0 at Kirkham in Lancashire in about 1846. (British Rail.)

From 1837 he was Locomotive Superintendent on the London & Birmingham Railway at Wolverton, until succeeded by McConnell on 1st January 1847 when he was appointed to the Great Northern Railway as Locomotive Engineer. His work so impressed the management that in 1849 he was appointed General Manager. He resigned this post in 1850.

The Liverpool Works closed down in 1850. Two Bury engines survive today, the Furness Railway 0–4–0 No. 3 at the Museum of British Transport, Clapham, London, and the 2–2–2 No. 36 of the Great Southern & Western Railway at Cork (Kent) Station, Ireland.

Nicholas Wood (1795–1865), as Colliery Viewer at Killingworth near Newcastle upon Tyne, became associated with George Stephenson and the earliest steam locomotives. One of three built by Stephenson and Wood for the Hetton Colliery, County Durham in 1822 is preserved in the York Railway Museum. It worked (rebuilt) until 1912 and led the Railway Centenary Procession from Darlington to Stockton under its own steam in 1925. In 1825 Wood published an important treatise giving the results of his experiments in the use of fixed and locomotive engines for railways. In 1829 he was appointed one of the Judges at the Rainhill Trials. He made great contributions to improvements in the working and ventilation of coal-mines in the Newcastle area.

Matthias W. Baldwin (1795–1866), founder of the famous Baldwin Locomotive Works in Philadelphia, U.S.A., the largest in the world.

He was born in Elizabethtown, New Jersey, and became first a watchmaker, then a toolmaker and then a machinist. This brought him into contact with stationary steam-engines and then locomotives. His first locomotive *Old Ironside* was built in 1832, and remained in service for over twenty years. His second locomotive, the 4–2–0 *E. L. Miller*, was a great advance and it introduced many features which became standard American practice. In 1838 he instituted standardisation using templates and gauges and by 1840 he was using metallic packing for glands. His first European engine was built for Austria in 1841. Horizontal cylinders in identical castings including half the smokebox saddle were introduced in 1858 and soon became standard in America. In England, nearly half a century later, they were adopted by Churchward on the Great Western Railway.

When he died in 1866 his firm's annual output was 120 engines; also in that year the 2–8–0 was introduced, becoming the most numerous type in America. The last Baldwin steam-engine was built for India in 1955, bringing the total to about 75,000.

John Dixon (1796–1865) was the founder of the profession of Civil Engineer and friend of George Stephenson. He assisted Stephenson in the survey of the Stockton & Darlington Railway in 1821. In 1827 he left the S. & D. and began the difficult task of surveying for the Liverpool & Manchester Railway across Chat Moss for which George Stephenson devised his famous method of "floating" the line across the bog on a mattress of brushwood. Dixon returned to the S. & D. in 1845 and from then until his death, two years after the S. & D. had become part of the North Eastern Railway, he occupied the position of Consulting Engineer.

John Braithwaite (1797–1870) began training in his father's engineering works. Following the death of his father John in 1818 and his brother Francis in 1823, John Braithwaite carried on the business himself, taking up the manufacture of high-pressure steam-engines. In 1827 he became acquainted with the Stephensons and with Captain John Ericsson with whom he constructed a locomotive, *Novelty*, which was entered in the Rainhill Trials. It was the first engine to run a mile in under a minute. At the same time Braithwaite achieved distinction by manufacturing the first steam fire-engines. From 1834 he began to practise as a civil engineer working with Vignoles on the 5 ft gauge Eastern Counties Railway. With J. C. Robertson he was joint founder of the *Railway Times* in 1837, one of the earliest railway periodicals. In 1836–38 he and Ericsson fitted up a canal boat with a steam-engine and screw-propeller in which they made a circuit of canals between London and Manchester. In 1844–46 Braithwaite surveyed several railways in France.

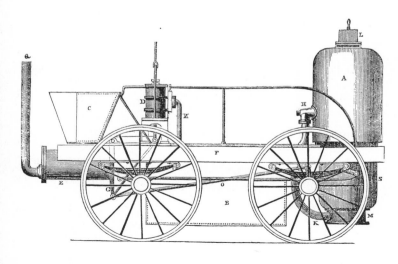

The Novelty *of 1829, the first inside-cylinder engine.* (The Engineer, *9th January 1925.*)

William Bridges Adams (1797–1872), son of the Staffordshire coachbuilder who invented the C-spring. His early life was spent in Chile until 1837 when he returned to England. In 1838 he invented a rail-brake, acting on the sides of the rail, but the idea was first applied by J. B. Fell on the centre brake on his Mont Cenis Railway in 1868.

In 1843 Adams established the Fairfield Engineering Works at Bow, London (now Bryant & May's Match Factory), and here in 1847 he built the very first railcar, the *Express*, for the Eastern Counties Railway. He also built the extraordinary 7 ft gauge railcar *Fairfield* in 1848 for the Bristol & Exeter Railway. His "light locomotive" idea was taken up by several other firms.

He invented the radial axlebox, first used on some 2–4–2 tanks on the St. Helens Railway in 1863. Perhaps his most famous invention was the rail fishplate.

George Hudson (1800–1871) was known as the "Railway King". He achieved considerable success as a draper in York and at the age of twenty-seven he received a bequest of £30,000 which he invested in North Midland Railway shares. He quickly rose to important positions in the town, becoming Lord Mayor of York in 1837. In that year he was appointed Chairman of the York & North Midland Railway, opened in 1839, and he became closely associated with George Stephenson. He next became actively engaged in extending the railway from York to Newcastle upon Tyne. He was instrumental in the formation of the Midland Railway by the amalgamation of several companies in 1844 and became Chairman of the company.

During the rush of railway speculation in 1844 he was in control of 1,016 miles of railway. This was the period of his greatest success and despite his rough North Country accent and uncultivated manners his acquaintance was sought by the leading persons in the country, even the Prince Consort.

However, as his power increased his financial dealings became questionable and after paying dividends to the extent of £294,000 out of Eastern Counties Railway capital his fall was rapid.

To his credit, however, it must be said that he was the first person in control of railways who attempted to guide their development according to an over-all plan, though his rule to "mak' all t' railways cum t' York" did not always lead to the best routes being chosen. The railway which suffered his most powerful opposition, the Great Northern, was in the end the one which really put York "on the railway map".

George Bradshaw (1801–1853) was born in Salford, Lancashire. On leaving school he was apprenticed to an engraver and in 1821 he established an engraving business in Manchester where he specialised in the engraving of maps, his first being a map of his native county. In 1830 he produced the first of his maps of canals and inland navigation. In 1838, soon after the introduction of railways, he produced the first of his railway maps.

His famous railway timetable first appeared in 1839. In 1840 this became *Bradshaw's Railway Companion* with maps, price one shilling, and in December 1841 *Bradshaw's Monthly Railway Guide*. Among other publications were: *Bradshaw's Continental Railway Guide* from 1847 and *Bradshaw's General Railway Directory and Shareholders' Guide* from 1849.

While still a young man Bradshaw joined the Society of Friends and was very prominent in philanthropic work. The last Bradshaw timetable was No. 1521 published in June 1961. An almost complete collection was handed over to Manchester Public Library. Blacklock's Printing Works, successor to Bradshaw & Blacklock, closed in 1971.

Robert Stephenson (1803–1859) ranks with Brunel, Locke and Vignoles as one of the greatest of early railway engineers. In 1814 his father, George, was able to send him to school in Newcastle upon Tyne. In 1823, when only twenty, he was placed in charge of the locomotive works in Newcastle upon Tyne which his father had founded under the name of Robert Stephenson & Company.

In 1824 he visited South America for three years and there met Richard Trevithick, penniless, whom he helped to repatriate.

Under Robert Stephenson's direction the famous *Rocket* was built for the Rainhill Trials. He assisted his father on the Liverpool & Manchester, Leicester & Swannington and other railways and in 1833 was appointed Engineer of the London & Birmingham Railway, completed in 1838.

It is for his great bridges, however, that he is best remembered. Famous examples are the High Level Bridge, Newcastle (1846–49), Royal Border Bridge over the Tweed at Berwick (1850), and his great bridges built on the tubular system devised in conjunction with William Fairbairn at Conway (1846–48) and the Menai Strait (1846–50, damaged by fire on 23rd May 1970 and now being rebuilt) and the Victoria Tubular Bridge over the St. Lawrence at Montreal (1854–59).

Robert Stephenson's Victoria Tubular Bridge built over the St. Lawrence River at Montreal in Canada in 1854–59.

Joseph Mitchell (1803–1883), Engineer of the Highland Railway, Scotland. He trained under Thomas Telford, later becoming Engineer of roads and bridges in the Scottish Highlands. He also erected forty churches in the Highlands. In 1844 he laid out the Scottish Central Railway (Perth–Falkirk) and in 1845 the Perth–Inverness line of the H.R. This was considered impracticable at the time and it was not finished until 1863, to Forres, on the Inverness & Aberdeen Junction Railway, over the highest main-line summit in Britain, 1,484 ft at Druimuachdar. In the meantime he had surveyed most of the other H.R. lines, including that to Wick and Thurso. This was completed in 1874, seven years after Mitchell had retired following a paralytic disease. A member of the Institution of Civil Engineers from 1837, it was he who first established the Minutes of Proceedings of that Institution.

John Ericsson (1803–1889) the famous inventor was born in Sweden and, after spells in the Army and Navy, in 1826 went to London. Here he continued his experiments towards an engine which would use heat more economically than a steam-engine. In 1828 he designed a steam fire-engine with a 12 in diameter cylinder and a boiler with a forced draught, which was built by John Braithwaite. In 1829 he designed his only railway locomotive, also built by Braithwaite, the *Novelty*, which was entered for the Rainhill Trials. But for an unfortunate breakdown it might have won the prize. On 13th July 1836 he took out a patent for a screw-propeller and built a screw-vessel in 1837. Failing to interest anyone in his work in Britain he moved to America, where he remained until his death in New York.

Joseph Hamilton Beattie (1804–1871) is famous for being the first to devise a means of burning coal on a locomotive without producing smoke, and for his feed-water heating apparatus. Details of his early career are obscure, but by 1839 he was Assistant Engineer on the London & Southampton Railway under Locke.

In 1850 he succeeded J. V. Gooch as Locomotive Superintendent on the London & South Western Railway (successor to the L. & S.R.) at Nine Elms, London.

The first locomotive to be fitted with his coal-burning firebox and feed-water heater was a 6 ft 6 in single-wheeler named *The Duke* in 1853. The firebox was in two parts, one of which burnt coal and the other coke. It was the coke fire which burnt the smoke from the coal. This complicated arrangement was, however, made obsolete by the firebox with brick arch and baffle-plate in 1860.

The trouble with the feed-water heater was that injectors would not work so that crosshead-driven boiler feed-pumps had to be used.

His 2–4–0 with outside cylinders achieved renown, two examples even being built for the East Lancashire Railway in 1857. Three examples of the tank version of this type, built in 1874–75 and much rebuilt since, survived in use at Wadebridge, Cornwall until 1962.

Joseph Locke (1805–1860) was another of the principal early railway civil engineers. Born near Sheffield and educated at Barnsley Grammar School, he was articled to George Stephenson in 1823 and worked with him on the Liverpool & Manchester Railway. It was during the construction of the tunnel down to Wapping under Liverpool that Locke proved errors in Stephenson's survey which led to an estrangement.

Locke's principal works were the Grand Junction (Birmingham–Warrington—begun by Stephenson), 1835–37; the London–Southampton, 1836–40; the Sheffield–Manchester, 1838–40; the Lancaster–Preston, 1837–40; the Greenock–Paisley–Glasgow, 1837–41; the Paris–Rouen, 1841–43; the Rouen–Havre, 1843; the Barcelona–Mattaro, 1847–48; and the Dutch Rhenish Railway, 1856.

In 1840 Locke entered a partnership with John Edward Errington (1806–1862) and together they constructed the Lancaster & Carlisle, 1843–46; the East Lancashire and the Scottish Central, 1845; the Caledonian (Carlisle–Glasgow), 1848; and other Scottish lines.

Locke was noted for his avoidance of tunnels. For instance there is no tunnel between Birmingham and Glasgow, despite the heavy climbs over Shap and Beattock. He was also noted for the low cost of his lines, some of which proved, however, expensive to operate due to the steep gradients.

Thomas Brassey (1805–1870), one of the most famous railway contractors, born and educated in Cheshire and articled to a land surveyor at the age of sixteen. In 1834 he became acquainted with George Stephenson and through him obtained a contract for Penkridge Viaduct on the Grand Junction Railway. This was followed by other G.J. contracts under Locke.

Following his marriage in 1831, his wife persuaded him to take up a career as a railway contractor and by 1850 he had works in progress throughout Britain and Europe. Other works were the Grand Trunk Railway, Canada, 1852–59; the Crimean Railway, with Peto and Betts, 1854; Australian railways, 1859–63; Argentinian railways, 1864; several Indian railways, 1858–65; and Moldavian railways, 1862–68.

He was remarkable for his punctuality and thoroughness in his contracts, his power of mental calculation, skill in organisation, his ability to delegate responsibility to his subordinates and for his humane treatment of the navvies working under him. He was a man of unfailing courtesy and kindness, and scrupulous honesty.

Isambard Kingdom Brunel (1806–1859) was the son of Marc Isambard Brunel (1769–1849) who was Engineer of the Thames Tunnel, begun in 1825 and completed in 1843 and later adapted by John Hawkshaw as part of the East London Railway. I. K. Brunel worked with his father in the tunnel. His first major work was the Clifton Suspension Bridge, Bristol, although this was not completed until after his death. In March 1833, when only twenty-seven, he was appointed Engineer to the Great Western Railway between London and Bristol, laying out the line with bold engineering works and to the unprecedented gauge of 7 ft. The Box Tunnel, 1·75 miles long, was laid out on such a line that it was penetrated by the sun's rays only on 9th April—his birthday. He continued as Engineer of the Bristol & Exeter, the South Devon (where he experimented unsuccessfully with the atmospheric system of propulsion) and the Cornwall railways, also the line from Swindon to Gloucester and South Wales. For this he devised a combination of tubular, suspension and truss bridge to carry the line over the Wye at Chepstow and developed this design in his famous Saltash Bridge over the Tamar near Plymouth. This was completed just before his death in 1859. Besides railways, Brunel designed and built steamships, the most famous being the *Great Western* of 1838 and the *Great Britain* of 1845. His greatest ship, the *Great Eastern* was built for the Eastern Navigation Company in 1858. The anxieties connected with this broke his health and he died the following year.

The 1·75 mile long Box Tunnel on the Great Western Railway is penetrated by the sun at 05.16 hours on the 9th April, Brunel's birthday.

George Parker Bidder (1806–1870) is best remembered for his extraordinary calculating ability. In 1834 he became associated with Robert Stephenson on the London & Birmingham Railway. This brought him into Parliamentary work where he achieved a reputation as a formidable opponent in committees, through his powers as a mental calculator. He was engaged in numerous railway works at home and abroad, but his most important construction work was the Victoria Docks, London. He was the originator of the railway swing-bridge, the first of which he designed and erected at Reedham on the Norwich & Lowestoft Railway, and was one of the founders of the Electric Telegraph Company. He was President of the Institution of Civil Engineers in 1860–62.

Edward Fletcher (1807–1889) was a locomotive engineer. In 1825 he was appointed to Robert Stephenson & Company at Newcastle upon Tyne, where, in 1829 he made much of the machinery for the *Rocket*. In 1830 he went to the Canterbury & Whitstable Railway where he drove the locomotive *Invicta* on the opening day.

After working on the construction of the York & North Midland Railway from 1837, he became Locomotive Superintendent of the Newcastle & Darlington Railway and in 1854 assumed the same office on the newly formed North Eastern Railway at Gateshead, providing the company with a stud of simple, robust engines. When he retired in 1882 he had completed forty-seven years in the service of the N.E.R. and its predecessors.

Thomas Cook (1808–1892), the founder of the great English firm of Thomas Cook & Son Limited. He was born in Melbourne, Derbyshire, and after a succession of occupations he became interested in the Temperance Movement and on 5th July 1841 he ran a Temperance excursion on the Midland Counties Railway. The success of this led to others and to the establishment of a business in Leicester which, in 1865, was transferred to London. In 1866 he arranged his first tours to the U.S.A. and there followed many to other parts of the world, all at reduced rates. Since 1948 control of Thomas Cook & Son has been vested in the British Transport Commission.

Samuel Morton Peto (1809–1889) stands second only to Brassey as one of the greatest of railway contractors. He inherited his father's firm of Grissell & Peto which was responsible for many important buildings in London, including the Nelson Column in 1843. His first major railway contracts were on the Great Western Railway in 1840 and the South Eastern Railway in 1844. In 1846 the firm of Grissell & Peto was dissolved, Peto retaining the railway contracts. These included works on the Chester & Holyhead, the London & South Western and, in partnership with E. L. Betts (1815–1872), the Great Northern, the Oxford, Worcester & Wolverhampton, the Hereford & Gloucester, the Oxford & Birmingham, the South London & Crystal Palace, and the Great Eastern railways in England; also railways in South America, Russia, North Africa and Norway. In conjunction with Thomas Brassey he constructed lines in Australia, the Grand Trunk Railway in Canada, including Robert Stephenson's Victoria Tubular Bridge at Montreal, and in France. From 1847 to 1854 he sat in Parliament as Liberal Member for Norwich. He was knighted in 1855 following work on a railway in the Crimea. Like Brassey he was noted for his humane treatment of his workers.

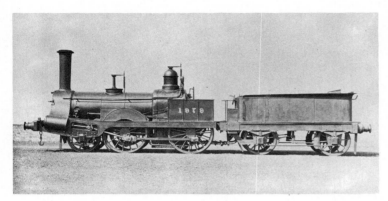

*The Allan/Buddicom
Crewe-type locomotive.
(British Rail.)*

Alexander Allan (1809–1891), a locomotive engineer who shares with Buddicom the credit for the Crewe-type engine introduced about 1842, with the cylinders mounted in an outside framing and with the smokebox sheeting continuing in a curve over the cylinders. Allan pioneered the balanced slide-valve in 1844 and his straight-link valve gear in 1856. This became widely used throughout the world. In 1860 he introduced the first successful steel firebox.

Nathaniel Worsdell (1809–1896) was the eldest son of Thomas Clarke Worsdell, builder of the tender for Stephenson's *Rocket*. In 1828 he began work on the Liverpool & Manchester Railway and with his father designed and built the earliest passenger coaches. In 1836 he succeeded his father as Superintendent of the Carriage Department of the L. & M.

In 1837 he invented the apparatus for picking up and depositing mail-bags on railways which was patented in 1838, but he never received any remuneration for this. He is also credited with the invention of the screw-coupling, but using a single right-hand thread only.

The year his son Thomas William was born, 1838 (see page 57), he built the "Experience" coach for the L. & M., consisting of three horse-carriage bodies on a railway-carriage frame, so establishing the design upon which future compartment coaches in Great Britain and Europe were based.

When the Locomotive and Carriage Departments were transferred from Liverpool to Crewe in 1843 he moved there and played an important part in the development of the new town. He retired in 1880.

He was a Quaker, like his father, and was renowned for his integrity. It was said of him that he would speak the truth if he had to die for it. His two brothers, Thomas and George, became noted railway engineers and of his five sons Thomas William and Wilson became Locomotive Engineers on the North Eastern Railway, Henry worked on railways in India, and Robert also on the N.E.R.

Henry Meiggs (1811–1877) was the engineer and contractor responsible for what is surely the most wonderful railway in the world, the Central of Peru. He was born in New York State and was an outstanding mathematician. He had an astute business sense, an ability to select the right men to serve under him, and was a man of dauntless courage and optimism. After making several fortunes, not always honestly, and losing them, he settled in Chile in 1854 where he constructed the Santiago Railway. In 1867 he moved to Peru where he began work on the Oroya Railway from Lima to Oroya in the

The track beneath the south end of the Cacray Zigzag on the Central Railway of Peru, where Henry Meiggs took the old river-bed for the road-bed and diverted the Rimac River through a tunnel seen on the right. There has never been any flooding here. (Brian Fawcett, M.I.L.E.)

A double zigzag on the Oroya Railway, later the Central Railway of Peru showing how Meiggs carried the line up into the Andes. (Brian Fawcett, M.I.L.E.)

Andes, the highest railway in the world. He died before the railway was completed but the rest of the route was fully worked out.

He had great generosity and was the first big contractor in North or South America to treat the imported Japanese coolies as humans.

John Hawkshaw (1811–1891) was responsible for the greatest number of major engineering works of the foremost nineteenth-century engineers. He was born in Yorkshire and trained with C. Fowler and later with Alexander Nimmo.

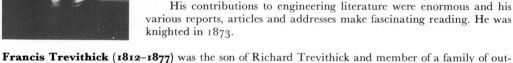

He constructed a large portion of the Lancashire & Yorkshire Railway between 1845 and 1853, including some tremendous viaducts in Yorkshire, and was the first engineer to demonstrate conclusively that steam locomotives on smooth rails were capable of surmounting gradients steeper than 1 in 50.

Other railway works included the Charing Cross and Cannon Street railway bridges and stations, London; the East London Railway utilising Marc Brunel's Thames Tunnel; and the Severn Tunnel.

With Sir James Brunlees he was Engineer to the original Channel Tunnel project from 1872 to 1886.

Abroad he reported on the Suez and Panama canal projects and from 1862 to 1876 was Engineer to the Amsterdam Ship Canal.

His contributions to engineering literature were enormous and his various reports, articles and addresses make fascinating reading. He was knighted in 1873.

Francis Trevithick (1812–1877) was the son of Richard Trevithick and member of a family of outstanding engineers. In 1840 he began as Resident Engineer on the Grand Junction Railway between Birmingham and Crewe and in 1841 was appointed Locomotive Superintendent at Edge Hill, Liverpool, following the resignation of Buddicom.

It was under Francis Trevithick that the Locomotive Works were established at Crewe in 1843, where the G.J.R. was joined by the Manchester &. Birmingham and the Crewe & Chester lines.

Upon the formation of the London & North Western Railway in 1846 he was responsible for the locomotives of the Northern Division, with Headquarters at Crewe. Ramsbottom remained in charge of the North Eastern Division locomotives at Longsight, Manchester, until the Divisions were amalgamated in 1857 when Trevithick resigned and Ramsbottom took over at Crewe.

William Henry Barlow (1812–1902), civil engineer, trained at Woolwich Dockyard and London Docks. After six years on engineering works in Turkey he returned to England in 1838 and became Assistant Engineer on the Manchester & Birmingham Railway, in 1842 he became Resident Engineer on the Midland Counties Railway and in 1844 on the North Midland Railway. On the formation of the Midland Railway in 1844 he became Chief Civil Engineer. In 1849 he patented the saddle-back form of rail which bore his name (it was much used on the Great Western Railway) and between 1844 and 1886 he took out many patents relating to permanent way. In 1862–69 he laid out the extension of the Midland Railway from Bedford to London and designed the great roof of St. Pancras Station (opened on 1st October 1868).

With Sir John Hawkshaw in 1860 he completed the Clifton Suspension Bridge at Bristol, begun by I. K. Brunel. Barlow was closely connected with the Tay and Forth bridges.

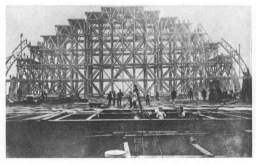

St. Pancras Station under construction in 1867 showing a travelling gantry and first girder. (British Rail.)

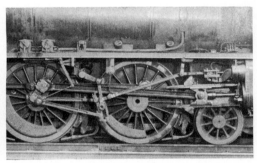

Howe/Stephenson link motion fitted outside the frames on the London, Midland & Scottish Railway Class "5" 4–6–0 No. 44767, which was built in 1947. (John Marshall.)

William Howe (1814–1879) was the inventor of the steam-engine valve gear known as "Stephenson's link motion". He was born in County Durham and trained under Hackworth at New Shildon, then at the Vulcan Foundry, Lancashire and at Liverpool.

In 1840 he removed to Gateshead and joined Robert Stephenson & Company and it was here in 1842 that he devised the reversing gear using two eccentrics and a curved link. His original model of this gear can be seen in the Science Museum, London.

It was immediately adopted by Stephenson who gave Howe full credit for the invention, and it was soon in universal use. It seems probable, however, that the gear was used at first as a reversing gear only, and that its use in expansive working by cutting off the steam to the cylinder before the end of the piston stroke was discovered later.

John Ramsbottom (1814–1892) is best remembered as the inventor of the water-trough and the safety-valve named after him. About 1839 he entered the Locomotive Works of Sharp, Roberts & Company, Manchester and in 1842 became Locomotive Superintendent of the Manchester & Birmingham Railway with his works at Longsight, Manchester.

In 1846 the M. & B. became a part of the newly formed London & North Western Railway and in 1857 Ramsbottom succeeded Francis Trevithick as Locomotive Superintendent of the entire Northern Division of the L.N.W.R. at Crewe. He invented the water-trough in 1859, to enable locomotives to pick up water while in motion. In 1862, with the ending of locomotive work under McConnell at Wolverton, Crewe became the Locomotive Headquarters for the entire railway. Ramsbottom retired from the L.N.W.R. in 1871, but in 1883 he became connected with the Lancashire & Yorkshire Railway and was partly responsible for the establishment of the L.Y.R. Works at Horwich, near Bolton.

William Barber Buddicom (1816–1887) is best remembered for the famous Crewe-type engine with outside cylinders, in which Alexander Allan also possibly had a share. The type was much used on the London & North Western, the Highland and the Caledonian railways.

He was born in Liverpool and from 1831 to 1836 served an apprenticeship with Mather, Dixon & Company, Liverpool. In 1836 he began work on the Liverpool & Manchester Railway for two years, then becoming Resident Engineer of the Glasgow, Paisley & Greenock Railway. In 1840 he was appointed Locomotive Superintendent of the Grand Junction Railway which had amalgamated with the L. & M., with his Headquarters at Edge Hill, Liverpool. It was Buddicom who prepared the plans and estimates for the new Works at Crewe, carried out under his successor Francis Trevithick.

In 1841 he went to France to superintend the construction of rolling stock for the Paris & Rouen Railway then being built by Thomas Brassey and MacKenzie and of which Joseph Locke was Engineer. A company was formed under the name of Allcard, Buddicom & Company until 1851 when it became Buddicom & Company. When the Sotteville Works at Rouen were ready in 1842 Buddicom's firm entered into a contract for running the railway.

Thomas Russell Crampton (1816–1888) must rank as one of the most courageous and original of early locomotive engineers. He was born at Broadstairs, Kent and from 1839 to 1844 he worked under Marc Brunel and afterwards with Daniel Gooch on the Great Western Railway at Swindon for a very short time. It was while here that he conceived his famous design for a locomotive with a large low boiler and a pair of large driving-wheels behind the firebox.

In 1845 the first two of his engines of this type were built and others followed for the London & North Western Railway and other lines. The biggest was the *Liverpool*, a 6–2–0 built by Bury, Curtis & Kennedy in 1848. It weighed 35 tons and had the largest boiler on any locomotive of that date. Its 8 ft driving-wheels and general majestic appearance earned it a Gold Medal at the Great Exhibition of 1851.

The largest number of Crampton engines was in France, the first twelve being built for the Northern Railway of France in 1848–49 by Derosne, Cail et Cie. Hundreds more were built in France and Germany. One of the French Cramptons, *Le Continent* built in 1852 for the Paris–Strasbourg Railway, has been preserved for use on special trains.

Crampton steam locomotive and carriages of the same period. (French Railways Limited, London.)

Daniel Gooch (1816–1889), the most distinguished member of a great family of engineers. He was born in Bedlington, Northumberland, the son of John Gooch, Manager of Bedlington Ironworks, and Anna, daughter of Thomas Longridge of Newcastle upon Tyne. He was apprenticed at Robert Stephenson's Works at Newcastle upon Tyne and, after some experience with Tayleur at the Vulcan Foundry in Lancashire, and in Scotland, in 1837 he applied to I. K. Brunel for the post of Locomotive Superintendent of the Great Western Railway.

After some preliminary brushes with Brunel, whose misguided specifications for locomotives had resulted in some wretched specimens being obtained, Gooch ordered engines of his own design from Newcastle upon Tyne which at once achieved a reputation for speed and reliability. His 8 ft single-wheeler design of 1847 remained in production until 1878 and examples survived to the end of the broad gauge in 1892.

Gooch took a leading part in the establishment of the new Locomotive Works at Swindon from 1843, and made an active contribution to the development of the new town.

In 1864 he resigned from the post of Locomotive Superintendent so as to lay the first Atlantic cable from Brunel's steamship *Great Eastern*. The first telegraph messages were sent across the Atlantic in 1866; and Gooch was made a baronet.

The same year he returned to the G.W.R. as Chairman, remaining in this position until the last year of his life. During his chairmanship he guided the G.W.R. through difficult times and in his last years threw all his energies into the Severn Tunnel project, which was completed in 1887.

His brothers Thomas Longridge (1808–1882) and John Viret (1812–1900) were both distinguished engineers. The first was Resident Engineer of the Manchester & Leeds Railway and the second was Locomotive Superintendent of the London & South Western and Eastern Counties railways.

James Brunlees (1816–1892) was a civil engineer, responsible for some outstanding railway works. He learned surveying under Alexander Adie on the Bolton & Preston Railway and later with Locke and Errington on the Caledonian Railway. On the completion of the latter in 1844 he became Acting Engineer under

Hawkshaw on lines forming the Lancashire & Yorkshire Railway until 1850.

He then became responsible for a succession of major railway projects: the Ulverston & Lancaster Railway, 1851, including viaducts across the Kent and Leven estuaries; the São Paulo Railway, Brazil with its amazing rope-worked inclines, 1856; the Fell Railway over Mont Cenis Pass (between France and Italy), 1865; the Solway Junction Railway including the viaduct over the Solway Firth, 1865–69; the Cleveland Extension, Yorkshire with the 180 ft high Skelton Beck Viaduct. With Douglas Fox he built the Mersey Railway Tunnel. On the completion of this in 1886 Brunlees and Fox were knighted.

From 1872 to 1866 Brunlees was Engineer with Hawkshaw to the original Channel Tunnel Company.

Ernst Werner von Siemens (1816–1892) was born at Lenthe, Hanover. In 1834 he entered the Prussian Artillery and in 1844 took charge of the Artillery Workshops, Berlin.

He is best remembered in railway circles for having built the first practical electric railway, for the Berlin Trades Exhibition of 1879, operated from 31st May to 30th September on a track about 600 yd long.

He was responsible for the Portrush–Giant's Causeway Tramway in Ireland, the first railway in the world to be run on hydroelectric power, opened on 28th September 1883.

John Fowler (1817–1898) was born at Sheffield and trained under J. U. Rastrick on the London & Brighton Railway, as a civil engineer. Later he became Resident Engineer of the Stockton & Hartlepool Railway on the completion of which in 1842 he was appointed Engineer, General Manager and Locomotive Superintendent. From 1844 he worked on the lines from Sheffield to the east coast, which became the Manchester, Sheffield & Lincolnshire Railway and from 1898 the Great Central Railway.

He designed the Pimlico Railway Bridge, the first across the Thames at London, finished in 1860. From 1860 he was engaged, with B. Baker, on the Metropolitan Railway, London, the first section of which opened in 1863. For this he devised the first fireless locomotive which, however, was not a success.

In 1870 he was appointed to a commission to advise on narrow-gauge railways in India and also visited Norway in this capacity.

From 1875 he entered into partnership with Baker and from 1883 to 1890 supervised the construction of the Forth Bridge in Scotland. In 1890, with Baker, he was knighted.

Charles Easton Spooner (1818–1889), the most famous name in the history of narrow-gauge railways. He was born at Maentwrog, Wales, where his father James Spooner had engineered the narrow-gauge tramway over the embankment to Portmadoc.

When the Act of Parliament for the Festiniog Railway was obtained in 1832 C. E. Spooner was only fourteen but he assisted in the construction of this 1 ft 11·5 in gauge railway from the slate-quarries of Blaenau Festiniog down to the coast at Portmadoc. When his father died in 1856 Spooner became Engineer and Manager.

In 1863 powers were obtained to work the line with locomotives instead of horses (ascending) and gravity (descending) and at the same time the line was improved. In 1865 it opened for passengers, becoming

The Festiniog Railway 1 ft 11·5 in gauge 0–4–0 Princess. This was the first narrow-gauge steam locomotive. (Festiniog Railway Company.)

the world's first passenger-carrying narrow-gauge line. It was visited by engineers from all over the world.

The first 0–4–0 engines were built by George England but in 1869 the first of the Fairlie double engines appeared. Several of the engines still in operation today are original.

Alfred Belpaire (1820–1893) was the inventor of the famous locomotive firebox which bore his name. He was born in Ostend, Belgium, and in 1840 gained his Engineering Diploma in Paris. In that year the Belgian State Railways entrusted him with charge of the Locomotive Shops at Malines where his contemporary Egide Walschaerts began work. In 1850 he was appointed Director of the Rolling Stock Department at Brussels.

To achieve greater efficiency from the low-grade fuel burnt on Belgian locomotives he produced his famous firebox in 1860, in a round form which was tested on the 2–4–0 No. 1. In 1864 he abandoned this type and adopted the familiar square form which facilitated the use of vertical and horizontal stays. It was used on all the Belgian State Railways engines from 1864 to 1884. At the end of 1884 he introduced new details, increasing both length and width of the grate, the area of which reached 73·8 ft² on some express engines on the Luxemburg line.

He also invented a combined screw and lever reverse for locomotives. In 1878 he invented a steam rail-carriage, the precursor of the rail-motor. He designed large numbers of locomotives.

The Belpaire firebox was first used in Britain on the 0–6–2 tanks designed by Harry Pollitt and built in 1891 for the Manchester, Sheffield & Lincolnshire Railway. The first to be constructed in Britain were by Beyer Peacock & Company of Manchester in 1872 for some 2–4–0s for the Malines–Terneuzen Railway in Belgium, and it was through the Chief Draughtsman of the M.S. & L. who had been with Beyer Peacock, that it was used on that railway. It was adopted as standard by G. J. Churchward on the Great Western Railway, and his designs influenced others right down to the series of standard engines built by British Railways from 1950 to 1959.

Egide Walschaerts (1820–1901), inventor of one of the most efficient and widely used valve gears on steam locomotives. He was born in Belgium and started work as a mechanic on the Belgian State Railways at Malines. In 1844 he invented his famous valve gear which was first fitted to an inside-cylinder 2–2–2 at Brussels in 1848, with great success. It was used on the Crampton engines, Nos. 165–70, of the Northern Railway of France built in 1859. In Belgium it was applied to all outside-cylinder engines, but the Stephenson link motion was preferred for inside cylinders. The first locomotive in Britain to have the Walschaerts valve gear was a 0–4–4 tank built in 1878 by the Fairlie Engine Company, London, for the Swindon, Marlborough & Andover Railway.

Thomas Bouch (1822–1880) trained as a civil engineer under Larmer on the Lancaster & Carlisle Railway. In 1849 he became Engineer of the Edinburgh & Northern Railway, designing the mechanism for loading and unloading wagons on the world's first train ferries, across the firths of Forth and Tay. On the South Durham & Lancashire Union Railway, later part of the North Eastern

The first Tay Bridge from the south in 1878.

The North Eastern Railway "Q6" No. 63455 on goods from Weatherhill, County Durham, crossing Hownes Gill Viaduct. (John Marshall.)

Railway, he built the great iron viaducts at Belah (highest in England), Deepdale and Barnard Castle, which gave good service until dismantled in recent years. In 1877–78 he completed a bridge 2 miles long across the Tay at Dundee. He was knighted in 1879, but shortly afterwards, on 28th December, the bridge blew down while a train was crossing. He never recovered from the shock, and died the following year.

His permanent monument remains, however, in his tremendous 150 ft high Hownes Gill Viaduct, which was built in fire-bricks for the Stockton & Darlington Railway near Consett, County Durham. It was first used on 1st July 1858.

David Joy (1825–1903) is best remembered for his radial valve gear for steam-engines, but he had many other inventions to his credit. He was born in Leeds and served an apprenticeship with Fenton, Murray & Jackson, the world's first locomotive-building firm. When this closed in 1843 he transferred to Shepherd & Todd, also in Leeds, and in 1846 to the Railway Foundry. Here he worked on the design for the *Jenny Lind* 2–2–2 engine, forerunner of a famous type.

In 1850 he left to take charge of the Nottingham & Grantham Railway, then just opened, later becoming Locomotive Superintendent of the Oxford, Worcester & Wolverhampton Railway, where he remained until 1856 when he returned to the Railway Foundry.

In 1857 he patented a compound marine engine. He also patented a steam reversing gear, the first in the world, and at the same time took out the first of his three patents for hydraulic organ-blowers. In 1860 he invented a pneumatic hammer.

The 2–2–2 Jenny Lind *built by E. B. Wilson at the Railway Foundry, Leeds in 1847. (*The Engineer, *13th March 1925.)*

From 1862 to 1876 he ran a business of his own at Middlesborough. He then became Secretary to the Barrow Ship Building Company and it was here, in 1879, that he invented his famous radial valve gear.

Its first use on a locomotive was in 1880 when F. W. Webb had it fitted to a 0–6–0 built at Crewe. The gear became standard on the London & North Western Railway and from 1886 on the Lancashire & Yorkshire Railway.

The valve gear has been criticised as mechanically unsound because it involved boring the main connecting-rod but on all but the largest locomotives it gave excellent results.

Robert F. Fairlie (1831–1885), the inventor of the Fairlie articulated locomotive, familiar on the Festiniog Railway in Wales. He patented the arrangement in 1863, either one or both bogies being powered, with either a single or double boiler. The first engine in 1865 had a double boiler with back to back fireboxes. In all a considerable range of varieties was produced under his patent.

The Festiniog Railway No. 7 Little Wonder, *the first of the narrow-gauge double Fairlies. (Festiniog Railway Company.)*

David Jones (1834–1906). The name of Jones is inseparably associated with the first 4–6–0s to run on a British railway, the famous "Jones Goods" of the Highland Railway. He was born in Manchester and at the age of thirteen began an apprenticeship under John Ramsbottom on the London & North Western Railway, first at Longsight, Manchester, and then at Crewe.

In 1855 he went to the Highland Railway and in 1870 he was appointed Locomotive Superintendent at Inverness. His first locomotive followed the traditional design established on the L.N.W.R. by Buddicom and Alexander Allan, with sloping cylinders set in outside framing. He continued with the spacious cabs provided by his predecessor William Stroudley.

While on the H.R. he acted also as Consulting Engineer for railways in Australia, South America and India and he had some influence in the design of the "L" Class 4–6–0s built in 1880 by Dübs & Company, Glasgow, for the Indus Valley State Railway.

His famous "Big Goods" 4–6–0 was clearly based on this type. The first, No. 103, appeared in 1894 (it is preserved today in the Glasgow Transport Museum) and was an immediate success. Fourteen others were built. Before he retired in 1896 he had prepared designs for a similar 4–6–0 for passenger trains. This was built by his successor, Peter Drummond, becoming the "Castle" Class. Surprisingly, although nineteen were built for the H.R., no less than fifty were built for the French State Railways in 1911.

Anatole Mallet (1837–1919) is famous as the inventor of the Mallet-type articulated engine, first patented in 1884 as a four-cylinder compound arrangement with the low-pressure cylinders on the front engine frame. It was first used in 1887 on light railways, to spread the load on light rough track. In 1890 it was introduced on European main lines and in 1904 appeared in America where it developed to its greatest extent. The Virginia Railroad 2–10–10–2 of 1918 had 48 in low-pressure cylinders, the largest ever used on a loco-motive. A triplex type, with a third unit under the tender, was also produced. These had two high-pressure and four low-pressure cylinders all of equal size. Three 2–8–8–8–2s were built for the Erie Railroad in 1914 and one 2–8–8–8–4 for the V.R. in 1916. Mallet opposed the introduction of simple expansion types, but none the less several types were built. Mallets developed into the world's biggest engines, examples being the Chesapeake & Ohio Railroad 2–6–6–6s, the Northern Pacific Railroad 2–8–8–4s and the Union Pacific Railroad 4–8–8–4 "Big Boys", all over 500 tons. The last, however, being simple expansion engines, are not true Mallets.

Thomas William Worsdell (1838–1916), the eldest son of Nathaniel Worsdell of the Liverpool & Manchester Railway, trained mainly on the London & North Western Railway at Crewe under John Ramsbottom. In 1865 he joined the staff of the Pennsylvania Railroad in the U.S.A. as Master Mechanic at the Altoona Works. However, after six years he returned to Crewe where he became Works Manager.

In February 1872 he was appointed Locomotive Superintendent of the Great Eastern Railway at Stratford, London, and while there he patented his two-cylinder compound locomotive in conjunction with A. von Borries of the Hanover State Railways, Germany.

In 1885 he became Locomotive Superintendent of the North Eastern Railway at Gateshead where many locomotives were built on his compound principle. He was succeeded by his brother Wilson in 1890 and remained as Consulting Engineer until he retired in 1893.

William Arrol (1839–1913) was born near Paisley, Scotland. At fourteen he began work with a local blacksmith and in 1863, after some years as a journeyman smith, he obtained employment with Blackmore & Gordon of Port Glasgow. By 1868 he had saved £85, half of which he spent on a boiler and engine and with which he started a small works of his own near Glasgow. Three years later this formed the nucleus of the great Dalmarnock Works.

Bridge-building was added to his work and his first contract was for bridges on the Hamilton Branch of the Caledonian Railway, including a long multi-span bridge over the Clyde at Bothwell. The C.R. then

The Forth Bridge from the top of the North Cantilever, built by William Arrol to designs by Benjamin Baker and John Fowler. The pier of Thomas Bouch's abandoned suspension-bridge project can be seen beside the back of the Inchgarvie Tower, surmounted by a lighthouse. (John Marshall.)

The Highland Railway "Jones Goods" No. 103 at Keith Junction Station—the first 4–6–0 to run in Britain. (N. Fields.)

Inverness train at Kyle of Lochalsh on the Highland Railway. (From a painting by J. D. Goffey in the collection of Colonel Rixon Bucknall.)

entrusted him with the bridge over the Clyde into Central Station, Glasgow, in 1875.

In 1873 he had undertaken construction of a railway suspension bridge over the Firth of Forth to designs by Thomas Bouch and work actually began, but it was halted after the collapse of the first Tay Bridge in 1879. His next important contract was the bridge carrying the North British Railway over the South Esk on the Montrose line. On this he gained experience which served him well when he undertook the second Tay Bridge, to designs by W. H. Barlow, begun in 1882 and completed in 1887. It is the longest railway bridge in Europe.

His greatest contract was the Forth Bridge of 1882–90, after which he was knighted by Queen Victoria.

Other great works included the steelwork for the Tower Bridge, London; the first Redheugh Bridge, Newcastle upon Tyne; three bridges over the Nile at Cairo; the Queen Alexandra Bridge, Sunderland; the Scherzer Lifting Bridge at Barrow and the second portion of the Clyde Bridge into Glasgow Central Station.

Benjamin Baker (1840–1907) was a civil engineer, born in Somerset. From 1856 to 1860 he served an apprenticeship at Neath Abbey Ironworks, South Wales and in 1860 he worked as Assistant to W. Wilson on the Grosvenor Railway Bridge and Victoria Station, London. In 1861 he joined the staff of John Fowler and was his partner from 1875 until Fowler's death in 1898.

From 1861 he was engaged on the construction of the Metropolitan and District (Inner Circle) railways, London and the extension to St. John's Wood. Later he was one of the engineers responsible for the first London "tubes", the City & South London opened in 1890 and the Central Line opened in 1900. In these Baker adopted a method suggested to him in 1875, of making the line drop out of one station and rise into the next to assist starting and stopping. In 1896 he acted as Joint Engineer with W. R. Galbraith for the Bakerloo Line.

From the early years of his career Baker had made a deep study of long-span bridges and in 1872 he evolved the cantilever system which he adapted in his design for the Forth Bridge, in Scotland, begun in 1882 and opened in 1890. For this he was knighted in 1890.

In addition, Baker was responsible for many other works in Britain, Egypt and America.

The Du Bousquet-Mallet 0–6–2–2–6–0 tank. (French Railways Limited (S.N.C.F.).)

Gaston du Bousquet (1840–1910). Famous French locomotive engineer. He worked with de Glehn on the first four-cylinder compound of 1886 and in the later 4–4–0, 4–4–2, 4–6–0 and 4–6–2 designs. From 1890 until his death he was Locomotive Engineer on the Northern Railway of France. In 1901 he introduced a class of successful 4–6–0 tandem compound tank engines on the Ceinture Railway of Paris. For the freight traffic he introduced the Du Bousquet-Mallet tank engines of 0–6–2—2–6–0 type with centrally mounted cylinders and with buffing and draw-gear mounted on a separated frame. He was working on a very advanced type of 4–6–4 express engine when he died.

Walter Mackersie Smith (1842–1906). British locomotive engineer. From 1874 to 1883 he was the first Locomotive Superintendent of the Imperial Japanese Government Railway. In 1883 he joined the North Eastern Railway under T. W. and Wilson Worsdell at Gateshead, England. In 1887 he produced his piston-valve design and in 1899 his three-cylinder compound 4–4–0 which formed the basis of the celebrated Midland Railway design of Samuel Johnson. In 1906 he produced his masterpiece, the four-cylinder compound 4–4–2.

George Westinghouse (1846–1914), American engineer, inventor of the most successful compressed-air brake widely used on railways. He began working this out in 1866, first producing the non-automatic "straight air" brake. The automatic brake (which applied itself if the train broke apart) was developed in 1872–73. Further improvements were made in 1886–87 to enable a more rapid brake application. From the beginning Westinghouse insisted on a rigorous standardisation of details so that Westinghouse fitted stock from any railways can be coupled. The Westinghouse Electric Company was formed in 1886, other works later being established in England and Europe. The principal British railways using the Westinghouse brake were the Great Eastern, the North Eastern, the North British and the Caledonian. Other companies used the vacuum-brake.

Alfred George de Glehn (1848–1936). Son of Robert von Glehn who settled in London from the Baltic provinces. When Alfred was quite young the family moved to France and changed its name to de Glehn. After training as an engineer, Alfred de Glehn became Technical Head of the Société Alsacienne at Belfort and here he was responsible for the design and construction of the first four-cylinder compound engine, the Northern Railway of France No. 701, in 1886. This engine had two low-pressure cylinders inside driving the first crank-axle, and two high-pressure cylinders outside driving the rear driving-wheels by outside cranks. The driving-wheels were not coupled.

The first four-cylinder De Glehn compound engine No. 701 of the Northern Railway of France, now preserved. (French Railways Limited (S.N.C.F.).)

In its fully developed form as an "Atlantic" the De Glehn compound became used throughout France. The Great Western Railway in England bought three of these compound "Atlantics". The De Glehn system was subsequently applied to a wide range of locomotive types. Some very large De Glehn compound "Atlantics" and "Pacifics" were built for the Bengal & Nagpur Railway in India.

A four-cylinder De Glehn compound engine "Pacific" No. 808 of the Bengal & Nagpur Railway, India. This was built by the North British Locomotive Company of Glasgow in 1929. (John Marshall.)

Wilson Worsdell (1850–1920), the son of Nathaniel Worsdell, grandson of Thomas Clarke Worsdell and younger brother of T. W. Worsdell, all mentioned earlier. He was educated at the Quaker School at Ackworth and at the age of seventeen began training at the Altoona Works of the Pennsylvania Railroad where his brother was working as Master Mechanic. In 1871 he and his brother returned to England and after some years at Crewe, Stafford and elsewhere on the London & North Western Railway he was appointed in 1883 as Assistant to Alexander McDonnell, Locomotive Superintendent of the North Eastern Railway at Gateshead.

From 1886 he assisted his brother T. W. Worsdell until 1890 when he became Locomotive Superintendent of the N.E.R., a post he held for twenty years. He was the first to introduce the 4–6–0-type engine for passenger work in England, his "S" Class in 1899. His 4–4–0 "M" Class achieved distinction in the Races to Edinburgh and Aberdeen in 1895. It was under Worsdell that the Tyneside electrification of the Newcastle upon Tyne suburban services was carried out in 1904, opening on 29th March 1904 and so achieving the distinction of being the first suburban electrification scheme in England by beating the Lancashire & Yorkshire Railway Liverpool to Southport line by one week. Most of his engines were of excellent design, mechanically and aesthetically, and gave many years of useful service. A particular feature was the large side-window cab, clearly influenced by Worsdell's experience in the U.S.A. Examples of his 0–6–0s and 0–8–0s achieved the distinction of being the last pre-Grouping engines on British railways and are still represented on the North Yorks Moors Railway near Whitby. Worsdell was outstanding in his ability to delegate responsibility to his subordinates, giving them great freedom while retaining absolute command.

Henry Alfred Ivatt (1851–1923) was born in Cambridgeshire and at seventeen was apprenticed under John Ramsbottom and later F. W. Webb at Crewe on the London & North Western Railway. After serving in various situations on the L.N.W.R. he was appointed in 1877 as District Superintendent at Cork on the Great Southern & Western Railway in Ireland. In 1882 he became Works Manager at the Inchicore Works of the railway, at Dublin, and

H. A. Ivatt. (British Rail.)

in 1886 he was made Locomotive Engineer in succession to J. A. F. Aspinall. In 1895 Ivatt was appointed Chief Locomotive Engineer on the Great Northern Railway at Doncaster, England. The first British "Atlantic", his No. 990, appeared in 1898 and was an immediate success. It was followed by twenty similar engines and in 1903 by No. 251, the first of the large-boilered "Atlantics" which introduced the wide firebox into Britain. Ivatt's other engines included 4–4–0, 4–4–2, 0–8–0 and 0–6–0 tender engines and 4–4–2, 0–6–2 and 0–8–2 tanks.

"Atlantics" Nos. 990 and 251 are preserved at York Railway Museum.

Magnus Volk (1851–1937) was born in Brighton, the son of a German clock-maker, and was builder of the first electric railway in Great Britain. In 1881 he gained a Gold Medal for a street fire-alarm system and the following year he equipped his house with the first telephone and first electric light in Brighton.

In 1883 he completed the installation of electric light in the Brighton Pavilion and at the same time built a 2 ft gauge railway along the beach making use of a Siemens dynamo and a 2 hp Crossley gas-engine. The first section of the railway opened on 4th August 1883, eight weeks before the Portrush–Giant's Causeway Tramway in Ireland.

In 1884 the line was extended and the gauge changed to 2 ft 9 in and the rebuilt line opened on 4th April 1884.

His most extraordinary venture was the Brighton & Rottingdean Seashore Electric Tramroad, with a car like a ship on long legs which ran through the sea at high water. The line was about 2·75 miles long and was opened on 28th November 1896 and ran until January 1901.

Opening of Magnus Volk's Electric Railway in Brighton, England on the 4th August 1883.

August von Borries (1852–1906) was the pioneer of locomotive compounding. He studied in Berlin. From 1875 to 1902 he was Chief Mechanical Engineer of the Prussian State Railways. His first two-cylinder compound was built in 1880 and his first four-cylinder in 1899. Among his numerous innovations in German locomotives was the use of nickel-steel for boilers in 1891. From 1902 until his death he was Professor of Transport and Machinery at the Berlin Technical School. He wrote extensively on locomotive matters.

Samuel M. Vauclain (1852–1940). American engineer, trained at the Baldwin Locomotive Works in Philadelphia from 1883. In 1889 he produced his famous compound design in which the high- and low-pressure piston-rods on both sides of the engine were connected to common crossheads, driving two cranks. Later four-crank arrangements were produced. Up to 1907 over 2,000 Vauclain compounds were built.

Richard von Helmholz (1854–1934). German locomotive engineer, from 1884 to 1917 Chief Designer at Kraus Locomotive Works, Munich. In 1884 he produced a straight-link version of the Walschaerts valve gear, and in 1888 the Kraus-Helmholz truck in which the leading carrying-wheels and coupled wheels formed a bogie, as on the Flamme 2–10–0 in Belgium. He was one of the originators of the locomotive booster, or auxiliary engine.

George Jackson Churchward (1857–1933) was possibly the greatest of British locomotive engineers. At the age of sixteen he was articled to John Wright, Locomotive Superintendent of the South Devon Railway at Newton Abbot. In 1876, when this became part of the Great Western Railway, Churchward transferred to Swindon under Joseph Armstrong. However, the following year Armstrong died and Churchward continued under William Dean. In 1895 he became Assistant Locomotive Works Manager and Manager in 1896, and soon afterwards Chief Assistant to Dean. In this position he was given freedom to experiment with new boiler designs incorporating a high Belpaire firebox which appeared on most of the later Dean engines, including the famous *City of Truro*. In 1902 Dean retired and Churchward became Chief Mechanical Engineer. He had already produced his first 4–6–0, named *William Dean*. It was the forerunner of the famous "Saint" Class and later the "Halls" and "Granges". Churchward adopted a system of standard components such as boilers, cylinders, etc., combinations of which could be worked into a wide range of different locomotive designs. He was so impressed by the work of the De Glehn compound

The De Glehn compound 4–4–2 No. 102 La France *was bought by the Great Western Railway from France in 1903. (British Rail.)*

4–4–2s in France that in 1903 he persuaded the G.W.R. to buy one of these for trials. Two more were bought in 1905. For comparison Churchward designed a four-cylinder simple 4–4–2, later rebuilt into a 4–6–0, and the forerunner of the "Stars", "Castles" and "Kings" and of his greatest engine *The Great Bear*, the first British "Pacific" of 1908. From the French engines he adopted the high pressure of 225 lb/in² and the generous bearing surfaces and from American practice the front-end arrangement with long travel-valves, the tapered boiler and cylindrical smokebox. Another innovation was his superheater at a time when the merits of superheating were still doubted on other railways. He retired at the end of 1921 but continued his close association with Swindon until, on a misty morning on 19th December 1933, he was walking across the main line when he was struck and instantly killed by the 10.30 Fishguard express.

Britain's first "Pacific", the Great Western Railway No. 111 The Great Bear *designed by G. J. Churchward in 1908. (British Rail.)*

Wilhelm Schmidt (1859–1924). German engineer, the inventor of the high-degree superheater which revolutionised steam-locomotive design. The standard fire-tube design with the elements housed in a large flue-tube was first used in Belgium in 1901. It was first used in Britain on the Lancashire & Yorkshire Railway in a series of 0–6–0s introduced at Horwich in 1906 by George Hughes.

Karl Gölsdorf (1861–1916). Austrian locomotive engineer. His father Adolf was Locomotive Engineer of the Austrian Southern Railway from 1885 to 1907. As Locomotive Engineer of the Austrian State Railways from 1893 until his death he produced over sixty designs, of great elegance and ingenuity. In 1893 he introduced the two-cylinder Austrian compound and in 1901 his first four-cylinder compound. His first ten-coupled engine appeared in 1900. He designed the first 2–6–2 (1904), 2–6–4 (1908) and 2–12–0 (1911) in Europe, the last two being entirely new, and a 0–12–0 tank for the Abt rack system in 1912. He introduced a new valve gear which dispensed with the expansion link, and is remembered particularly for his conveniently arranged footplate controls and his system of locomotive numbering which was widely used.

Herbert William Garratt (1864–1913), inventor of the Garratt articulated locomotive developed in conjunction with Beyer Peacock & Company of Manchester, England. It consisted of two engine units with the boiler mounted between them. The first was a 2 ft 6 in gauge engine built for Tasmania in 1909. South Africa became the largest user. In all some 2,000 were built.

Herbert Nigel Gresley (1876–1941) is famous as the engineer responsible for the world's fastest steam locomotive. From 1893 to 1897 he served an apprenticeship under F. W. Webb on the London & North Western Railway at Crewe, and completed his training on the Lancashire & Yorkshire Railway under J. A. F. Aspinall. In 1905 he was appointed Carriage and Wagon Superintendent on the Great Northern Railway at Doncaster, and in 1911 succeeded H. A. Ivatt as Chief Mechanical Engineer. He was the first to introduce articulated carriages in Britain, in 1907, using one bogie to

H. N. Gresley. (British Rail.)

support the ends of two coaches. His bow-ended teak carriages were among the smoothest riding ever built.

He remained in charge at Doncaster until his death, becoming Chief Mechanical Engineer of the London & North Eastern Railway at the Grouping of companies in 1923.

Most of the locomotives designed under him did good work, though some suffered from structural or mechanical defects which became prominent as maintenance standards declined during the Second World War.

His most famous achievements were the "Silver Jubilee" and "Coronation" streamlined trains in the mid 1930s. On 3rd July 1938 his "A4" Class 4–6–2 No. 4468 *Mallard* achieved a world record speed, for a steam locomotive, of 126 mile/h which has never been exceeded. It was not attained without risk, and it has never been established that no other locomotive could do better on the same stretch of line. *Mallard* is at present preserved at the Museum of British Transport, Clapham, London.

Arturo Caprotti (1882–1938). Italian engineer, designer of a locomotive valve gear employing vertical poppet-valves operated from a rotating cam-shaft as in automobile practice. It was first used on a 2–6–0 goods engine on the Italian State Railways in 1921. Its first application in Britain was on the London & North Western Railway 4–6–0 No. 5908 *Claughton* in 1926, resulting in a coal economy of 20·76 per cent.

The London, Midland & Scottish Railway Class "5" 4–6–0 No. 44686, fitted with Caprotti valve gear. (John Marshall.)

Oliver Bulleid (1882–1970) was one of the last and in many ways the most original of steam-locomotive engineers. He was born in New Zealand and after graduating at Leeds and Sheffield Universities he was apprenticed at the Doncaster Works of the Great Northern Railway. From 1912 to 1937 he worked with H. N. Gresley, making many contributions to locomotive and carriage design.

In 1937 he became the last Chief Mechanical Engineer of the Southern Railway for which he designed the extraordinary "Merchant Navy"-type "Pacific" with its numerous novel features such as chain-driven valve gear working in an oil-bath, American-type Boxpok wheels and welded boiler with steel firebox and thermic siphon. The success of this boiler greatly influenced the design of the boiler for the British Railways standard "Pacifics". Bulleid's "Pacifics" had tremendous power but poor adhesion, leakage of oil from the valve gear being the major cause of this.

The first of the "Pacifics" came out in 1940. In 1945 a lighter version, the "West Country" type, appeared for use on lines west of Exeter where weight restrictions ruled out the use of the "Merchant Navy" type.

His other locomotive design for the S.R. was a 0–6–0 of unconventional appearance, but of tremendous power. At the end of his term of office on the S.R. he worked out his most revolutionary design of all, the "Leader"-type 0–6–6–0 with six cylinders and sleeve-valves. It was produced in a hurry in a race against Nationalisation in 1948 and there was too little time to attend to the numerous snags which arose.

Following this expensive failure he went to Ireland in 1949 to become Chief Mechanical Engineer of Coras Iompair Ereann where he designed a locomotive to burn turf. It worked, but with the advent of the diesel-electric locomotive it was soon eclipsed. He retired in 1958 and died in Malta. Though a century later than George Stephenson, he was no less a pioneer.

André Chapelon (b. 1892) is one of the most famous names in the history of the steam locomotive, developing the French compound engine to a high degree of efficiency. After the First World War he joined the Paris–Lyon–Méditerranée Railway; in 1925 the Paris–Orléans Railway and in 1936 he became Chief Experimental Engineer. In co-operation with M. M. Kylala in 1926 he perfected the Kylchap double blast-pipe which gave greater freedom to the locomotive exhaust. His first "Pacific" rebuilt in 1929 and a 4–8–0 in 1932 incorporated improvements which doubled the power output.

On the formation of the Société Nationale des Chemins de fer Français (S.N.C.F.) in 1938 he was appointed to the Department of Steam Locomotive Studies of which he became Chief. He retired in 1953, but characteristically he continues to produce calculations which, could they still be applied, would result in even greater steam-locomotive efficiency.

The Chapelon-rebuilt compound "Pacific" on the Northern Railway of France.

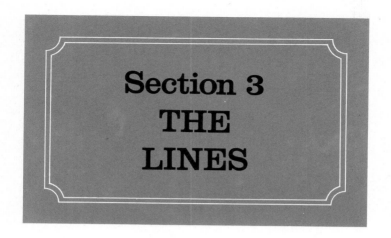

Section 3
THE
LINES

RAILWAY GAUGES
or measurement between the inner edges of the rails

Standard gauge, 4 ft 8·5 in or 1·435 m, is used in Great Britain, North America including Mexico, Europe (except Spain, Portugal, Finland and the U.S.S.R.), North Africa, the Near Eastern countries, the Australian Commonwealth and New South Wales, China and South Korea. Also some lines in Japan, Western Australia and Victoria.

Other principal gauges:
Wide gauges

5 ft 6 in (1·676 m) India, Pakistan, Ceylon, Spain, Portugal, Argentina and Chile.
5 ft 3 in (1·6 m) Ireland, South Australia, Victoria and Brazil.
5 ft 0 in (1·524 m) the U.S.S.R. and Finland.

Sub-standard gauges

3 ft 6 in (1·067 m) Queensland, South and West Australia, Tasmania, New Zealand, South Africa, Rhodesia, Malawi, Ghana, Nigeria, Sudan, Japan, Indonesia, Newfoundland and some lines in Norway and Sweden.
3 ft 5·25 in (1·05 m) Algeria, Syria, Lebanon and Jordan.
3 ft 3·375 in (1 m) Secondary lines in Switzerland, Portugal, India, Pakistan, South America and Iraq. Principal lines in Burma, Thailand (Siam), Vietnam, Malaysia, East Africa, West Africa and Cambodia.

At Crewe, England, there were three gauges at first. The Grand Junction Railway (1838) was 4 ft 8·5 in; the Crewe & Chester Railway (1840) was 4 ft 8·75 in; and the Manchester & Birmingham Railway (1842) was 4 ft 9 in.

The metre gauge holds second place in the world's route mileage. Out of about 700,000 route miles (1930) about 70,000 miles were in metre gauge. Third place is held by the 3 ft 6 in gauge, with a route mileage of 47,000.

For narrow gauges (less than 1 m) see "Narrow Gauge" in *Miscellany*.

Australia has three different gauges. Of its 25,000 miles or more, nearly half is 3 ft 6 in gauge and the remainder is almost equally divided between 4 ft 8·5 in and 5 ft 3 in.

The 5 ft 3 in gauge was the result of employing an Irish engineer, F. W. Shields; the 3 ft 6 in gauge was adopted as an economy measure. Plans to unify the system have been discussed since 1897.

I. K. Brunel adopted a gauge of 7 ft for the Great Western Railway, England (see *The Pioneers*).

Four brakes of gauge on one particular journey. (Australian News & Information Bureau.)

The last railway to be built to the 7 ft gauge was the 4·25 mile branch of the West Cornwall Railway from St. Erth to St. Ives, England, opened on 1st June 1877.

The last broad-gauge trains of the Great Western Railway ran on 20th May 1892. Gauge conversion was completed by 23rd May.

The last of the Great Western Railway broad-gauge engines awaiting scrapping at Swindon in 1892. (British Rail.)

TRACK

The first steel rails were made by Robert Forester Mushet and were laid experimentally at Derby Station on the Midland Railway early in 1857, on a heavily used line. They remained in use until June 1873.

The first steel rails on the London & North Western Railway were laid at Chalk Farm, London in 1862.

The first steel rails in Canada were used about 1875. In 1876 it was reported that there were 2,273·75 miles of steel rails in Canada, about 45 per cent of the main routes.

British Rail consumes about 2,500,000 sleepers or ties annually. Each timber sleeper measures 8 ft 6 in × 11 in × 5 in.

The number of sleepers per mile in Britain is from 2,112 to 2,464 according to loadings, foundations, curves, etc. The maximum British axle load is 25 tons, but in America where loads can be up to 34 tons per axle, 3,000–3,500 ties are used per mile.

In Britain there are about 9,000,000 pre-stressed concrete sleepers in use. They measure 8 ft 3 in long and weigh 588 lb with fastenings, compared with 237 lb for a chaired and creosoted wooden sleeper. They have an estimated life of from forty-four to fifty years, more than double that of a wooden sleeper, but are brutally heavy to handle, though mechanised handling has largely overcome this. They became popular during the wartime timber shortage.

Steel sleepers are extensively used on the continent of Europe and other parts of the world. Steel sleepers can last from forty to fifty or even eighty years.

In Switzerland 70 per cent of the Federal system and the whole of the Rhaetian and other metre-gauge systems are laid with steel sleepers. Greece, Congo Republics, systems in West, East and South Africa use steel sleepers for 90–100 per cent of the track.

In Britain steel sleepers are little used, partly because of the climate which stimulates rapid rust deterioration, although this can be minimised by resilient tar coatings or the addition of a small percentage of copper to the steel.

The standard British flat-bottomed rails (Vignoles section) measure 6·25 in high, 5·5 in wide across the foot, 2·75 in across the head and weigh 109·75 lb/yd. They are rolled in 60 ft lengths. In Germany 30 m, or 98 ft 5 in, is common. They are then welded into continuous lengths first at the depot (into 600 ft, 720 ft, 900 ft or 1,320 ft) and into greater lengths at the site.

London Transport use a 95 lb/yd "bull-head" rail in chairs, mounted on sleepers of jarrah on underground lines.

The longest stretch of unbroken four-track line in the world is 342·5 miles—between Castleton and Dunkirk, New York, U.S.A. Except for a 2 mile break at Dunkirk, the four-track line extends from Castleton to Collinwood, Cleveland—473·75 miles.

The longest continuous four-track line in Britain is on the former Midland Railway between London and Glendon North Junction, 75 miles, though the two pairs of lines separate between Souldrop Box and Irchester South Junction (about 3 miles), the freight lines passing through Sharnbrook Tunnel, 1 mile 100 yd.

Another section on the same system extends from Kilby Bridge, Wigston, to Tapton Junction, Chesterfield—53 miles.

The second longest four-track line in Britain is the 60 miles from London (Euston) to Roade, formerly the London & North Western Railway.

Other long sections of four-track line are:

London (Paddington)–Steventon, on the Great Western Railway—56·5 miles; London (Waterloo)–Battledown Junction, Basingstoke—51 miles. The former Great Northern Railway out of London (King's Cross) has more of its first 100 miles quadrupled than any other similar length in Britain, but it is broken at Welwyn, Arlesey, Huntingdon and Holme.

LONGEST STRAIGHTS

The world's longest straight stretch is on the standard-gauge Transcontinental Railway in the Commonwealth of Australia, 297 miles across the Nullarbor Plain.

A standard-gauge (4 ft 8·5 in) railway stretching for 2,461 miles across Australia to link Sydney on the coast of the Pacific Ocean with Perth on the shore of the Indian Ocean. It was completed on the 29th November 1969. (Australian News & Information Bureau.)

The Buenos Aires & Pacific Railway, Argentina, is dead straight, and almost level for 205 miles between Junin and MacKenna, on the 5 ft 6 in gauge line from Buenos Aires to Mendoza where it connects with the metre-gauge South Transandine line.

In the U.S.A. the longest straight is the 79 miles on the Seaboard Air Line Railway between Wilmington and Hamlet, North Carolina.

In Rhodesia is a 70 mile straight between Sawmills and Dett on the Bulawayo–Waukie main line.

In Russia the Moscow & St. Petersburg (Leningrad) Railway is almost straight and level for 400 miles. It was begun in 1843 and opened on 13th November 1851. It was the first Russian railway to adopt the 5 ft gauge.

In England the longest straight is 18 miles on the former North Eastern Railway Selby–Hull line (opened by the Hull & Selby Railway on 1st July 1840). Next is the 16 miles on the former Great Northern Railway Boston–Grimsby line between Boston and Burgh-le-Marsh, Lincolnshire, opened throughout on 1st October 1848.

The former South Eastern Railway between Tonbridge and Ashford, opened throughout on 1st December 1842, is nearly straight for 24 miles, but has a slight deviation at Headcorn near Staplehurst.

FLYING JUNCTION

The first "flying junction" was on the London & North Western Railway at Birdswood (later Weaver) Junction in Cheshire where the Runcorn line, opened on 1st April 1869, joined the former Grand Junction main line.

GRADIENTS

The steepest railway in the world is the Swiss funicular (cable-worked) incline between Piotta and Piora (Lake Ritom) in Canton Ticino, with a gradient of 1 in 1·125 (88 per cent). It is closely approached by the Châtelard–Barberine funicular south of Martigny, Switzerland, with a gradient of 1 in 1·15 (87 per cent). Both lines were built for transport of materials for hydro-electric schemes and were later adapted for passengers.

The world's steepest rack railway is the Pilatus Railway in Switzerland with a gradient of 1 in 2 (see "Mountain and Rack Railways" in *Miscellany*).

The steepest incline worked by adhesion is 1 in 11, between Chedde and Servoz, on the electric Chamonix line of the South-Eastern Region of the French National Railways.

The steepest adhesion incline in Great Britain was the 1 in 14 Hopton Incline on the Cromford & High Peak Railway in Derbyshire, opened in 1831 and closed in 1967. It was originally cable-worked.

Hopton Incline Top on the Cromford & High Peak Railway showing 1 in 14 on the gradient post. (John Marshall.)

The steepest gradient over which standard-gauge passenger trains were worked in Great Britain was on the Chequerbent Incline on the Kenyon–Leigh–Bolton Branch of the London & North Western Railway in Lancashire. Mining subsidence had affected the incline making a short stretch as steep as 1 in 19·5. "Officially" the gradient was 1 in 33! At this place one end of a coach was 3 ft higher than the other end.

From Middleton Junction to Oldham the branch of the Lancashire & Yorkshire Railway opened in 1844 rose for 0·75 mile at 1 in 27. Passenger services ended in 1958 and the line was closed completely on 7th January 1963.

The line was part of the original Bolton & Leigh Railway, the first railway in Lancashire, opened on 1st August 1828. Passenger services ran from 13th June 1831 to 3rd March 1952.

No. 48178 descending Chequerbeat Incline, 1 in 19·5 at the signal post. (John Marshall.)

The slightest gradient in Britain indicated on a gradient-post is 1 in 13,707 between Sturt Lane Junction and Farnborough, Hampshire, on the former London & South Western Railway.

The steepest gradient in Britain over which passenger trains work today is 1 in 27 on the Mersey Railway, on the section from the bottom of the Mersey Tunnel up to James Street Station, Liverpool.

From Middleton Junction to Oldham the branch of the Lancashire & Yorkshire Railway opened in 1844 rose for 0·75 mile at 1 in 27. Passenger services ended in 1958 and the line was closed completely on 7th January 1963.

At the summit of the 1 in 27 incline at Oldham, Lancashire, England. (John Marshall.)

In Scotland the Causewayend Incline near Manuel, about 2 miles west of Linlithgow, Stirlingshire, included 880 yd at 1 in 23. The Commonhead Incline near Airdrie, Scotland, included a short stretch of 1 in 23. Passenger trains ran until 1st May 1930 on both these lines.

On the former Brecon & Merthyr Railway, Wales, in the 7·25 miles from Talybont-on-Usk to Torpantau the line climbed 925 ft on gradients of 1 in 38–40.

The Canterbury & Whitstable Railway in Kent, opened on 3rd May 1830, included 594 yd at 1 in 28.

The self-acting inclined plane in which descending loaded wagons pull empties up was invented by M. Menzies who took out a patent in 1750.

The first use of a steam winding engine to draw wagons up an incline was about 1805.

The world's toughest and longest gradient is on the standard-gauge Central Railway of Peru. In 107 miles the line rises 15,665 ft. This gives an *average* gradient of 1 in 36 but this includes stations and reversing switches. The normal gradient is 1 in 25 with long stretches of 1 in 20 or 19. The line was begun by Henry Meiggs (see *The Pioneers*) in 1870 and completed in 1893.

On the Burma State Railways the line between Mandalay and Lashio climbs for 12 miles continuously at 1 in 25. This section includes the Gokteik Viaduct (see p. 97).

Zigzags originated on the Great Indian Peninsula Railway, but Henry Meiggs used the idea extensively on the Central Railway of Peru, which had twenty-one of them (two have now been by-passed). This view is of the Cacray Zigzag; the lower end can be seen on the right. (Brian Fawcett, M.I.L.E.)

La Cima at 15,806 ft above sea-level is not now the highest point on the Central Railway of Peru. A mine branch peeling off at this point climbs still higher to 15,848 ft, the highest point of any railway anywhere. La Cima itself is now higher than any point on any other railway as the old highest summit on the Collahuasi Branch of the F.C.A.B. in Chile has been abandoned.

THE WORLD'S HIGHEST RAILWAY SUMMITS*

Summit	Railway	Gauge	Altitude ft
La Cima, new branch	Central (Peru)	4 ft 8·5 in	15,848
Montt	Antofagasta & Bolivia	metre	15,817
La Cima	Central (Peru)	4 ft 8·5 in	15,806
Condor (Potosí Branch)	Antofagasta & Bolivia	metre	15,705
Galera Tunnel	Central (Peru)	4 ft 8·5 in	15,694
Cumbre Pass	La Paz–Yungas	metre	15,270
Caja Real	Yauricocha (Peru)	4 ft 8·5 in	15,100
Chaucha	Yauricocha (Peru)	4 ft 8·5 in	14,974
Km 41	Yauricocha (Peru)	4 ft 8·5 in	14,888
Chorrillos	Argentine Railways (North Transandine)	metre	14,682
Crucero	Southern (Peru)	4 ft 8·5 in	14,666
Yuma	Antofagasta & Bolivia	metre	14,440
Alcacocha	Cerro de Pasco (Peru)	4 ft 8·5 in	14,385
Cerro	Cerro de Pasco (Peru)	4 ft 8·5 in	14,208
La Raya	Southern (Peru)	4 ft 8·5 in	14,153
Jeneral Lagos	Arica–La Paz	metre	13,963
La Cima	Cerro de Pasco (Peru)	4 ft 8·5 in	13,822
Cuesta Colorada	Bolivian Government	metre	13,573
El Alto	Guaqui–La Paz	metre	13,471
Escoriani	Bolivian Government	metre	13,310
Between Potosí and Sucre	Bolivian Government	metre	13,231
Comanche	Arica–La Paz	metre	13,225
Kenko	Antofagasta & Bolivia	metre	13,134
Munano	Argentine Railways (North Transandine)	metre	13,120
Ascotan	Antofagasta & Bolivia	metre	12,120
Socompa	Antofagasta–Salta (Chile)	metre	12,822
San Antonio de los Cobres	Argentine Railways (North Transandine)	metre	12,379
Cachinal	Argentine Railways (North Transandine)	metre	12,264
Oruro	Antofagasta & Bolivia	metre	12,125
Tres Cruces	Argentine Railways (Ex C.N.A.)	metre	12,116
Pumahuasi	Argentine Railways (Ex C.N.A.)	metre	11,674
Incahuasi	Argentine Railways (North Transandine)	metre	11,654
Villazon	Villazon–Atocha (Bolivia)	metre	11,308
Iturbe	Argentine Railways (Ex C.N.A.)	metre	10,965
Diego de Almagro	Argentine Railways (North Transandine)	metre	10,840
La Cumbre	Chilean Transandine	metre	10,466 (rack approach)
La Cima	National Railways of Mexico	4 ft 8·5 in	10,020
El Oro	National Railways of Mexico	4 ft 8·5 in	9,977
Timboroa	East African	metre	9,131
Cachinal	Taltal (Chile)	3 ft 6 in	8,840
Nanacamilpa	National Railways of Mexico	4 ft 8·5 in	8,400
Acocotla	National Railways of Mexico	4 ft 8·5 in	8,337
Sherman	Union Pacific (U.S.A.)	4 ft 8·5 in	8,013
Cerro Summit	Denver & Rio Grande	4 ft 8·5 in	7,968
Las Vigas	National Railways of Mexico	4 ft 8·5 in	7,923
Kikuyu	East African	metre	7,857
Asmara	Eritrean	metre	7,854

* North American summits over 10,000 ft are listed under "Some American Facts and Feats" in *The Lines*.

The 2 ft 7·5 in gauge
Snowdon Mountain Railway
with trains at the summit.
(John Marshall.)

The North Eastern Railway
0–8–0 BR No. 63394
near Waskerley on the
former Stanhope & Tyne
Railway. (N. Fields.)

Summit	Railway	Gauge	Altitude ft
Addis Ababa	Franco Ethiopian	metre	7,703
Quezaltenango	Guatemala State	4 ft 8·5 in	7,650
Raton Pass	Santa Fé (U.S.A.)	4 ft 8·5 in	7,586
Ghoom	North Eastern (India) (formerly Darjeeling Himalayan Railway)	2 ft	7,407
Bernina Hospice	Rhaetian (Switzerland)	metre	7,403
Asit	Turkish State	4 ft 8·5 in	7,401
	Nilgiri (India)	metre	7,275 (rack)
Nurabad	Trans-Persian (Southern Section)	4 ft 8·5 in	7,274
Furka Tunnel	Furka-Oberalp (Switzerland)	metre	7,098 (rack approach)
Gaduk	Trans-Persian (Northern Section)	4 ft 8·5 in	6,929
Oberalp Pass	Furka-Oberalp (Switzerland)	metre	6,711 (rack approach)
Belfast	South African	3 ft 6 in	6,463
Nederhorst	South African	3 ft 6 in	6,871
Kandapola	Ceylon Government Railways	2 ft 6 in	6,316
Pattipola	Ceylon Government Railways	5 ft 6 in	6,226
Albula Tunnel	Rhaetian (Switzerland)	metre	5,981
	Beyrout–Damascus	3 ft 6 in	5,885 (rack approach)
Kolpore	Mushkaf–Bolan (North-Western Railway, Pakistan)	5 ft 6 in	5,874
Puerto de Navacerrada	Spanish National	5 ft 6 in	5,777
Johannesburg	South African	3 ft 6 in	5,735
Arosa	Rhaetian (Chur–Arosa)	metre	5,715
Mullar Tunnel	Northern Pacific (U.S.A.)	4 ft 8·5 in	5,560
Bozemar Tunnel	Northern Pacific (U.S.A.)	4 ft 8·5 in	5,560
Marandellas (near)	Rhodesia Railways	3 ft 6 in	5,538
Zermatt	Brig–Visp–Zermatt	metre	5,415
Wolfgang	Rhaetian (Switzerland)	metre	5,358
Great Divide	Canadian Pacific	4 ft 8·5 in	5,335
	Peking–Suiyuan (China)	4 ft 8·5 in	5,200
Taurus	Turkish State	4 ft 8·5 in	4,900
La Molina	Spanish National	5 ft 6 in	4,659
Kalaw	Burma State	metre	4,610
La Cañada	Spanish National	5 ft 6 in	4,526
Brenner	Austrian Federal	4 ft 8·5 in	4,496
Ben Lomond	New South Wales Government Railways (Australia)	4 ft 8·5 in	4,473
Mont Cenis Tunnel	Italian State	4 ft 8·5 in	4,284
Arlberg Tunnel	Austrian Federal	4 ft 8·5 in	4,275
Taugevatu, near Finse	Bergen–Oslo, Norwegian State	4 ft 8·5 in	4,265
Tauern Tunnel	Austrian Federal	4 ft 8·5 in	3,881
St. Gotthard Tunnel	Swiss Federal	4 ft 8·5 in	3,780
Maan	Hedjaz	3 ft 5·25 in	3,700
Pokaka	New Zealand Railways	3 ft 6 in	2,671
Waiouru	New Zealand Railways	3 ft 6 in	2,670

ALTITUDES

The highest railway in Great Britain is the summit terminus of the 2 ft 7·5 in gauge Snowdon Mountain Railway—3,540 ft.

The second highest is the summit of the 3 ft 6 in gauge Snaefell Mountain Railway, in the Isle of Man —2,034 ft. The Fell centre rail is used for braking.

Car on the Snaefell Mountain Railway approaching the summit. (John Marshall.)

The highest summit on British Rail is at Druimuachdar, 1,484 ft, between Dalnaspidal and Dalwhinnie on the former Highland Railway main line from Perth to Inverness, opened in 1863.

In 1902 a 7·25 mile branch was opened from the Caledonian Railway Glasgow–Carlisle main line, at Elvanfoot, to Wanlockhead, the highest village in Scotland, reaching a height of 1,498 ft. It closed in January 1939.

On the Great Western Railway, England, the terminus of the branch to Princetown on Dartmoor was at a height of 1,373 ft. It was closed on 5th March 1956. Stainmore Summit on the former Stockton & Darlington Kirkby Stephen line was 1,370 ft above sea-level. It was opened in 1861 and closed on 22nd January 1962.

Stainmore Summit. (John Marshall.)

Driving the last spike to join the Canadian Pacific Railway and Union Pacific Railway.

The "Western Endeavour", the first and only steam train to travel the new Australian Indian Pacific rail route from Sydney to Perth in August 1970. (Australian News & Information Bureau.)

At Weatherhill, County Durham, on the former Stanhope & Tyne Railway, later the North Eastern Railway, the rails stood at 1,378 ft. From here a private mineral branch, opened in 1846, ascended to about 1,670 ft at the top of the incline down to Rookhope. *This was the highest point reached by standard-gauge rails in Britain.* A private passenger service operated over it until about 1921.

The summit of the Rookhope Incline and ruins of Bolts Law Engine-house, the highest point reached by standard-gauge lines in Britain (about 1,670 ft). (B. Roberts.)

The lowest point on British Rail is the bottom of the Severn Tunnel, 144 ft below Ordnance Datum.

The lowest point reached by any railway in the world was Jisr el Majame near Samakh (Zemach), 700 ft below sea-level, where the 3 ft 5·25 in gauge line from Haifa in Israel to Derraa crossed the River Jordan just south of the Sea of Galilee. At Derraa it joined the Hedjaz Railway from Damascus to Medina. It was begun in 1901 and opened through to Medina on 31st August 1908. The Haifa–Derraa section is at present out of use for political reasons.

TRANSCONTINENTAL RAILWAYS

The longest railway in the world is the Trans-Siberian, from Moscow to Vladivostok—5,801 miles. It was opened in sections. By ferry across Lake Baikal and via the Chinese Eastern Railway through Manchuria, through communication was established on 3rd November 1901. In 1904 while Lake Baikal was frozen over, rails were laid across the ice, but the first locomotive plunged through a gap and was lost.

The Circum Baikal line, round the south of the lake, was opened on 25th September 1904. The 1,200 mile Amur line, opening up through travel entirely on Russian soil, was begun in 1908 and completed in 1916.

The "Trans-Siberian Express" covers the journey in 9 days 3 hours.

The first big step towards an American transcontinental railroad was taken on 21st April 1856 when trains first crossed the Mississippi between Rock Island, Illinois, and Davenport, Iowa.

On the route of the Canadian National transcontinental line through the Rockies. (Canadian National Railways.)

The first American transcontinental railroad was completed on 10th May 1869 when the last spike was driven at Promontory, north of the Great Salt Lake, Utah, uniting the Central Pacific and Union Pacific railroads. Because the point of joining had not been previously established, rival grading gangs passed one another and the U.P. gangs went on constructing 225 miles of parallel grading until they were officially stopped. They were being paid by the Government on a mileage basis. The railway ran from Omaha, Nebraska, to Sacramento, California, 1,725 miles. The old Western Pacific Railroad had been opened from Sacramento to Oakland opposite San Francisco, a further 92 miles, in 1862. Passengers crossed by ferry to San Francisco.

Through communication between the Atlantic and Pacific coasts was finally established in 1877 when the first bridge was opened across the Missouri near Omaha. The present bridge, 1,750 ft long, was built in 1886.

The Lucin Cut-off across the Great Salt Lake, totalling 103 miles, was opened on 8th March 1904 and shortened the journey between Ogden and Lucin by 42 miles, making the original Promontory route redundant. The old line, however, with its curves equivalent to eleven completed circles, was not abandoned until 1942.

A short section at Promontory was relaid in 1969 for the enactment of the centenary celebrations. For the benefit of crowds of visitors the "last spike" suffered numerous drivings and extractions.

Driving the last spike on the Canadian Pacific Railway at Craigellachie on 7th November 1885. (Canadian Pacific Rail.)

The first railway across Canada, the Canadian Pacific, was completed at a place named Craigellachie in the Eagle Pass when the Eastern and Western Sections were joined on 7th November 1885. The original contract was signed on 21st October 1880 by which year 700 miles had been already built. The C.P.R. was incorporated on 16th February 1881 and its completion within ten years was a condition of British Columbia entering the Confederation. Construction began on 2nd May 1881, and throughout 1882 2·5 miles of track were laid every day. The Prairie Section was finished on 18th August 1883 and the Great Lakes Section on 16th May 1885. The section through

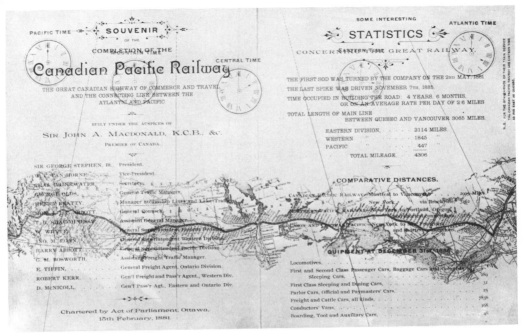

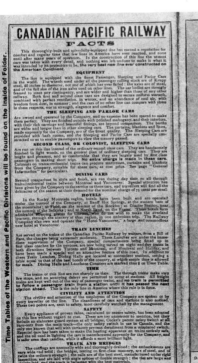

The Canadian Pacific Railway completion souvenir. (Canadian Pacific Rail.)

Facts about the Canadian Pacific Railway—Folder A. (Canadian Pacific Rail.)

*The Canadian Pacific
Railway 4–4–0 No. 371,
built in 1886, with the first
through transcontinental
scheduled train at Port
Moody, British Columbia
on 4th July 1886.
(Canadian Pacific Rail.)*

the rock and muskeg north of Lake Superior was the toughest going of the
whole route. Services between Montreal and Port Moody began on 28th
June 1886 and were extended to Vancouver in 1887. From Montreal to
Vancouver, 2,879 miles, the journey takes three days on the "Canadian"
transcontinental train.

An alternative route through the Rockies at Crow's Nest Pass,
through a rich coal region close to the border with the U.S.A. was completed in 1914. It crosses the great viaduct at Lethbridge, 314 ft high over
the Belly River, and another 147 ft high over Old Man River at Macleod.

*Climbing the "Big Hill" in
the Kicking Horse Pass on
the Canadian Pacific
Railway—on 4·1 miles of
1 in 22·25 before the spiral
tunnels were built in 1909.
(Canadian Pacific Rail.)*

Canada's other transcontinental railway, now the Canadian National, is an amalgamation of
various systems (see "Some Canadian Facts and Feats" in *The Lines*). The
Grand Trunk Pacific Railway was begun in 1905 and reached Edmonton
from Winnipeg in September 1909. The entire route was completed on
9th April 1914 at a point 374 miles east of Prince Rupert, establishing
through-rail communication between there and Sydney, Nova Scotia,

Transcontinental train on the Canadian National Railways in steam days. (Canadian National Railways.)

4,118·2 miles, the longest journey on a single railway system in the Americas and second longest in the world. The Canadian Northern Extension to Vancouver, sharing the Fraser River Canyon with the C.P.R., was completed in 1915.

In the U.S.A. there is no single railroad from coast to coast. The first through sleeping-car service between the Atlantic and Pacific coasts began on 31st March 1946. Before that a change had to be made at Chicago or St. Louis.

The principal routes with years of completion are:

From New York to Chicago; via New York Central; the Pennsylvania; the Baltimore & Ohio.

From Chicago to Seattle there are three main routes: the Great Northern completed in 1893; the Northern Pacific completed in 1888; and the Chicago, Milwaukee, St. Paul & Pacific (the "Milwaukee Road") completed in 1909—2,232 miles. From Chicago to Omaha and on to San Francisco via the Union Pacific and Central (now Southern) Pacific (1869); via the Chicago, Burlington & Quincy, the Denver & Rio Grande Western and the Western Pacific (1911). From Chicago to Los Angeles and San Francisco via the Atchison, Topeka & Santa Fé (1884); via the Chicago, Rock Island & Pacific and the Southern Pacific (1883).

Canadian National Railway at Cisco in the Fraser River Canyon. (Canadian National Railways.)

Eastbound "Atlantic Express" on the first Stoney Creek Bridge in about 1887. The timber trestle, then the world's highest, was built in 1886. It had two spans of 200 ft and one about 100 ft. It was replaced in 1893–94. (Canadian Pacific Rail.)

The first South African transcontinental railway linked Cape Town and Durban at Heidelberg in the Transvaal on 10th October 1895.

Another African transcontinental route was completed in 1928. It runs from Benguela, Angola, via the Congo and Rhodesia to Beira in Portuguese East Africa.

The first Trans-Australian Railway from Port Augusta to Kalgoorlie, 1,052 miles, all 4 ft 8·5 in gauge, was opened on 22nd October 1917. Across the Nullarbor Plain it traverses the world's longest straight stretch—297 miles long. The "Indian Pacific Express" was inaugurated on 1st March 1970 by the opening of the new standard-gauge line between Sydney, New South Wales, and Perth, Western Australia.

A Trans-Australian Railway goods train on its 2,461 mile journey from Sydney to Perth, Western Australia. As it skirts the edge of the arid and treeless Nullarbor Plain the train will run for 300 miles without bend or rise on the longest straight stretch of railway line in the world. (Australian News & Information Bureau.)

The Transandine Railway between Valparaiso, Chile, and Mendoza, Argentina, was opened on 5th April 1910. It is metre gauge with Abt triple-rack sections, and climbs to an altitude of 10,466 ft (3,191 m) at the 3,463 yd long La Cumbre Tunnel.

At Mendoza it connects with the 5 ft 6 in gauge line from Buenos Aires; total distance 900 miles.

The Transandine Railway showing Abt triple rack. (Brian Fawcett, M.I.L.E.)

The Northern Transandine Railway from Antofagasta, Chile, to Salta a distance of 562 miles, is metre gauge and was completed in 1948. It reaches 14,682 ft (4,475 m), at Chorrillos; 13,120 ft (4,000 m) at Muñana; and over 10,000 ft at four other summits. At Salta it connects with the metre-gauge main line from Buenos Aires.

TRANSALPINE RAILWAYS

The first transalpine railway was the line over the Brenner Pass, opened on 24th August 1867, between Austria and Italy. It is the only main line which crosses the Alps without a major tunnel, but its altitude of 4,496 ft (1,370 m) makes it one of the highest main lines in Europe.

North end of the 3 mile 1,134 yd long Albula Tunnel on the Rhaetian Railway, Switzerland. (John Marshall.)

The only metre-gauge transalpine route was opened on 1st July 1903 and is operated by the Rhaetian Railway in Switzerland. From Chur to St. Moritz the railway passes through the Albula Tunnel, 3 miles 1,134 yd long, at an altitude of 5,981 ft (1,823 m).

From St. Moritz to Tirano in Italy the Bernina Railway, opened on 5th July 1910, crosses the Alps in the open at an altitude of 7,403 ft (2,257 m), the highest through railway in Europe.

Spirals on the Albula Section of the metre-gauge Rhaetian Railway, Switzerland. (M. Meerkämper, Davos-Platz, Graubünden, Switzerland.)

The North end of the 8 mile 555 yd long Mont Cenis Tunnel. (La Vie du Rail, Paris.)

The first railway across the main range of the Alps was opened over the Mont Cenis Pass on 15th June 1868. It operated with the centre-rail friction-drive system invented by J. B. Fell. It worked until 18th September 1871 when the Mont Cenis Tunnel was opened. This, the first of the major Alpine tunnels, was begun on 31st August 1857 and took fourteen years to complete. It is 8 miles 555 yd long and links the Italian and French railway systems but is operated by the Italian State Railways.

The St. Gotthard Railway and Tunnel were opened to passenger trains on 1st June 1882. The tunnel, 9 miles 562 yd with double track, was begun on 13th September 1872. The engineer Louis Favre died of a heart attack inside the tunnel on 18th July 1879. The two bores met on 28th February 1880.

New northern entrance of the St. Gotthard Tunnel at the Göschenen with Schöllenenbahn on the right-hand side. The left-side tunnel was opened in 1959 for car-ferry service and joins the old tunnel about 200 yd inside. (John Marshall.)

The principal railway through the Alps from east to west is the Arlberg Railway in Austria. It was completed with the opening of the Arlberg Tunnel for double track, 6 miles 650 yd long, on 20th September 1884. It traverses a greater distance through magnificent mountain scenery than any other railway in Europe.

The east end of the Arlberg Tunnel in Austria. It is 6 miles 650 yd long and was opened on 20th September 1884. (John Marshall.)

The Simplon Railway between Switzerland and Italy was completed with the opening of the first single-line Simplon Tunnel, 12 miles 537 yd long, on 1st June 1906. The second tunnel was opened on 16th October 1922 and is 12 miles 559 yd long.

The Simplon Tunnel at Brig, Switzerland, The Bo Bo No. 11472 "Brig" leaving on goods. (John Marshall.)

The second railway between Austria and Italy was opened by the Austrian Federal Railways on 7th July 1909 after the completion of the Tauern Tunnel, 5 miles 551 yd long, under Bad Gastein.

The value of the Simplon route was greatly increased by the opening of the single-track Berne–Lötschberg–Simplon Railway on 15th July 1913. It included the double-track Lötschberg Tunnel under the Bernese Oberland Mountains, 9 miles 140 yd long. The tunnel deviates from a straight line to avoid a section where, on 24th July 1908, an inrush of water and rock caused the loss of twenty-five lives.

The Lötschberg Railway is now being doubled.

The Berne–Lötschberg– Simplon Railway 1 C C 1 No. 206 entering the Lötschberg Tunnel at Goppenstein, Switzerland. (John Marshall.)

THE LIMITS

The most northerly railway in the world is a 1·5 mile long 2 ft 11 in gauge line at King's Bay, Spitsbergen, on latitude 79° N only 750 miles from the North Pole. It connects coal-mines with the harbour, and is used in summer only. It was built in 1917 and has five German 0–4–0 tank engines. The line was closed in 1929 but was reopened in 1945.

The most northerly "main-line" railway in the world is at Pechenga in Murmansk Oblast, north-west Russia, 205 miles north of the Arctic Circle, latitude 69.33° N. The most northerly point reached is by an extension of 20 miles to a wharf at Litsnayamari, but this carries no passenger service.

At Narvik in Norway the Lapland iron-ore railway, opened in July 1903, is about 130 miles north of the Arctic Circle.

The most northerly railroad in North America is at Fairbanks, Alaska, northern terminus of the standard-gauge Alaska Railroad, 470 miles long from Seward, opened in June 1923. Fairbanks is just south of latitude 65, about 130 miles south of the Arctic Circle. **The Alaska Railroad is also the most westerly line in North America at Anchorage, on longitude 150° W.**

The furthest west in Europe reached by rail was shared by Valencia Harbour, Ireland, the terminus of the 5 ft 3 in gauge branch of the Great Southern & Western Railway from Killorglin opened on 12th September 1893, and by Dingle, the terminus of the 3 ft gauge Tralee & Dingle Railway, opened on 31st March 1891, both in County Kerry. Both are now abandoned. The honour now belongs to Cascais, about 18 miles west of Lisbon, Portugal.

Valencia Harbour in Ireland, the furthest west reached by rail in Europe. (National Library of Ireland.)

The most westerly railway in Africa is at Dakar, on the metre-gauge Senegal Railways, longitude 17.24° W. The line from Dakar via Thiès to Saint-Louis was opened in 1885. The extension from Thiès to Kayes (Mali) was begun in 1907 but not completed until 1924.

The most southerly railway in the world is at the Atlantic port of Deseado in Argentina, latitude 47.45° S, terminus of the 5 ft 6 in gauge railway from Colonia Las Heras.

Furthest south by rail in Europe is Algeciras near Gibraltar, Spain, southern terminus of the 5 ft 6 in gauge branch from Bobadilla.

The most southerly point in Asia reached by rail is Bentjulak on the island of Java, on the 3 ft 6 in gauge Indonesian State Railways, latitude 8·0° S.

The furthest east in North America is operated by the Canadian National Railways. The standard-gauge Cape Breton line to Sydney, Nova Scotia, longitude 60.11° W, was opened on 1st January 1891, and the 3 ft 6 in gauge railway to St. John's, Newfoundland, longitude 52.54° W, was opened in 1896.

Furthest east in Asia by rail is the 3 ft 6 in gauge line at Nemuro on the island of Hokkaido, Japan, longitude 145.34° E.

The limits of British Rail are:

North, at Thurso on the Highland Railway, opened on 28th July 1874.
South, at Helston on the Great Western Railway, opened on 9th May 1887.
East, at Lowestoft Central on the Great Eastern Railway, opened on 3rd May 1847.
West, the West Highland Railway between Arisaig and Morar, opened on 1st April 1901, longitude 5.53° W.

Lowestoft Central Station, Suffolk, the furthest east reached by British Rail. (British Rail.)

Thurso Station in Scotland, the furthest north reached by British Rail. (John Marshall.)

This is almost equalled by the Highland Railway branch from Dingwall to Kyle of Lochalsh, opened on 2nd November 1897, longitude 5.43° W near Kyle, and by Penzance, Great Western (West Cornwall) Railway, opened on 11th March 1852, longitude 5.33° W.

RAILWAY BRIDGES

The world's highest railway bridge is the Fades Viaduct over the Sioule River on the original Paris & Orléans Railway from Clermont-Ferrand to Montluçon, now the South-West Region of the French National Railways (S.N.C.F.).

The central span of 473 ft carries the rails at a height of 435 ft. It was completed in 1909.

Fades Viaduct in France, which is the world's highest railway bridge at 435 ft. (French Railways Limited, London.)

In Africa the Victoria Falls Bridge over the Zambezi in Rhodesia is 420 ft high, with a single steel span of 500 ft. It was designed by G. A. Hobson and was built in 1904 by the Cleveland Bridge & Engineering Company Limited, Darlington, England.

The French engineer Gustav Eiffel (1832–1923), whose tower in Paris is world famous, built the steel Garabit Viaduct on the main line from Neussargues to Béziers on the South-West Region of the S.N.C.F. It is 1,755 ft long with a central arch of 541 ft span and is 400 ft high. It was completed in 1884.

The Garabit Viaduct in France was built by Gustav Eiffel in 1884 and is 400 ft high. (French Railways Limited, London.)

The 380 ft high Viaur Viaduct in France was built in 1896–1902. (La Vie du Rail, Paris.)

The steel Viaur Viaduct at Tanus between Rodez and Albi on the South-West Region of the S.N.C.F., built in 1896–1902 by Bodin, is 380 ft high with a main cantilever span of 722 ft.

The highest railway bridge in South America is the Loa Viaduct on the metre-gauge Antofagasta & Bolivia Railway in Bolivia, it is 336 ft high and 800 ft long, at an elevation of 10,000 ft above sea-level. The railway was completed from Antofagasta, Chile, to Uyuni, Bolivia, in 1889 and to Oruro in 1893.

The highest railroad bridge in North America is the Pecos Bridge carrying the Southern Pacific Railroad 321 ft above the Pecos River a few miles above its confluence with the Rio Grande, 219 miles west of San Antonio, Texas. The original bridge, which took 103 days to build, was opened in October 1891. It replaced the earlier line, opened 5th January 1883 which ran down into

Pecos Bridge in Texas is the highest railway bridge in North America and was built in 1900. (Southern Pacific Railways.)

A Canadian Pacific Railway diesel-electric train at Ottawa on 26th June 1970. (John Marshall.)

The Canadian National Railway diesel-electric locomotives Nos. 6786 and 6787 on "Toronto Express" at Ottawa. (John Marshall.)

The westbound Canadian Pacific Railway freight leaving Red Sucker Tunnel on the north side of Lake Superior. (Canadian Pacific Rail.)

the Rio Grande gorge and across the Pecos by a low-level bridge built in 1882. The present bridge, opened in December 1944, is a continuous cantilever steel structure 1,390 ft 6 in long with seven spans, the longest being 374 ft 6 in. It carries a single line.

The Oregon Grand Trunk Railroad was carried across the Crooked River Canyon at a height of 320 ft by a single steel arch span of 340 ft.

The highest railway bridge in Canada is the Lethbridge Viaduct carrying the Southern route of the Canadian Pacific Railway over the Belly River, Alberta, at a height of 314 ft. It was opened in 1914 and is 1 mile 16 yd long with thirty-four spans on steel towers; it consumed 12,000 tons of steel and is dead straight.

The Lethbridge Viaduct over the Belly River, in Alberta is the highest railway bridge in Canada. (Canadian Pacific Rail.)

The highest railway bridge in Asia is the Faux-Mau-Ti Bridge, built in 1910, on the metre-gauge Yunnan Railway in China. It is 335 ft high with a clear span of 180 ft 6 in.

The Faux-Mau-Ti Bridge in China is 335 ft high and thus the highest railway bridge in Asia.

The Gokteik Viaduct, Burma, carries the metre-gauge Lashio line 825 ft above the River Nam Pan Hse. The tallest of the eighteen steel towers stands on a natural tunnel over the river and is 320 ft high. The viaduct was built in 1900 by the Pennsylvania Steel Company of the U.S.A., it is 2,260 ft long, consisting of sixteen spans of 40 ft, seven spans of 60 ft and ten spans of 120 ft.

On the Hellenic State Railways, Greece, the viaduct at Assopos is 330 ft high.

The highest railway bridge in New Zealand is the steel trestle Mohaka Viaduct on the Napier–Gisborne Extension in North Island—908 ft long and 318 ft high. It was built in 1936–42.

Mohaka Viaduct, New Zealand's highest railway bridge. (New Zealand Railways Publicity.)

The highest masonry bridges in Europe are both on the metre-gauge Rhaetian Railway, Switzerland. The Wiesen Bridge, built in 1908–09, crosses the Landwasser River at a height of 298 ft with a span of 180 ft. The Solis Bridge over the Albula, built in 1902, is 292 ft high.

The Solis Bridge on the Albula Section of the Rhaetian Railway in Switzerland was built 292 ft high above the Albula River. (Swiss National Tourist Office, London.)

The Wiesen Bridge over the Landwasser River in Switzerland, on the metre-gauge Rhaetian Railway, was built in 1908–09. Its height is 298 ft and the span of the main arch is 180 ft. (John Marshall.)

The highest railway bridge in Great Britain was the iron Crumlin Viaduct in Wales, built by T. W. Kennard for the Newport, Abergavenny & Hereford Railway and opened in June 1857. It was 200 ft high with a total length of 1,658 ft. It was demolished in 1965.

The Crumlin Viaduct, built in 1856–57 was the highest railway bridge in Britain. It was demolished in 1965. (John Marshall.)

The highest railway bridge in England was the Belah Viaduct in Westmorland on the South Durham & Lancashire Union line of the former Stockton & Darlington Railway. It was built by Thomas Bouch (see *The Pioneers*) in 1859 and was 1,040 ft long and 196 ft high. It was closed in 1962 and dismantled in 1963.

The Belah Viaduct in Westmorland was built in 1859 and demolished in 1963. (John Marshall.)

The world's longest concrete arch span railway bridge is the Esla Viaduct, Spain on the single-line 5 ft 6 in gauge Sierra de la Culebra Railway between Zamora and Pueblo de Sanabria near Andavias. It is 526 yd long, with a main arch over the River Esla of 645 ft span, and 275 ft 7 in high. It was opened in 1940.

*The Esla Viaduct in Spain
—the main span is 645 ft.
(Spanish National
Railways (R.E.N.F.E.).*

Next in order are: Plougastel Bridge at Brest, France, opened in 1929, with a span of 612 ft; Stockholm, Sweden, opened in 1935, with a span of 593 ft—both these carry rail and road. Lorraine Bridge over the Aare at Berne, Switzerland, with a main span of 495 ft was built in 1937–41 to replace the former lattice-girder steel spans, and carries four tracks into Berne Station.

Previously, the record was held by the Langwies Bridge on the metre-gauge Chur–Arosa Section of the Rhaetian Railway in Graubünden, Switzerland, built in 1912–13. This has a span of 315 ft and a height of 203 ft.

*Langwies Bridge on the
metre-gauge Chur–Arosa
Section of the Rhaetian
Railway in Switzerland has
a span of 315 ft and a
height of 203 ft. (John
Marshall.)*

The largest masonry arch railway bridge is the central span of Ballochmyle Viaduct over the River Ayr on the Glasgow & South Western main line from Glasgow to Carlisle, in Scotland. It was begun in March 1846 and finished in March 1848. The arch has a semicircular span of 181 ft (only 1 ft longer than Wiesen Bridge, Switzerland) and carries the line 169 ft above the river-bed. **This is now the highest railway bridge in Great Britain.**

The Ballochmyle Viaduct over the River Ayr on the Glasgow & South Western Railway was built in 1846–48.

The first railway suspension-bridge was built in 1830 to carry the Middlesborough Extension of the Stockton & Darlington Railway over the Tees. Its lack of rigidity caused its early replacement. Originally T. Hackworth had designed a plate-girder bridge, but it was an untried design and the Directors made the unwise choice of the suspension-bridge. The type has rarely been used since for railways, except for light rapid-transit systems.

The first iron railway bridge in the world carried the Stockton & Darlington Railway over the River Gaunless at West Auckland. It was built in 1825 and was replaced in 1901. It has been re-erected in York Railway Museum.

The world's first iron railway bridge, over the River Gaunless on the Stockton & Darlington Railway, was built in 1825. (British Rail.)

The earliest of the long railway bridges was the Victoria Bridge across the St. Lawrence River at Montreal. The original bridge, begun in 1854 and opened on 17th December 1859, was a single-line tubular structure designed by Robert Stephenson. It was 1 mile 1,668 yd long and carried the Grand Trunk Railway, later part of the Canadian National Railways. It had a central span of 350 ft and twenty-four other spans of 242 to 247 ft.

The smoke nuisance and increasing traffic led to its reconstruction under engineer Joseph Hobson as an open girder bridge carrying double track and two roadways on the original piers. When reopened on 13th December 1898 it was named the "Victoria Jubilee Bridge".

The Victoria Jubilee Bridge, Montreal, Canada during reconstruction on 18th August 1898, showing the new girder bridge constructed round Robert Stephenson's Tubular Bridge. The first tube has already been removed. (Canadian National Railways.)

The world's longest railroad bridge is the Huey P. Long Bridge, New Orleans, U.S.A., with a length of 4 miles 705 yd. It was opened on 16th December 1935 and belongs to the New Orleans Public Belt Railroad. It is used by the Southern Pacific, the Missouri Pacific, and the Texas & Pacific railroads and as a road. The eight river spans total 3,524 ft with a central cantilever span of 790 ft.

The Bay Bridge linking San Francisco with Oakland, California, U.S.A. viewed from the San Francisco end.

An electric inter-urban train from Oakland to
San Francisco crossing the Bay Bridge.

The Bay Bridge linking San Francisco and Oakland, California, carried electric inter-urban railway cars, as well as road traffic. It has a total length of 4 miles 533 yd but is in two portions separated by a tunnel of 180 yd through Yerba Buena Island. The West Bay Section includes two suspension spans of 2,310 ft and four of 1,160 ft. The East Bay Crossing includes a cantilever span of 1,400 ft. It was opened on 12th November 1936.

The Lower Zambezi Bridge, Mozambique, Portuguese East Africa is 2 miles 501 yd long, made up of thirty-three main spans of 262 ft 5 in, seven secondary spans of 165 ft, six approach spans of 66 ft at the east end and a steel trestle viaduct at the west. It was opened in 1934 and carries the 3 ft 6 in gauge line from Marromeu to Tete.

The longest railway bridge in Europe is the Tay Bridge in Scotland. It is 2 miles 1,093 yd long and it carries the Edinburgh–Aberdeen line across the Estuary at Dundee. The original single-line bridge designed by Thomas Bouch (see *The Pioneers*) was opened on 1st June 1878. It was badly constructed, and on 28th December 1879 the centre spans were blown down in a gale while a train was crossing. Of the seventy-eight passengers and crew there were no survivors.

The present double-track bridge, designed by W. H. Barlow and built by William Arrol, was opened on 20th June 1887.

In Denmark the Storstrøm Bridge, opened on 26th September 1937, is only 8 yd under 2 miles long and carries both road and rail.

Tay Bridge seen from the north. This is the longest railway bridge in Europe. The stumps illustrated are of Thomas Bouch's first Tay Bridge. (John Marshall.)

The longest railway bridge in Asia is the Upper Sone Bridge on the Grand Chord route between Calcutta and Delhi, India. Opened on 27th February 1900, it is 1 mile 1,591 yd long.

Also in India is the Godavari Bridge over the River Godavari between Calcutta and Madras, opened on 6th August 1900. It is 1 mile 1,272 yd long.

The Hardinge Bridge over the Ganges north of Calcutta was opened on 4th March 1915. It has fifteen steel spans of 350 ft and a length of 1 mile 207 yd between abutments. The main piers are carried down to a depth of 160 ft below the lowest water-level and were the deepest foundations of their kind in the world. It consumed more than 38,860,000 ft^3 of masonry and 1,700,000 rivets. The engineer was R. R. Gales.

It carried the main line northwards from Calcutta to Siliguri at the foot of the Himalayas.

Other long Indian railway bridges are the Mahanadi Bridge on the South Eastern Railway, opened on 11th March 1900—1 mile 544 yd long; and the Izat Bridge over the Ganges at Allerhabad on the North Eastern Railway—1 mile 367 yd long, with forty spans of 150 ft.

The longest bridge in China is the Hwang-Ho or Yellow River Bridge, of 102 spans, opened in November 1905, on the Peking & Hankow Railway.

Other long bridges in China are the Great Bridge, 1 mile 99 yd long, opened in 1957, and the Nanking–Pukow Bridge, 1,749 yd long, opened on 1st October 1969. Both carry a double-track railway with a road above.

The greatest of all railway bridges, and the oldest railway cantilever bridge is the Forth Bridge, Scotland, opened on 4th March 1890. It was designed by John Fowler and Benjamin Baker and built by William Arrol. The three cantilever towers are 361 ft high and the double-line railway is carried 156 ft above high water. The two main spans are 1,710 ft and the total length of the bridge is 1 mile 1,005 yd.

Forth Bridge viewed from the south-east. (John Marshall.)

The world's first successful railway suspension-bridge was built across the Niagara Gorge below the Falls by Charles Ellet in 1848. In 1855 it was strengthened by John A. Roebling and an upper deck added to carry a railway, to connect the Great Western of Canada with the American lines. It was 821 ft 4 in between the towers, and carried a double-track railway on the upper deck and a road beneath. After forty years use it was replaced by a steel arch bridge in 1897.

The world's largest railroad suspension-bridge is the Delaware River Bridge connecting Philadelphia and Camden, New Jersey, U.S.A., opened on 1st July 1926. The total length is 1 mile 1,107 yd; the main structure measures 3,536 ft and the central span 1,750 ft. Besides a roadway it carries the rapid-transit trains of the Philadelphia elevated and underground railways.

New York has more large bridges than any other city. Its railroad bridges include:
Queensboro Bridge opened in 1909, 1 mile 723 yd long with a main cantilever structure 3,725 ft long and a channel span of 1,182 ft. It carries only light rapid-transit electric cars, not main-line stock.

Queensboro Bridge, New York, U.S.A., opened in 1909. (A. Barlow.)

Williamsburg Bridge, a suspension-bridge, opened on 19th December 1903 with a channel span of 1,600 ft, two side spans of 596 ft and a total length of 1 mile 676 yd. It has two decks.

Brooklyn Bridge, also a suspension-bridge, opened on 24th May 1883. It has an over-all length of 1 mile 419 yd, its main structure is 3,470 ft long, it has a channel span of 1,595 ft and two side spans of 930 ft. The New York approach is 1,563 ft and the Brooklyn approach 971 ft.

Brooklyn Bridge, looking towards New York from Brooklyn in 1894. (M. Cohn.)

Hell Gate Bridge, New York, U.S.A., opened in 1917. (A. Barlow.)

The Hell Gate Bridge opened in 1917 is a steel arch structure with a main span of 977 ft over the East River and with long approach viaducts at each end. It is the longest span steel arch railway bridge in the U.S.A.

The largest steel arch span in the world is the Sydney Harbour Bridge in Australia, with a main span of 1,650 ft. It was opened on 19th March 1932 and carries four tracks, a 57 ft road and two 10 ft footways at a height of 170 ft. Its total length is 3,770 ft.

Sydney Harbour Bridge, Australia, opened on 19th March 1932. (Australian News & Information Bureau.)

The world's largest cantilever span is the Quebec Bridge over the St. Lawrence River, Canada, opened on 3rd December 1917, by the Canadian National Railways. The total length of 3,238 ft includes a main span of 1,800 ft and shore spans of 562 ft 6 in. The central suspended span of 675 ft is the second one to be built. The first collapsed, causing the loss of ten lives while being hoisted into position on 11th September 1916 and now lies at the bottom of the river.

The first attempt by the Phoenix Bridge Company of Pennsylvania to erect a bridge here ended in disaster on 29th August 1907 when the south cantilever collapsed, killing seventy-five of the eighty-six men working on it.

Quebec Bridge, Canada, opened 3rd December 1917. (Canadian National Railways.)

Arthur Kill vertical-lift bridge in New York, U.S.A. The span of 558 ft is the longest of its kind in the world. (A. Barlow.)

The longest railroad vertical-lift bridge span carries the Baltimore & Ohio Railroad connection to the Staten Island Rapid Transit across Arthur Kill, New York. It was opened on 25th August 1959 and replaces the earlier swing-bridge. The centre span, 558 ft long, is suspended from two 215 ft steel towers. It can be raised to its maximum height of 135 ft, or lowered to its closed position 31 ft above the water, in two minutes. The second longest carries the New York, New Haven & Hartford Railroad across the Cape Cod Canal, Massachusetts. It was built in 1933–35. The 544 ft span can be raised from 7 ft to 135 ft in two and a half minutes.

Britain's longest viaduct is the original London & Greenwich Railway, the first railway in London. It is 3·75 miles long and consists of 878 brick arches. It was designed by Lieutenant-Colonel G. T. Landmann (later Engineer of the Preston & Wyre Railway) and was opened in December 1836, first to an intermediate station at Deptford on 14th December.

The Harringworth Viaduct in Rutland was opened in 1880. (British Rail.)

The longest masonry viaduct across a valley in Britain is the Harringworth Viaduct in Rutland on the former Midland Railway. It is 1,275 yd long with eighty-two brick arches of 40 ft span and a maximum height of 60 ft. It was opened in 1880.

The earliest and largest "elastic arch" railway bridge in Britain is at West Wylam on the North Wylam Branch of the North Eastern Railway, Northumberland. It was designed by William George Laws on the principle of Leather's bridge over the Aire at Leeds, and has a span of 245 ft. It was built by the Scotswood, Newburn & Wylam Railway and was opened in October 1876, becoming part of the North Eastern system in 1880. It was the "father" of the arch bridges at Newcastle upon Tyne, Sydney, the Hell Gate in New York, and others.

The wrought-iron arch bridge over the Tyne at West Wylam has a span of 245 ft and was built in 1876. (John Marshall.)

Britain's second largest railway cantilever-bridge, and the only other besides the Forth Bridge, is across the entrance to Loch Etive, Scotland. It was designed by Sir John Wolfe Barry and erected by Sir William Arrol and opened on 21st August 1903. It carried the Ballachulish Branch of the Caledonian Railway and a road. The main span is 524 ft and the total length of the 2,600 tons of steelwork is 735 ft. The railway was closed on 28th March 1966 and the bridge is now used only by road traffic.

Cantilever-bridge carrying the Ballachulish Branch of the Caledonian Railway over Loch Etive at Connel Ferry. (John Marshall.)

The Solway Viaduct was designed by James Brunlees (see *The Pioneers*) and was begun in March 1865 and completed in July 1868. It was part of the Solway Junction Railway between Dumfriesshire in Scotland and Cumberland in England, opened on 1st September 1869 for freight and on 8th July 1870 for passengers. Until the Tay Bridge was built it was the longest railway bridge in Europe —5,790 ft long. The rails were 34 ft above the bed of the Solway. In January 1881 forty-five piers were demolished by ice-floes causing thirty-seven spans to fall. The bridge was reopened on 1st May 1884. The last train crossed on 21st August 1921 and the viaduct was dismantled in 1934–35 after a period during which Scottish drinkers used it as a footpath to English pubs on Sundays.

The Solway Viaduct from the north side. It was designed by James Brunlees and built from March 1865 to July 1868. Its length between the abutments was 5,790 ft, and the maximum height above the river-bed was 34 ft. It was last used on 21st August 1921 and dismantled in 1934–35. (Cumberland News, Carlisle.)

The Severn Bridge on the Severn & Wye Railway (Great Western and Midland Joint railways) between Lydney and Sharpness in Gloucestershire, England, was 4,162 ft long, with twenty-one iron spans of which two were 327 ft long, and 39 ft deep. At the south end a swing span of 197 ft crossed the Gloucester & Berkeley Canal. It was opened on 17th October 1879 and remained in use until a barge collided with a pier in fog and demolished two spans on 25th October 1960. The bridge was subsequently dismantled.

The 4,162 ft long Severn Bridge near Lydney, Gloucestershire, on the Severn & Wye Railway (Great Western & Midland Joint railways) from the south end showing the 197 ft swing span over the Gloucester & Berkeley Canal. It was opened on 17th October 1879 and closed after a barge collided with a pier on 25 October 1960. The bridge was subsequently dismantled. (British Rail.)

SOME AMERICAN BRIDGE RECORDS

The world's highest "railroad over-bridge", and also the world's highest bridge, is the suspension-bridge over the Royal Gorge near Cañon City, Colorado. It was opened on 8th December 1929 and had a span of 880 ft and was 18 ft wide, at a height of 1,053 ft above the Arkansas River. Through the gorge, beside the river, runs the old main line of the Denver & Rio Grande Western Railroad, opened in 1880 with 3 ft gauge. Standard gauge was laid in 1890.

Royal Gorge, Colorado, on the Denver & Rio Grande Western Railroad. The train is passing beneath the world's highest bridge.

The largest railroad cantilever-bridges in the U.S.A.

Bridge	Location	Main span	Year
Richmond	San Francisco Bay	(2) 1,070 ft	1957
Baton Rouge	Mississippi	848 ft	1940
Cornwall	St. Lawrence	843 ft	1899
Vicksburg	Mississippi	825 ft	1930
Huey P. Long	New Orleans	790 ft	1935
Memphis (Harahan)	Mississippi	790 ft	1916
Memphis	Mississippi	790 ft	1892

America's longest draw-bridge span of 525 ft forms part of the Atchison, Topeka & Santa Fé Railroad bridge over the Mississippi at Iowa, Illinois, opened in 1926.

The longest swing spans on American railroads are at Fort Madison over the Mississippi of 525 ft, completed in 1927; the Willamette River Bridge at Portland, Oregon of 521 ft, completed in 1908; and the East Omaha Bridge over the Missouri of 519 ft, completed in 1903.

The longest simple-truss span on American railroads is the 720 ft of the Chicago, Burlington & Quincy Railroad Metropolis Bridge over the Ohio River, opened in 1917. The truss is 110 ft deep.

The Metropolis Bridge over the Ohio River on the Paducah & Illinois Railroad, U.S.A. operated by the Chicago, Burlington & Quincy Railroad. It is the longest simple-truss span in the world.

The longest continuous-truss railroad-bridge span in the U.S.A. is the 775 ft of the Sciotville Bridge, also over the Ohio River, opened in 1918.

TUNNELS

The world's first railway tunnel was an underground line at Newcastle upon Tyne, England, built in 1770 (see "Underground Railways" in *Miscellany*).

Chapel Milton Tunnel on the Peak Forest Tramway, Derbyshire, England, was opened on 1st May 1800. This was a plateway with L-section rails. At Ashby de la Zouch, Leicestershire, England, a tunnel 308 yd long was built for the Ticknall Tramway (also using L-section rails) in 1800–05. It was enlarged by the Midland Railway for the Ashby–Melbourne Branch opened on 1st January 1874. Passenger trains ran until 22nd September 1930. Hay Hill (or Haie Hill) Tunnel on the Forest of Dean Tramroad, Gloucestershire, England, was opened in September 1809 and was 1,064 yd long. In 1854 it was enlarged by Brunel to accommodate the 7 ft gauge Forest of Dean Branch from the South Wales Railway to Cinderford. It was converted to standard gauge in 1872 and was closed on 1st August 1967.

Talyllyn Tunnel on the Brecon & Hay Railway in Breconshire, Wales, was opened on 7th May 1816 and was 674 yd long. In 1860 it became part of the Brecon & Merthyr Railway and was enlarged in 1862. It was closed on 2nd May 1964.

The first railway tunnel to be used for passenger traffic was the Tyler Hill Tunnel on the Canterbury & Whitstable Railway opened on 4th May 1830. It was 828 yd long. Passenger traffic ended on 1st January 1931 and the line closed completely on 1st December 1952.

The second was the Glenfield Tunnel on the Leicester & Swannington Railway opened on 17th July 1832. It was 1,746 yd long. Passenger trains ran until 24th September 1928 and the tunnel was closed completely on the 4 April 1966.

The first underwater railway tunnel was the Thames Tunnel on the East London Railway. The two parallel bores were built by Marc Brunel, begun in 1825 and opened on 25th March 1843 for pedestrian traffic. They were incorporated in the E.L.R., opened on 7th December 1869. As on the Severn Tunnel later, the Engineer was Sir John Hawkshaw. The railway now forms part of the London Transport system.

The longest underwater tunnel in the world is the Severn Tunnel built by the Great Western Railway between England and Wales and opened on 1st September 1886, after fourteen years' work. It is 4 miles 628 yd long. The Engineer was Sir John Hawkshaw.

The Severn Tunnel seen from the English end. (British Rail.)

The longest underwater tunnel in America is the Bay Area Rapid Transit (BART) Trans Bay Tube carrying rapid-transit trains beneath San Francisco Bay at San Francisco, which is 3·6 miles long. The railway is still under construction. The 2,009 yd St. Clare Tunnel, linking Canada and the U.S.A. under the St. Clare River between Sarnia and Port Huron was opened on 27th October 1891 for freight and on 7th December for passengers. It cost $2,700,000. In 1908 it was electrified with single-phase a.c. 3,300 V 25 c/s. The tunnel became part of the Canadian National system in 1958 and with the coming of the diesels the electrification was dismantled.

The Channel Tunnel between England and France first came into prominence in 1874 when the South Eastern Railway (England) obtained Parliamentary powers to sink experimental shafts and in 1881 to acquire lands between Dover and Folkestone. The Submarine Continental Railway Company Limited, incorporated on 12th December 1881, took over the S.E.R. works, and drove a pilot tunnel about 2,100 yd out under the sea. The Chief Engineer was Sir John Hawkshaw. Work was suspended in 1883, largely for military reasons. In 1875 a Channel Tunnel company and a French submarine railway company obtained powers and the latter drove a 1·5 mile gallery under the sea from Sangatte. In 1886 the English company was absorbed by the Submarine Continental Company and in 1887 the name became the "Channel Tunnel Company". The original S.E.R. interests are now held by the British Railways Board.

In Japan the Seikan undersea railway tunnel, under construction, will be 30–35 miles long and will pass 330 ft below the ocean-bed in badly faulted granite containing water-filled seams of broken rock. It will connect Yoshioka on the island of Hokkaido with Miumaya on Honshu. Work began in 1964 on shafts and pilot tunnels. It is hoped to complete it by 1980. The rails in the centre will be about 788 ft (240 m) below sea-level.

The highest railway tunnel in the world is the Galera Tunnel on the Central Railway of Peru, opened in 1893. It is 1,287 yd long at an altitude of 15,688 ft.

The east portal of the Galera Tunnel, under the Continental Divide at Galera Station on the Central Railway of Peru. This is the highest tunnel in the world, its peak being 15,688 ft above sea-level. Its length is 3,860 ft and it has a maximum grade of 4 per cent. (Brian Fawcett, M.I.L.E.)

The highest tunnel in Britain was at Torpantau on the Brecon & Merthyr Railway in Wales which was 666 yd long. The west portal was 1,313 ft above sea-level, and it was opened on 1st May 1863 and closed on 2nd May 1964.

The world's longest continuous railway tunnel is on the London Underground railway system, from East Finchley to Morden via The Bank—17 miles 528 yd. There are, however, twenty-four stations and three junctions in the tunnel.

The longest ordinary railway tunnel is the 12 mile 559 yd long Simplon Tunnel, between Switzerland and Italy (see "Transalpine Railways", page 90).

The longest double-track railway tunnel is the Apennine Tunnel in Italy on the Diretissima line from Florence to Bologna. It was opened on 22nd April 1934 and is 11 miles 892 yd long.

The eleven Asian tunnels over 3 miles long are all in Japan. The longest are the:

Hokuriku, 8 miles 1,089 yd, opened on 10th June 1962.

Shin-Shimizu, 8 miles 684 yd, opened in 1961.

Kubiki, 7 miles 10 yd, opened in 1970.

Shimizu, 6 miles 50 yd, opened on 1st September 1931.

New Tanna, 4 miles 1,663 yd, opened on 1st October 1964.

Old Tanna, 4 miles 1,493 yd, opened on 1st December 1934.

Five other Japanese tunnels are over 3 miles long.

The longest tunnel in North America is the 7 miles 1,387 yd long Cascade Tunnel (see "American Tunnels", page 118).

The longest tunnel in France is the Somport Tunnel, actually between France and Spain. It is 4 miles 1,572 yd long and was opened on 18th July 1928. It carries a single line and is operated by the French National Railways (S.N.C.F.).

The Somport Tunnel,
between France and Spain.
*(*La Vie du Rail, *Paris.)*

The longest railway tunnel in Russia is the Suran Tunnel, nearly 2·5 miles long, on the Poti–Baku line in the Caucasus.

Norway has the three longest tunnels in northern Europe. These are the:

Kvineshei Tunnel of 5 miles 1,112 yd.

Haegebeostad Tunnel of 5 miles 467 yd.

Gyland Tunnel of 3 miles 972 yd.

All these were opened under the German Occupation, on 17th December 1943. Full traffic began on 1st March 1944.

The Ulrikken Tunnel of 4 miles 1,338 yd, was opened on 1st August 1964 to improve the route from Bergen to Oslo.

Top: The Norwegian State Railways loading buses at Finneid, north of the Arctic Circle, to be taken by rail to Sulitjelma, because there is no road between the two places. (N. Fields.)

Above: The Railway Museum at Hamar in Norway showing the first locomotive in Norway, the Neilson 2–4–0 engine No. 16. (N. Fields.)

Left: The North British Railway "Glen" Class 4–4–0 No. 256 Glen Douglas at Garelochhead on the West Highland Railway. (N. Fields.)

The longest tunnel in the Southern Hemisphere is the single-track Rimutaka Tunnel in South Island, New Zealand, on the railway from Wellington to Masterton. It was opened on 3rd November 1955 and is 5 miles 821 yd long. It was built to replace the line over the Rimutaka Ranges involving the famous Fell Incline of 3 miles at 1 in 14–16.

The Otira Tunnel in North Island, New Zealand, between Christchurch and Greymouth, is 5 miles 564 yd long and was opened on 4th August 1923. It is electrically worked, at 1,500 V d.c. A new 5·5 mile long tunnel through the Kaimai Hills in North Island is being constructed as part of a new line between Tauranga and Rotorua.

The Rimutaka Tunnel—official train emerging from eastern portal during the opening ceremony in 1955. (New Zealand Railways Publicity.)

The Otira Tunnel, with the 1,285 hp "Ea" Class Bo Bo electric locomotive emerging from the Otira portal. (New Zealand Railways Publicity.)

The record for the most "be-tunnelled" train in Great Britain was held in 1946 by the 10.00 London (St. Pancras) to Glasgow (St. Enoch) via Nottingham, Derby, Sheffield and Leeds. In all it passed through forty tunnels totalling about 15 miles.

The total number of tunnels in Great Britain was 1,049 in 1938. By then several lines had been abandoned and the total could have been about 1,060. The total includes "long bridges" classed as tunnels.

The railway with the greatest number of tunnels is the Sierra de la Culebra Railway, Spain. Between Puebla de Sanabria and Carballino, a distance of 107·5 miles, there are 182 tunnels amounting to 48·5 miles, the longest being the 3 mile 1,226 yd Padornelo Tunnel, opened in 1957–59.

It is closely followed by the Bergen–Oslo line in Norway with 178 tunnels in a distance of 305·75 miles amounting to 22·5 miles. It was opened on 1st December 1909.

SOME AMERICAN FACTS AND FEATS

Gauges

Over one hundred years ago, in 1871, there were nineteen different gauges in use in the U.S.A., ranging from 3 ft to 6 ft. Subsequently many 2 ft gauge lines were built.

Between 1867 and 1871 it was possible to travel from New York to St. Louis on 6 ft gauge tracks via the present Erie route to Dayton, Ohio, and the present Baltimore & Ohio through Cincinnati to St. Louis. In 1868 the Missouri Pacific Railroad was converted from 5 ft 6 in to standard, and in 1871 the Ohio & Mississippi (now the Baltimore & Ohio) Railroad from 6 ft to standard. These influenced other conversions, and so by 1887 nearly every important railroad in the U.S.A. was operating on standard gauge, the most outstanding exception being the Denver & Rio Grande Western Railroad which in 1888 operated a maximum of 1,673 miles of 3 ft gauge.

U.S. railroad mileages		Great Britain
Year	Miles	Miles
1830	23	
1840	2,818	1,484
1850	9,021	6,084
1860	30,626	9,069
1870	52,922	13,563
1880	93,267	15,557
1890	163,605	17,274
1900	140,313	18,665
1910	143,366	19,979
1916	254,000 (peak)	
1920	252,865	20,326
1930	249,619	20,445
1940	234,182	20,227
1950	224,331	19,790
1960	217,551	18,771
1970	209,001	11,799

In 1920 American railroads employed over 2,000,000 persons. In 1960 793,071 employees earned $4,956,902,360; in 1969 589,626 earned $5,450,830,724. However, since 1916 the U.S.A. has abandoned more than 50,000 miles of railroad. This is nearly 2·5 times the maximum railway mileage in Great Britain.

The longest continuous curve in the U.S.A. is probably the Pontchartrain Curve between Ruddock and Tunity in Louisiana on the Illinois Central Railroad, skirting the western shore of Lake Pontchartrain. It is 9·45 miles long with only slight changes of radius.

The Southern Railway shortly before entering New Orleans skirts the same lake on a curve nearly 9 miles long.

The longest uniform curve is on the Texas & Pacific Railroad between Alexandria and Cheneyville, also in Louisiana. It has a radius of 6·5 miles throughout its 5·7 miles.

AMERICAN SUMMITS

The highest adhesion-worked standard-gauge line was the Denver & Salt Lake Railroad or "Moffat Road" over Rollins or Corona Pass, at an altitude of 11,600 ft. It was opened in 1907 and used until the Moffat Tunnel was completed in 1928. It is now a road.

The record was then held by the branch of the Denver & Rio Grande Western Railroad from Leadville up to Ibex, Colorado, at an altitude of 11,522 ft. This closed in 1944.

The highest standard-gauge summit still in use on a through line is the 10,239 ft at Tennessee Pass north of Leadville, Colorado, on the Denver & Rio Grande Western Railroad.

The highest narrow-gauge summit in North America was on the Denver South Park & Pacific (later the Colorado & Southern) line, a subsidiary of the Chicago, Burlington & Quincy Railroad. This 3 ft gauge line reached 11,940 ft at the Alpine Tunnel on the Como–Gunnison Section, and 11,330 ft on the Fremont Pass north of Leadville. This line was opened in February 1844 and closed in 1937. A standard-gauge line from Leadville to Climax—11,319 ft—was laid in 1943. The 600 yd long Alpine Tunnel was built in 1881 and closed in 1917.

The remaining summits over 10,000 ft were on 3 ft gauge lines:
Marshall Pass, Colorado on the Denver & Rio Grande Western Railroad through Gunnison—10,856 ft;
Lizard Head Peak, Wyoming on the Rio Grande Southern Railroad—10,248 ft;
Colorado & Southern Leadville line—10,207 ft;
Monarch, Colorado on the Denver & Rio Grande Western Railroad—10,028 ft (now standard gauge);
Cumbres Pass, on the Denver & Rio Grande Western Railroad—10,015 ft.

AMERICAN TUNNELS

On its 254,000 miles of railroad, America had 1,539 tunnels, with a total length of 320 miles. This total number was only 50 per cent more than the total on 20,445 miles in Great Britain in 1930.

Part of a spectacular series of zigzags, which took the Great Northern Railway over the Cascade Mountains, U.S.A. between 1892 and 1900 while the first Cascade Tunnel was being built.

The longest tunnel in the U.S.A. is the Cascade Tunnel on the Great Northern (now Burlington Northern) main line from Spokane to Seattle in Washington State. It is 7 miles 1,387 yd long. It was opened on 12th January 1929 and replaced an earlier line which climbed to a summit tunnel 2·63 miles long. While this was being built trains crossed the summit on a spectacular series of zigzags in a line 12·25 miles long opened in 1892 and used until the tunnel was finished in 1900.

The second longest tunnel in the U.S.A. is the Flathead Tunnel in north-west Montana, also on the Great Northern, completed in October 1970. It is 10 ft over 7 miles long (36,970 ft), 18 ft wide and 23 ft 6 in high above rail-level, and is on a new 59·5 mile diversion necessitated by the Federal Government's Libby Dam project, which flooded much of the former main line. The east portal is closed by a door after the passage of a train, and two 103 in diameter fans clear the fumes from the tunnel in seventeen minutes.

The third longest tunnel is the Moffat Tunnel, 6 miles 373 yd under James Peak, Colorado, on the Denver & Salt Lake Railroad, the "Moffat Road". It was opened on 27th February 1928, at an altitude of 9,257 ft, and replaced the original line over Rollins or Corona Pass at an altitude of 11,600 ft. Moffat is a national tunnel, built with Government assistance, but it is operated by the Denver & Rio Grande Western Railroad.

With the Dotsero cut-off it shortened the route from Denver to Salt Lake City by 173 miles.

The most difficult tunnel in America was the Boston & Maine Railroad Hoosac Tunnel in Massachusetts, on the main line from Boston to Albany. It was begun in 1851 and took fourteen years to complete. It was opened on 9th February 1865. It is 4 miles 1,230 yd long and was electrified in 1911.

AMERICAN BRIDGES

The oldest stone viaduct in the U.S.A. is the Thomas Viaduct of eight arches carrying the Washington Branch of the Baltimore & Ohio Railroad across the Patapsco River. It was designed by Benjamin H. Latrobe and built in 1835, and is still in use.

The first iron tubular bridge in the U.S.A. was built in 1847 at Bolton, Maryland, on the Baltimore & Ohio Railroad.

The first iron truss-bridge was also built in 1847 near Pittsfield, Massachusetts, on the Boston & Albany Railroad.

The first all-steel bridge was opened in 1879 at Glasgow, Missouri, on the Chicago & Alton Railroad. It was 2,700 ft long.

The world's longest continuous railway bridge was the Great Salt Lake trestle-bridge on the Lucin Cut-off opened on 8th March 1904 and originally 22·94 miles long. Part of the viaduct was later filled in to form an embankment leaving 11·87 miles of trestle. This has since been replaced by embankment.

A railway which went out to sea was the 128 mile long Key West Extension, Florida. It was built by Henry Morrison Flagler (1830–1913), was begun in 1905, partly wrecked in a 125 mile/h hurricane in 1909, and was opened to Key West

View of the Long Key Viaduct and of the first passenger train to make the trip to Knights Key. The Viaduct is 2·7 miles long, built of reinforced concrete and the rails are 31 ft above mean high water. (South Florida Rail Sales, U.S.A.)

on 22nd January 1912. Between the mainland and Key West there were 17·25 miles of bridges and 20 miles of embankment through shallow water. The remainder was on the "keys". The longest bridge was the 7 mile long steel girder Little Duck Viaduct. The railway was closed after being damaged by a hurricane on 2nd September 1935 and has been replaced by a road. The rail journey took three and three-quarter hours.

The total number of bridges on American railroads in 1937 was 191,779 totalling 3,860 miles in a total mileage of 235,000.

SOME CANADIAN FACTS AND FEATS

At the time of the union of the Canadian Provinces on 1st July 1867 Canada had fifteen railways with some 2,495 miles of route, employing 9,391 persons. There were 485 locomotives, 310 First Class and 374 Second Class cars—which carried a total of 2,920,000 passengers in the year—and 4,214 freight cars which carried 2,260,000 tons.

Prince Edward Island entered the Confederation in 1873 while its railway system was under construction. The 210 miles of line were taken over by the Federal Government and opened for traffic in April 1875.

In 1882 the Grand Trunk and the Great Western railways which had 904 miles of track were amalgamated together with another 473 miles of line in Western Ontario.

Twenty years after Confederation, in 1887, Canadian railway mileage was 11,691 of which the Canadian Pacific system owned 4,174 miles and the Grand Trunk system 2,598 miles. There were 1,633 locomotives, 74 sleeping and parlour cars and 762 First Class and 514 Second Class cars. By 1888 some main-line cars were electrically lit.

The first train over the Sault Ste Marie Bridge entered Canada on 9th January 1888. The St. Lawrence was bridged at Lachine also in 1887 and at Coteau in 1890.

The first railway in Newfoundland from St. John's to Hall's Bay, was begun on 9th August 1881, against much local opposition and violence. The 547 miles of 3 ft 6 in gauge line, from St. John's to Port aux Basques, were completed in 1896.

The Newfie Bullet *on the Newfoundland 3 ft 6 in gauge main line. (Canadian National Railways.)*

The first iron railway bridge in Nova Scotia was built in 1877 to replace the timber bridge at Elmsdale. It was decided at the same time to replace all Canadian wooden bridges by iron.

By the end of the nineteenth century Canadian railway mileage had grown to 17,481 of which the Canadian Pacific Railway had 6,873 miles, the Grand Trunk Railway 3,138 miles and the Intercolonial Railway 1,511 miles.

One of the loneliest railways in Canada, the Temiskaming & Northern Ontario Railway, was completed to Moosonee on an estuary of James Bay in 1931.

The Canadian Northern and the Grand Trunk Pacific railways were completed in 1915 by which year Canada had three transcontinental routes. The C.N.R. ran from Quebec to Vancouver and the G.T.P.R., including the National Transcontinental Railway, extended from St. John, New Brunswick, to Prince Rupert, British Columbia.

The Canadian mileage was now 35,582, more than double that in 1900. In addition the Canadian Pacific Railway and the Grand Trunk Railway owned extensive mileage in the U.S.A.

The Canadian National Railways was formed in 1917, to acquire the Canadian Northern Railway. The Grand Trunk Pacific Railway was acquired in 1919 and the Grand Trunk Railway in 1921. In 1923, under an Order in Council, the control of all Government railways including the Grand Trunk and the Intercolonial railways passed to the Canadian National Railways, under a president and board of directors appointed by the Government.

In 1923 the C.N.R. had 20,573 miles of track, and the Canadian Pacific Railway 13,563, making them among the world's largest railway systems.

Newfoundland entered the Confederation in 1949 when its 705 miles of 3 ft 6 in gauge lines were absorbed by the Canadian National Railways system. Of this 547 miles are on the main "Overland route" from St. John's to Port aux Basques. In 1948 the Newfoundland lines carried 274,497 passengers and 856,560 tons of freight.

The longest tunnel in Canada is the 5 mile 39 yd long Connaught Tunnel on the Canadian Pacific Railway in the Selkirks. The double-track bore, opened on 6th December 1916, replaced the difficult route over the Rogers Pass which was threatened every winter with snow blockage despite many miles of snow-sheds.

Above left: Westbound Pacific Express *on the west side of Rogers Pass, descending to Glacier in British Columbia, Canada. (Canadian Pacific Rail.)*

Above right: Western portal of the Connaught Tunnel on the Canadian Pacific Railway in 1916. The original line over Rogers Pass can be seen above the trees. (Canadian Pacific Rail.)

Left: The eastern portal of the 5 mile 39 yd long Connaught Tunnel at the summit of the Selkirk Mountains in British Columbia. (Canadian Pacific Rail.)

The second longest tunnel is the 3 mile 268 yd Mount Royal Tunnel at Montreal, on the Canadian National Railways short route into the city, opened on 21st October 1918. It was built by the Canadian Northern Railway at a cost of $3,000,000. There are no other tunnels in Canada over 3 miles long.

The "Canadian" near the Great Divide and Mount Cathedral. (Canadian Pacific Rail.)

The highest railway summit in Canada is at the Great Divide on the Canadian Pacific Railway—5,335 ft.

Canadian railway mileage reached a maximum of 44,029 about 1960. Of this total Canadian National Railways owns 24,563 miles in addition to 704 miles of 3 ft 6 in gauge line in Newfoundland, and the Canadian Pacific Railway owns 16,268 miles.

Section 4
MOTIVE
POWER

LOCOMOTIVE TYPES

Steam locomotives are generally referred to by the Whyte system of wheel arrangement which can be easily worked out from the examples below. All locomotives are imagined facing to the left.

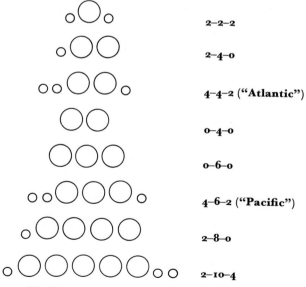

2–2–2

2–4–0

4–4–2 ("Atlantic")

0–4–0

0–6–0

4–6–2 ("Pacific")

2–8–0

2–10–4

The European countries use an axle system, thus in France a 4–6–2 is a 231.

Electric and diesel locomotives are referred to by a letter indicating the number of driving axles. A is one, B two, C three, D four.

A locomotive on two four-wheeled bogies with a motor to each axle is a Bo Bo. The small "o" indicates that the axles are not coupled. A locomotive on two six-wheeled bogies can be a C C if the acles are coupled, a Co Co if the axles are all driven but not coupled, or A1A, A1A if the centre axle of each bogie is undriven.

Electric locomotives with rod drive are, for example:

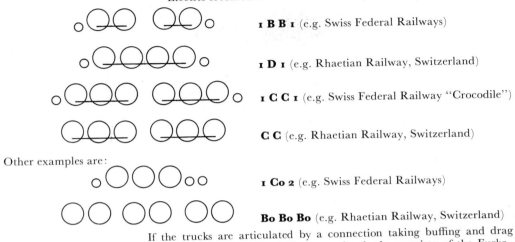

1 B B 1 (e.g. Swiss Federal Railways)

1 D 1 (e.g. Rhaetian Railway, Switzerland)

1 C C 1 (e.g. Swiss Federal Railway "Crocodile")

C C (e.g. Rhaetian Railway, Switzerland)

Other examples are:

1 Co 2 (e.g. Swiss Federal Railways)

Bo Bo Bo (e.g. Rhaetian Railway, Switzerland)

If the trucks are articulated by a connection taking buffing and drag stresses a plus sign is used; for example, the locomotives of the Furka–Oberalp and Brig–Visp–Zermatt railways, Switzerland, are Bo + Bo.

LOCOMOTIVE PROGRESS

The first locomotive to haul a load on rails was built by Richard Trevithick (see *The Pioneers*) in 1803 for the Penydarran plateway in South Wales. It had a single hori-

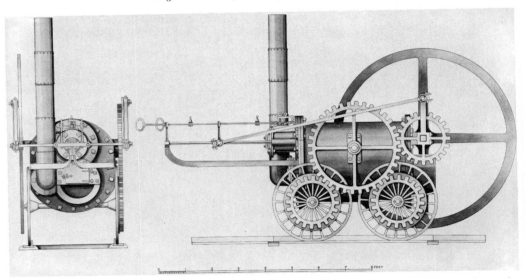

Trevithick's Coalbrookdale locomotive of 1803. It was probably intended for the tramway at Coalbrookdale Ironworks, Shropshire for there is no evidence that it actually ran. (The Science Museum, London.)

zontal cylinder mounted inside the boiler and ran on unflanged wheels. Its working life was short because it was too heavy for the L-section cast-iron plates.

The locomotive was introduced to Northumberland, England, by Christopher Blackett, Proprietor of Wylam Colliery and Member of Parliament. He ordered an engine on Trevithick's principle, through his Engineer John Steel and it was built at Gateshead, County Durham, by John Whinfield. However, when it was tried in 1804 it was too heavy at over 5 tons and was rejected. **It was the first locomotive to have flanged wheels.**

The short "D"-pattern slide-valve was introduced by Matthew Murray at Leeds, England, in 1806.

The first locomotive built entirely at Wylam, Northumberland, was built in 1811 by Timothy Hackworth and Jonathan Foster assisted by William Hedley. It ran on

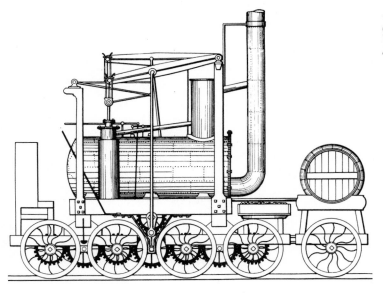

Drawing of Wylam 0–8–0. (The Baldwin Locomotive Works, Philadelphia, U.S.A.)

four flanged wheels and had a 4 ft diameter boiler 10 ft long. The two vertical cylinders at the rear drove the wheels through levers and connecting-rods to a centre jack-shaft geared to the two axles. It was known as the *Grasshopper*.

The next two engines built at Wylam in 1814–15 were of the same type but ran on eight wheels to spread the load on the light track until the cast-iron rails were replaced by wrought iron in 1830. Of these, *Puffing Billy* is now in the Science Museum, London, and *Wylam Dilly* is in Edinburgh Museum.

Two more "Grasshopper"-type engines on four wheels were built by Jonathan Foster and J. U. Rastrick at Stourbridge, Worcestershire, as late as 1828. One, named *Agenoria*, was put to work on the Shutt End Railway from Lord Dudley's Colliery at Kingswinford to the Staffordshire & Worcester Canal. It is now in York Railway Museum.

Puffing Billy, *built at Wylam Colliery, Northumberland, in 1814 by Hackworth, Foster and Hedley, is seen at work at a colliery about 1850 after reconversion to four wheels. (The Science Museum, London.)*

The other, named *Stourbridge Lion*, was sent to America where it was tried on the Carbondale–Honesdale Railroad on 8th October 1829, the day before the opening. (See "Early American Railroads", page 15.)

The first commercially successful locomotive was most probably that built by Matthew Murray in 1812 to an order by John Blenkinsop for the Middleton Colliery Railway, Leeds, England. It ran on four flanged wheels which were free and was propelled by a toothed wheel which engaged in a rack on the side of one rail. The two vertical 9 × 22 in cylinders drove cranks set at right angles and geared to the rack wheel. It weighed about 5 tons.

The spring-loaded safety-valve was introduced in 1812 by James Fenton at Leeds, England.

The locomotive bogie was patented by William Chapman in 1813.

In May 1813 William Brunton of the Butterley Ironworks, Derbyshire, secured a patent for a four-wheeled engine propelled by two legs working at the rear and pushing it along. It was known as *Brunton's Mechanical Traveller* and worked between 1814 and 1815. Its boiler then exploded, killing and injuring a number of people and causing considerable damage.

George Stephenson's first locomotive, named *Blücher*, was completed at Killingworth near Newcastle upon Tyne on 25th July 1814. It had a 2 ft 10 in diameter boiler, 8 ft long, in which the two 8 × 24 in cylinders were mounted vertically along the centre. They drove the wheels through counter-shafts geared to the two driving-axles.

In February 1815 Stephenson with Ralph Dodds, Viewer at Killingworth Colliery, patented an engine in which the wheels were driven directly and coupled by either rods or chains.

The first engine under this patent was built in 1815. Its wheels were coupled by rods working on cranked axles.

This was the first use of cranked axles in a locomotive, but they were abandoned as not strong enough and for a time wheels were connected by endless chains.

The loose-eccentric valve gear was introduced by George Stephenson in 1816 with the assistance of Nicholas Wood, and was used on the "Rocket"- and "Planet"-type engines until 1835.

Carmichael's valve gear with a single fixed eccentric was introduced in 1818. The end of the eccentric rod was fixed to two V-shaped "gabs" in the form of an X which could be raised to engage the forward valve-pin or lowered to engage the backward pin. These pins were at opposite ends of a centrally pivoted lever.

The first locomotive to have its wheels coupled by rods was *Locomotion*, No. 1 of the Stockton & Darlington Railway, built by George Stephenson in 1825. The two 9·5 × 24 in vertical cylinders were in line along the centre of the single-flue boiler and each drove one of the axles through rods and crank-pins on the wheels. Because these cranks were set at right angles one end of each coupling-rod had to be attached to a return crank.

Stephenson's Locomotion, *the Stockton & Darlington Railway No. 1, on a plinth at Darlington before being transferred to Darlington Station. (British Rail.)*

The first four-cylinder locomotive was built by Robert Wilson of Newcastle upon Tyne, England, and was sold to the Stockton & Darlington Railway at the end of 1825. The vertical cylinders were in pairs on each side of the engine and drove the rear wheels.

The multi-jet blast-pipe was introduced in 1826 by Sir Goldsworthy Gurney (1793–1875). The fusible plug (a soft metal plug in the firebox crown which melts if uncovered by water and allows steam to damp down the fire) and expansion valve gear (allowing steam to be used expansively) were also introduced by him in the same year.

The first six-coupled locomotive was Hackworth's *Royal George* built at Shildon, County Durham, in 1827. It was also the first engine in which the cylinders drove directly on to the wheels without intermediate gearing or levers. The piston-rods, however, were guided by Watt-type parallel motion, not a crosshead. Cylinders were 11 × 20 in and exhausted into a single blast-pipe. It weighed 8·4 tons.

The first locomotive in which the wheels were driven directly from the piston-rod working in a crosshead was Stephenson's 0–4–0 for the Bolton & Leigh Railway where it was named *Lancashire Witch* in 1828. The 9 × 24 in cylinders

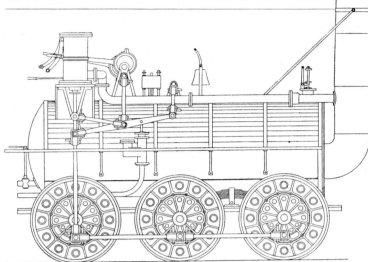

T. Hackworth's drawing of the Royal George, *built in 1827. (*The Engineer, *16th July 1920.)*

mounted on the rear of the boiler drove the front coupled wheels which were 4 ft diameter. This engine also incorporated expansion valve gear in a primitive form.

Stephenson's *Rocket* of 1829 incorporated the same arrangement of cylinders which, however, were only 8 × 16·5 in. It was the first engine to combine a multi-tubular boiler and a blast-pipe. Driving-wheels were 4 ft 8·5 in diameter and the weight of the engine only was 4 tons 5 cwt. It won the £500 prize at the Rainhill Trials. The design was mainly by Robert Stephenson.

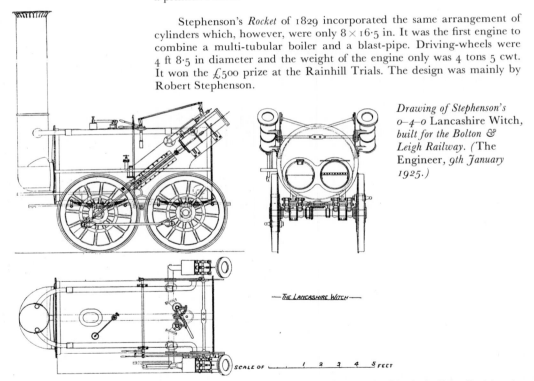

Drawing of Stephenson's 0–4–0 Lancashire Witch, *built for the Bolton & Leigh Railway. (*The Engineer, *9th January 1925.)*

THE LANCASHIRE WITCH

SCALE OF   1   2   3   4   5 FEET

The first "inside-cylinder" engine, driving on to a crank-shaft, was the *Novelty* built by Braithwaite to a design by Ericsson (see *The Pioneers*). It was also the first well-tank engine. The 6 × 12 in vertical cylinders drove the front axle through bell-cranks. It was entered in the Rainhill Trials in 1829, but failed.

The first locomotive powered by a horse walking on a moving platform was designed by T. S. Brandreth. In the Rainhill Trials on the Liverpool & Manchester Railway in 1829 *Cycloped* achieved a speed of 15 mile/h.

In the U.S.A. a similar locomotive was designed by D. C. Detmold for the South Carolina Canal & Railroad in 1830. It was named *Flying Dutchman* and won a $300 prize. On an experimental trip it pulled twelve passengers at 12 mile/h.

The bar-frame and Haycock firebox first appeared in the 0–4–0 *Liverpool* built by Edward Bury, largely to the designs of James Kennedy, and tried on the Liverpool & Manchester Railway in June 1830, two months before the line opened. It had 12 × 18 in cylinders beneath the smokebox driving on to a cranked axle.

It was a highly advanced engine at the time. The inside cylinders became standard British practice and the bar-frame standard American practice.

Stephenson's 2–2–0 engine *Planet* built in September 1830 for the Liverpool & Manchester Railway had inside cylinders enclosed within the smokebox and was **the first engine to be built with outside sandwich-frames and outside bearings**, a feature of British practice which survived in Stephenson's designs for many years. (The "sandwich"-frame consisted of a slab of oak or ash between two iron plates.)

Hackworth's first inside-cylinder 0–4–0 was built at Shildon in 1830 for the Stockton & Darlington Railway and named *Globe*. The 9 × 16 in cylinders were mounted beneath the driving-platform at the rear.

The first locomotive in which the outside cylinders were attached to the frame instead of to the boiler was the *Union* built by Rothwell, Hick & Rothwell of Bolton, Lancashire, in 1831 for the Bolton & Leigh Railway. It was a 2–2–0 with a vertical boiler, 9 × 18 in cylinders and 5 ft driving-wheels.

The first locomotive of Stephenson's "Planet"-type inside-cylinder 0–4–0 to be delivered to America was originally named *Stevens* in honour of John Stevens (see "Early American Railroads", page 15), but was renamed *John Bull*. It went into service on the Camden & Amboy Railroad on 12th November 1831, where a two-wheeled truck and pilot was fitted in front. It ran until 1865 and is now preserved in the Smithsonian Institution, Washington, D.C.

The inside-cylinder 0–4–0 Stevens, *built in 1831 by Robert Stephenson & Company of Newcastle upon Tyne, England for the Camden & Amboy Railroad, U.S.A., was later renamed* John Bull. *(Crown Copyright. Science Museum, London.)*

The first bogie locomotive in the world was a 4–2–0 designed by John B. Jervis and built in 1832 at the West Point Foundry, U.S.A., for the Mohawk & Hudson Railroad and named *Experiment*. In its day it was the fastest locomotive in the world, covering 14 miles in thirteen minutes. It was claimed that it reached 80 mile/h over a 1-mile stretch.

The classic British single-wheeler was established by Robert Stephenson in a patent on 7th September 1833. It was a development of the "Planet" type with a pair of wheels behind the firebox, becoming a 2–2–2, the success of the design resulting from the outside framing which allowed space for an adequate firebox.

The first engine, named *Patentee*, was built at Newcastle upon Tyne in 1833 for the Liverpool & Manchester Railway. It soon became widely adopted in Britain and abroad and was the design upon which the famous Gooch "Singles" of the Great Western Railway were based. It was developed also into the 0–4–2 and 0–6–0 goods engines.

First experiments with piston-valves were made by Robert Stephenson in 1832. A design was prepared for a locomotive for the Liverpool & Manchester Railway, but there is no evidence of their behaviour, or that they were in fact used.

The "petticoat" blast-pipe was also introduced by Robert Stephenson in 1832, by flaring the base of the chimney and extending it down into the smokebox to achieve a better smokebox vacuum.

The steam-whistle was introduced on the Leicester & Swannington Railway following an accident at a road-crossing on 4th May 1833.

The steam-brake was introduced by Robert Stephenson in 1833, and incorporated in his "patent"-type 2–2–2.

The first inside-cylinder 0–6–0, a development of the Stephenson "patent" type, was built by Robert Stephenson in 1833.

The bogie was first used on a British locomotive in 1833, on J. & C. Carmichael's 0–2–4 engine for the 4 ft 6 in gauge Dundee & Newtyle Railway.

The "gab motion" (valve gear) operated by four fixed eccentrics was first used by Forrester & Company, Liverpool in 1834–36 and by R. & W. Hawthorn of Newcastle upon Tyne in 1835. Robert Stephenson & Company used the gear first on the "patent"-type 0–4–2 *Harvey Combe* built in 1835.

Balanced slide-valves were first used by John Gray on the Liverpool & Manchester Railway in 1838.

John Gray's expansion valve gear was first used in 1839 on the North Midland Railway. It was a complicated gear known as the "Horse Leg" motion. Its purpose was to cut off the steam at varying positions of the piston stroke to allow the remaining work to be done by the expansion of the steam.

The variable blast-pipe was introduced by Peter Rothwell of Bolton, Lancashire, England, in 1839 (see *The Pioneers*). It was in the form of a hollow cone which could be raised or lowered inside the blast-pipe orifice from a lever on the footplate. It was used on Sharp's heavy goods engines of 1848–49.

The locomotive superheater was introduced by R. & W. Hawthorn of Newcastle upon Tyne in 1839.

French National Railways (S.N.C.F.) exchanging electric power for steam at Hazebrouck for the last part of the run to Calais. The steam-engine is one of the splendid American "141Rs". (Simon Marshall.)

A French National Railways (S.N.C.F.) diesel-electric locomotive at Nantes. (K. B. Smith.)

A French National Railways (S.N.C.F.) 4–8–2 "Mountain"-type engine at Le Mans Depot. (K. B. Smith.)

Long travel-valves, giving greater cylinder efficiency, were first used on the Hull & Selby
Railway by John Gray in 1840. They had about 6 in travel.

It was about 1900 before they were regularly used in England, on
the Great Western Railway by G. J. Churchward (see *The Pioneers*), and
it was more than another thirty years before they were universally adopted
in Britain.

Hall's brick arch in the firebox for smokeless combustion of coal was first tried in 1841.
Previously engines had burned coke, or, in North America, wood. It did
not come into general use for some years but is stated to have been used on
the Scottish North Eastern Railway by Thomas Yarrow from about 1857.

The Stephenson "long boiler" locomotive was introduced in 1841, with the *North Star* for the 5 ft
gauge Northern & Eastern Railway. To obtain a large heating surface
with a longer boiler, without increasing the wheelbase, the firebox was
placed behind the rear axle. Mainly 2–2–2s, 2–4–0s and 0–6–0s were
built to this design, but they were unsteady at speed.

The first application of sanding gear to sprinkle sand on the rails to help the driving-wheels to grip
was applied by Robert Stephenson in 1841.

The Howe/Stephenson link motion—valve gear with two fixed eccentrics (see *The Pioneers*)—was
first used on locomotives for the North Midland Railway by Robert
Stephenson in 1843.

The "stationary link" motion was first used by Daniel Gooch on the Great Western Railway and
by his brother John Viret (1812–1900) on the London & South Western
Railway in England in 1843.

The Walschaerts valve gear was invented by Egide Walschaerts in 1844 (see *The Pioneers*).

The pneumatic brake was invented by James Nasmyth and May in 1844.

The dial pressure gauge, replacing the mercurial gauge, was first proposed in Germany by Schinz
in 1845.

The first three-cylinder locomotive was built by Robert Stephenson for the Newcastle & Berwick
Railway in 1846.

The compounding of locomotive cylinders was invented by J. Nicholson, and in 1850 was first
tried on the Eastern Counties Railway. (See *The Pioneers*: Von Borries,
De Glehn, Du Bousquet, J. M. Smith.)

*The last compound engine
for the British railways, the
London & North Eastern
Railway 4–6–4 No. 10000,
was designed by H. N.
Gresley and built in 1930.
(British Rail.)*

The double-beat regulator valve was introduced by John Ramsbottom on the London & North Western Railway in 1850. His famous duplex safety-valve was introduced in 1856, together with the screw-reverser, instead of the hand-lever, and the displacement lubricator. (The screw-reverser may have been used on the Aberdeen Railway some years earlier.)

The drop grate, to facilitate fire-cleaning, was introduced by Edward Bury in 1852.

A smokebox superheater for steam locomotives was used in 1852 by J. E. McConnell (1815–1883) at Wolverton on the London & North Western Railway.

Feedwater-heaters were first tried in 1854 by Joseph Hamilton Beattie (1804–1871) on the London & South Western Railway and were first applied in 1855. His double firebox and combustion-chamber to enable engines to burn coal without producing smoke were introduced in 1859.

The straight link motion invented by Alexander Allan (see *The Pioneers*) was first used on the Scottish Central Railway locomotives in 1854.

The firehole deflector-plate to assist combustion was first applied by G. K. Douglas on the Birkenhead, Lancashire & Cheshire Junction Railway early in 1858.

The combination of brick arch and firehole deflector-plate was first used by Matthew Kirtley (1813–1874) in 1859 while Locomotive Superintendent of the Midland Railway. It enabled coal to be burnt without the complication of the Beattie firebox.

Steel locomotive tyres were introduced by Naylor and Vickers on the London & North Western Railway in 1859.

The steam-injector (for forcing water into a locomotive boiler against pressure) was invented by M. Giffard (1825–1882) and was first used on locomotives by Sharp Stewart & Company, Manchester, England, in 1859.

A steel locomotive firebox was first tried by Alexander Allan on the Scottish Central Railway in 1860. Steel fireboxes became general in American practice, but European engineers tended to continue with the copper firebox.

Steel boilers in place of wrought iron were first used by George Tosh on the Maryport & Carlisle Railway in 1862.

The first fireless steam locomotive was a 7 ft gauge 2–4–0 condensing tank designed by John Fowler (see *The Pioneers*) and built by Robert Stephenson & Company

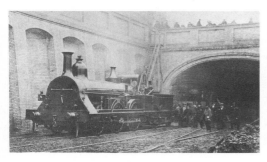

Fowler's Ghost, this 7 ft gauge 2–4–0 tank was built in 1861 by Robert Stephenson & Company of Newcastle upon Tyne for the Metropolitan Railway, London. (London Transport Executive.)

in 1861 for the Metropolitan Railway, London, for working in the tunnels. Steam was raised by red-hot firebricks heated by a small firebox which could be closed to prevent fumes escaping. It became known as "Fowler's Ghost", and in 1865, after attempts to make it go, it was bought by I. W. Boulton of Ashton-under-Lyne near Manchester. Boulton shut down his famous "Siding" before rebuilding was completed and the engine was sold to Beyer Peacock & Company who consigned it to scrap. So the "ghost" was exorcised (see *The Chronicles of Boulton's Siding*). The illustration shows it on the Metropolitan Railway.

The radial axlebox was invented by William Bridges Adams (see *The Pioneers*) and was first used on some 2–4–2 tanks for the St. Helens Railway, built by Cross & Company in 1863.

The counter-pressure brake in which the engine is reversed so that the cylinders act as compressors thereby absorbing power and avoiding wear on tyres and brake-blocks, especially on long inclines, was first used with water-injection by F. Holt on the South Staffordshire Railway in 1856. The Le Châtelier system using hot water was introduced on the London & North Western Railway in 1868.

The compressed-air brake was first used by the Caledonian Railway, Scotland, by Steel and McInnes in 1871.

The non-automatic vacuum-brake was introduced by J. Y. Smith on the North Eastern Railway in 1874.

The hydraulic brake was introduced by Francis William Webb (1835–1906) on the London & North Western Railway.

Gresham's automatic vacuum-brake was first used in 1878. By this system the brakes are automatically applied on both portions of a train if it breaks in two.

The "pop" safety-valve was patented in Britain by T. Adams in 1873 and was first used in 1874. A second patent in 1875 covered an annular pop chamber. It was much used in America long before it became popular in Britain.

The pop safety-valve of R. L. Ross was patented in 1902 and 1904 but it did not achieve extensive use in Britain until about twenty years later.

On the Lancashire & Yorkshire Railway a pop safety-valve was introduced by H. A. Hoy, Chief Mechanical Engineer, about 1900.

The advantage of the pop safety-valve was the small pressure difference, only about 1–2 lb/in², between opening and closing, compared with 5 lb/in² or more in the Ramsbottom type.

Speed-indicators for locomotives were first used by John Ramsbottom on the London & North Western Railway in 1861. A superior pattern was devised by William Stroudly (1833–1889), Locomotive Engineer of the London, Brighton & South Coast Railway, in 1874.

Steam reversing gear was first used by James Stirling (1800–1876) on the Glasgow & South Western Railway in 1874.

The Davies and Metcalfe exhaust-steam injector, making use of exhaust-steam for forcing water into the boiler, was introduced in 1876.

Steel plate-frames instead of wrought iron were first used by F. W. Webb on the London & North Western Railway in 1886. The plate-frame was peculiar to British steam-locomotive practice. American practice used the built-up bar-frame, first used by Edward Bury at Liverpool. Later American locomotive engineers developed the cast-steel locomotive bed which finally included cylinders, valve chests and smokebox saddle, representing a triumph of the pattern-maker's and foundryman's crafts.

Steam sanding gear, devised by Holt and Gresham, was introduced on the Midland Railway in 1886. By forcing sand beneath the driving-wheels it brought about a revival of the "single-wheeler" locomotive in Britain where it was built until about 1900 and lasted until the mid 1920s.

The British four-cylinder simple engine was introduced by James Manson on the Glasgow & South Western Railway in 1897, with the 4–4–0 No. 11.

The smoke-tube superheater was introduced in Germany by Wilhelm Schmidt in 1897. It was first used in Britain in May 1906 on the Great Western Railway two-cylinder 4–6–0 No. 2901 *Lady Superior* and on the Lancashire & Yorkshire Railway in two 0–6–0s (see *The Pioneers*).

A smokebox-type superheater was used by J. A. F. Aspinall, Chief Mechanical Engineer of the Lancashire & Yorkshire Railway, on his 4–4–2 No. 737 in 1899. **This was the first British superheated locomotive.**

The Lentz poppet-valve gear was first applied in Germany by Hugo Lentz (1859–1944) in 1905. It used the type of valves familiar in internal-combustion engines. In Britain it was applied by H. N. Gresley to several types of London & North Eastern Railway locomotives.

The Caprotti poppet-valve gear was first fitted to an Italian locomotive in 1920. (See Caprotti in *The Pioneers* for applications.)

The first locomotive to be fitted with roller-bearing axle-boxes throughout was the demonstration 4–8–4 No. 1111 constructed to the order of the Timken Company in 1930. After trials all over the U.S.A. it was purchased by the Northern Pacific Railroad for working through the Rockies.

The first British engine to be fitted with a booster was the Great Northern Railway "Atlantic"-type No. 1419 (later the London & North Eastern Railway No. 4419) in 1923. The booster, common in America, was tried only on the L.N.E.R. in Britain. It consisted of an auxiliary engine on the trailing truck which could be engaged and put into or out of operation as required.

The L.N.E.R. tried boosters also on two 2–8–2 freight engines, two North Eastern Railway "Atlantics" and a Great Central Railway 0–8–4 tank. The boosters were removed after a few years' trials.

NORTH AMERICAN LOCOMOTIVES

The archetypal American 4–4–0 was first patented in 1836 by Henry R. Campbell, Chief Engineer of the Philadelphia, Germantown & Norristown Railroad.

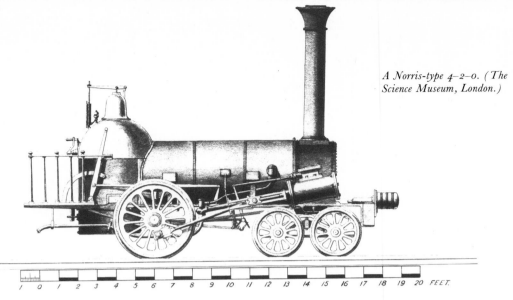

A Norris-type 4–2–0. (The Science Museum, London.)

The first American 4–4–0 was built in Philadelphia in May 1837. The "classic" American 4–4–0 with "three-point suspension" first appeared in 1839. It was a direct development of the Norris 4–2–0.

   About 1870 some 83–85 per cent of locomotives in the U.S.A. were of this type of 4–4–0. Between 1840 and 1890 about 20,000 were built.

The Canadian Pacific Railway 4–4–0 No. 144. (John Marshall.)

The first steam locomotive in Canada was the *Dorchester* built by Robert Stephenson & Company of Newcastle upon Tyne, England, in 1836 and delivered to the Champlain & St. Lawrence Railway (opened between St. John and La Prairie, Quebec, on 21st July 1836) where it worked until it blew up in 1867 and was scrapped.

   Wood was the standard fuel in nearly all Canadian locomotives. Apart from the three locomotives of the short coal line in Nova Scotia in 1839 (see *The Beginnings*) the first experiments with coal were made about 1858–60; but it was into the 1870s before coal became generally used.

   At first engines covered about 36 miles on a "cord" of wood, but by 1859 this had risen to 50 miles. A "cord" was a stack of wood $8 \times 4 \times 4$ ft.

The first engine to run on the Central Pacific Railroad, the Western Division of the first American transcontinental railroad was the 4–4–0 *Governor Stanford*, built in 1863. It had 4 ft 6 in driving-wheels.

America's early adoption of large numbers of driving-wheels was to obtain the necessary adhesion without excessive axle loading for the light track then in use.

Baldwin's first 0–8–0 type appeared in 1846 when seventeen were built for the Philadelphia & Reading Railroad. The two leading axles were mounted in a flexible truck.

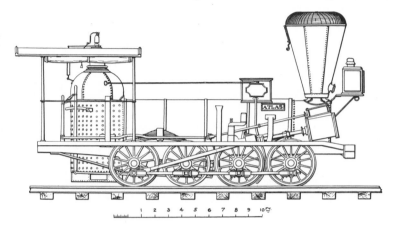

Drawing of a Baldwin 0–8–0. (The Baldwin Locomotive Works, Philadelphia, U.S.A.)

The world's first 4–6–0 was a Norris type built in the U.S.A. in 1847.

The first twelve-coupled locomotive was built in 1863 for the Philadelphia & Reading Railroad.

The first 2–6–0 was built in the U.S.A. in 1866 following a satisfactory design of a leading two-wheeled truck. It rapidly became a standard American type built in countless numbers for use at home and abroad.

The first 2–8–0 and 2–10–0 freight engines were built to designs by Alexander Mitchell for the Lehigh Valley Railroad, U.S.A., in 1866 and 1867.

Locomotive No. 1 of the Canadian Pacific Railway is an American-type 4–4–0 named *Countess of Dufferin*, built by Baldwin in 1872 (Baldwin No. 2660). After running as

The Countess of Dufferin *arrived in Winnipeg, Manitoba on 8th October 1877. It was the first locomotive on the prairies and is now preserved and exhibited at Winnipeg Station on Main Street. (Canadian Pacific Rail.)*

No. 56 on the Northern Pacific Railroad, U.S.A., it was bought by the contractor Joseph Whitehead and eventually, on 8th October 1877, it arrived by barge at Winnipeg. In 1883 it was bought by the C.P.R., becoming No. 151. In 1897 it was sold to a British Columbian lumber company but was bought back in 1910 and preserved as No. 1 outside Winnipeg Station.

The wide Wootten firebox was invented in 1877 by John E. Wootten when General Manager of the Philadelphia & Reading Railroad, U.S.A. It was designed to burn waste anthracite or "culm" which, because of its slow-burning qualities, required a larger area to give off the same heat as bituminous coal. It was first applied on the P. & R. 4–6–0 No. 411 in 1880. The grate area was 76 ft². The cab was mounted midway along the boiler. The fireman was carried on an open platform at the rear.

The first "Pacific"- or 4–6–2-type engine was built in 1886 at the Vulcan Iron Works, Wilkes Barr, Pennsylvania, to a design by George S. Strong for the Lehigh Valley Railroad, U.S.A. The class name "Pacific" did not come into use until many years later.

The first "Atlantic" or 4–4–2-type engine appeared in 1888, also built at the Vulcan Iron Works, Wilkes Barr to a Strong design for the Lehigh Valley Railroad. The class name "Atlantic" for the 4–4–2 type was suggested in 1894 by J. K. Kenly, General Manager of the Atlantic Coast Railroad, for a group of 4–4–2s built by Baldwin.

A Canadian Pacific Railway 4–4–2 "Atlantic"-type locomotive built at the C.P.R. De Lorimier Avenue Works, Montreal, in 1899. (Canadian Pacific Rail.)

The last, largest and fastest "Atlantics" were the streamlined engines built by the American Locomotive Company (ALCO) in 1934–35 to work the "Hiawatha" between Chicago and the Twin Cities (Minneapolis and St. Paul) on the Chicago, Milwaukee, St. Paul & Pacific Railroad. They ran at 100 mile/h daily.

The first all-welded boiler was fitted to a Delaware & Hudson Railroad 2–8–0 in 1934, and was given several years of trials before being passed as satisfactory by the Interstate Commerce Commission.

BRITISH AND EUROPEAN LOCOMOTIVE PROGRESS

The first British 4–4–0 was rebuilt from a Norris 4–2–0 of the Birmingham & Gloucester Railway between 1846 and 1850.

Daniel Gooch built ten 7 ft gauge 4–4–0s for the Great Western Railway in 1855, but with a rigid wheelbase.

The first British bogie 4–4–0s to be built new were two built by Robert Stephenson & Company for the Stockton & Darlington Railway in 1860 to William Bouch's design. They were followed by the London, Chatham & Dover and the Great North of Scotland railways in 1861. All these engines had outside cylinders.

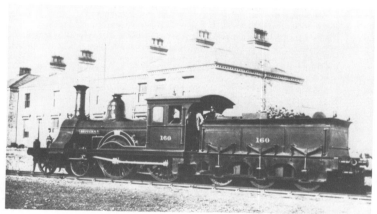

The Stockton & Darlington Railway 4–4–0 No. 160 Brougham, *built in 1860 by Robert Stephenson & Company at Newcastle upon Tyne to designs by William Bouch. This was the first 4–4–0 bogie engine in Britain and the first with the large American-type cab. (The Science Museum, London.)*

The typical British inside-cylinder inside-frame 4–4–0 was introduced by Thomas Wheatley on the North British Railway in June 1871. The first of these, No. 224, went down with the first Tay Bridge in 1879. It was recovered and ran until 1919.

The first British inside-cylinder 4–4–0, the North British Railway No. 224, built at Cowlairs, Glasgow in June 1871 to a design by Thomas Wheatley.

The 0–6–4 tank engine was introduced in 1876 on the Great Southern & Western Railway, Ireland, by Alexander McDonnell (1829–1924).

The type was also represented by the last steam locomotive built for Ireland, by Beyer Peacock & Company of Manchester, in 1948 for the Sligo, Leitrim & Northern Counties Railway and named *Lough Melvin.*

The first 2–6–0 or "Mogul" to be built and to run in Britain appeared on the Great Eastern Railway in 1878. Fifteen were built by Neilson & Company of Glasgow to the design of William Adams.

The first engine in service in Britain with a Belpaire firebox was the 0–6–2 tank No. 7 designed by Harry Pollitt and built by the Manchester, Sheffield & Lincolnshire Railway at its Gorton Works in September 1891, it was renumbered 515 on 24th October 1893. It became the London & North Eastern Railway No. 5515 "N5" Class in 1923, was renumbered 9250 in 1947 and was withdrawn in 1956 as British Railway No. 69250.

The first 4–6–0 to run on a British railway was introduced by David Jones on the Highland Railway (No. 103) in 1894. It was based on a design influenced by Jones, which had been built by British firms for use in India since 1880. It ran until 1934 and, after a short spell working special trains in the early 1960s, it was placed in the Glasgow Transport Museum.

The first 4–6–0 passenger engine in Britain was Wilson Worsdell's "S" Class on the North Eastern Railway in 1899.

Britain's first "Atlantic"-type locomotive was designed by H. A. Ivatt (see *The Pioneers*) and was built at Doncaster in 1898 by the Great Northern Railway. No. 990, later named *Henry Oakley* after the G.N.R. General Manager, had a narrow firebox and two 18·75 × 24 in outside cylinders.

The Great Northern Railway 4–4–2 No. 990 Henry Oakley. This express passenger locomotive was built at the G.N.R. Doncaster Works in 1898 to the design of the late H. A. Ivatt for work in the East Coast expresses between York and London. (The Museum of British Transport.)

It was closely followed by the giant inside-cylinder 4–4–2 of the Lancashire & Yorkshire Railway, designed by J. A. F. Aspinall and completed at Horwich Works in February 1899. It was remarkable for its 7 ft 3 in coupled wheels and high-pitched boiler.

Ivatt's large-boilered "Atlantic" with wide firebox first appeared in 1900. Its appearance startled the whole country, but its performance was sadly inferior until it was rebuilt with superheater and piston-valves.

The Great Northern Railway No. 251, designed by H. A. Ivatt and built at the G.N.R. Doncaster Works in 1902. (The Museum of British Transport.)

The first British "Pacific" locomotive was built at Swindon in 1908 to a design by G. J. Churchward (see *The Pioneers*) on the Great Western Railway. No. 111 *The Great Bear* was a large-boilered version of his very successful four-cylinder 4–6–0 and was built largely as a publicity stunt. Its weight restricted it to Brunel's London & Bristol Railway, and the design was not repeated. It was scrapped in 1923.

The first 4–6–4 engine was the last design produced by Du Bousquet, the "3.1102" Class on the Northern Railway of France. It had 6 ft 8·5 in driving-wheels and weighed 100 tons.

The 4–6–4 tender engine was not repeated until 1927 when large numbers were built in the U.S.A. The most famous were the New York Central Railroad "Hudsons".

Du Bousquet's masterpiece —the 4–6–4 of 1910–11. (French Railways Limited (S.N.C.F.).)

The first successful British "mixed traffic" locomotive, for passenger and goods trains, was the Great Western Railway 2–6–0 "Mogul" type, first built in 1911. It had 5 ft 8 in coupled wheels.

The Great Western Railway "Mogul"-type 2–6–0 No. 5361. This is the first type of British "mixed traffic" engine. (John Marshall.)

Only about 200 twelve-coupled engines were built in the whole world, and were represented by six different wheel types: 0–12–0, 0–12–2, 2–12–0, 2–12–2, 2–12–4 and 4–12–2.

The first twelve-coupled tender engine in Europe was Gölsdorf's 2–12–0 No. 100.01, built for the Austrian State Railways in 1911 for the long 1 in 40 grades on the Arlberg route.

The first four-cylinder tank engine in Britain was designed by J. A. Hookham for the North Staffordshire Railway and built in 1922. It was a 0–6–0 and was curious in having opposite pairs of cranks at 135 degrees to each other, so that it gave eight exhaust beats per turn of the wheels. It was converted into a tender engine in 1924.

This arrangement of the cranks was subsequently used on the Southern Railway "Lord Nelson" Class.

The only other four-cylinder tank engines in Britain were the ten Hughes 4–6–4s built at Horwich Works for the London, Midland & Scottish Railway in 1924.

The first British "Pacifics" to be produced as a class were designed by H. N. Gresley and built by the Great Northern Railway at Doncaster. No. 1470 appeared in April 1922 and No. 1471 in July. The third, No. 1472, appeared in January 1923 and was the first engine to be completed by the newly formed London & North Eastern Railway. It was renumbered 4472 and named *Flying Scotsman*, and on 30th November 1934 became the first steam locomotive to reach an authenticated speed of 100 mile/h.

The London & North Eastern Railway 4–6–2 No. 4472 Flying Scotsman, *which is privately preserved by Alan Pegler, at Manchester Central Station. (John Marshall.)*

Britain's first eight-coupled passenger engine was the London & North Eastern Railway 2–8–2 No. 2001 *Cock o' the North* designed by H. N. Gresley and built at Doncaster in 1934. It was built with Lentz rotary cam poppet-valve gear and was later rebuilt with Walschaerts valve gear and a streamlined front. With five other 2–8–2s it worked between Edinburgh and Aberdeen. In 1943–44 all six were rebuilt into 4–6–2s by Edward Thompson, Gresley's successor. They had 6 ft 2 in coupled wheels.

The London & North Eastern Railway 2–8–2 No. 2001 Cock o' the North, *designed by H. N. Gresley and built at Doncaster in 1934. It is shown as originally built with a Lentz rotary cam poppet-valve gear. Later it was rebuilt with Walschaerts valve gear and piston-valves and with a streamlined front. In 1943–44 it was rebuilt into a 4–6–2. (The Science Museum, London.)*

The only other eight-coupled engines to be regularly used on passenger trains in Britain were the Great Western Railway "4700" Class 2–8–0s, with 5 ft 8 in wheels.

The largest French express passenger engine was the "242A" Class three-cylinder compound 4–8–4, rebuilt by Chapelon in 1946. It had a starting tractive effort of 47,000 lb and could run up to 100 mile/h. The coupled wheels were 6 ft 4·75 in diameter.

The 4–8–2- or "Mountain"-type French express engine, the 241P Class four-cylinder compound, was developed by Chapelon in 1947–49 from the P.L.M. 4–8–2 of 1925. The inside high-pressure cylinders drove the third coupled axle and the outside low-pressure cylinders the second. The coupled wheels were 6 ft 7·5 in diameter.

The only 4–8–0 tender engines in the British Isles were the two built in 1905 for the 3 ft gauge Londonderry & Lough Swilly Railway. This railway also had the only two 4–8–4 tanks in the British Isles, built in 1912.

RUSSIAN STEAM LOCOMOTIVES

The world's tallest locomotives are in Russia where the loading gauge permits engines 17 ft high, 4 ft higher than in Great Britain. They can also be up to 11 ft 6 in wide.

The first Russian steam locomotive was probably a 2–2–0. It was built in 1833 at Nizhni-Tagil in the Urals by M. Cherepanov and it was run on a half mile long 5 ft 6 in gauge track.

The first locomotive in service in Russia was a 2–2–0 built by Hawthorns, Newcastle upon Tyne, England, in 1837, for the 14 mile long, 6 ft gauge line from St. Petersburg to Tsarskoe Selo, opened in 1836.

The largest steam locomotives built in Russia were the two "P38" simple expansion 2–8–8–4s built at Kolomna Works in 1954–55. They each weighed 214·9 tons and were 125 ft 6 in long. They were the last main-line steam-locomotive type built in Russia.

The only fourteen-coupled steam locomotive was a 4–14–4 built in Russia in 1934. Its use was severely restricted by its rigidity and it saw little service before it simply "disappeared".

THE LARGEST STEAM LOCOMOTIVES

The world's largest steam locomotives were the 4–8–8–4 "Big Boys" of the Union Pacific Railroad, U.S.A. With tenders they weighed 534 tons, and exerted a tractive force of 135,375 lb. On test they developed an indicated hp of 7,000. The firebox was 19 ft 7 in long by 8 ft 0·25 in wide, as big as a bus! The wheelbase of engine and tender was 117 ft 7 in. They were built by the American Locomotive Company (ALCO) in 1941–42. Two are preserved.

A Union Pacific Railroad 4–8–8–4 simple-articulated "Big Boy" Class steam locomotive, the world's largest and heaviest steam-locomotive type. (Union Pacific Railroad.)

The largest locomotives in Canada were the 2–10–4 "Selkirks", the "T1a" Class Nos. 5900–19 of the Canadian Pacific Railway. They were built by the Montreal Locomotive Works in 1929, followed by the "T1b" Class Nos. 5920–29 in 1938 and the "T1c" Class Nos. 5930–35 in 1949. They had 5 ft 3 in driving-wheels, a working pressure of 275 lb/in² and 25·5 × 32 in cylinders. They worked passenger and freight trains through the mountain section of the C.P.R. No. 5934 is preserved at Calgary and No. 5935 at the Canadian Railway Museum near Montreal.

A Canadian Pacific Railway "Selkirk"-type 2–10–4 locomotive. (Canadian Pacific Rail.)

The largest locomotives in New Zealand were the "K"-type 4–8–4s built, with slight variations, from 1931 to 1950. These 3 ft 6 in gauge engines with tenders measured 69 ft 11 in long and weighed 142·5 tons despite their over-all height of only 11 ft 3 in and width of 8 ft 6 in.

A "K"-type 4–8–4, the largest type of locomotive in New Zealand. (High Commissioner for New Zealand.)

The most powerful steam locomotive in Europe was the Chapelon-rebuilt 4–8–0 of the French National Railways, the "4701" Class, produced between 1932 and 1934. With an indicated hp of 4,170 and a weight of 107 tons it had the highest hp, of 39 per ton, of any European locomotive. It handled express passenger trains of up to 1,000 tons.

A French National Railways Chapelon-rebuilt 4–8–0. This was the most powerful steam locomotive in Europe on a horse-power basis.

The largest locomotives in South America were the 145 ton 2–10–4s built by Henschel of Germany, for the 5 ft 6 in gauge Central Railway of Brazil. The same railway also ran the largest metre-gauge engines in South America, the Henschel 2–8–8–4 Mallets.

The world's most powerful steam locomotive was a triplex articulated 2–8–8–8–4 Mallet-type compound, built by Baldwin, U.S.A. in 1916 for the Virginian Railroad (No. 700). It had a tractive effort of 166,300 lb working compound and 199,560 lb working simple.

The American Locomotive Company (ALCO) built a 2–10–10–2 "Mallet" in 1918, No. 802 for the Virginian Railway, weighing over 305 tons and over 100 ft long. The 48 in diameter low-pressure cylinders were the largest ever used on a locomotive. The high-pressure cylinders were 30 in and the stroke 32 in. The grate area was 108·7 ft². Starting simple the engine had a tractive effort of 176,600 lb and working compound had a tractive force of 147,200 lb. The engine hauled coal trains a mile long composed of 100 cars each carrying 218,000 lb, a total of over 10,000 tons.

The world's once largest locomotive was the Erie Railroad 2–8–8–8–2 No. 5014 *Matt H. Shay*, the first of three built in 1914–18 for banking freight trains up the 1 in 67 Susquehanna Incline in Pennsylvania. It pulled 250 freight cars weighing altogether 15,300 tons, and stretching for 1·6 miles, at a speed of 13·5 mile/h. They were withdrawn in 1929.

The most powerful British express passenger locomotive on a purely tractive-effort basis was the British Railways Eastern Region three-cylinder "A2" Class "Pacific" designed by Arthur H. Peppercorn (1890–1952), with a tractive effort of 40,430 lb. However, the London, Midland & Scottish Railway four-cylinder "Pacifics" designed by William Stanier were considerably larger and were, therefore, capable of a higher power output, despite the lower tractive effort of 40,300 lb for Nos. 6200–12 and 40,000 lb for Nos. 6220–57.

The British Railways Eastern Region three-cylinder "A2" Class "Pacific" No. 60528 at Dundee Engine-shed. This type, the most powerful British express passenger steam locomotive on a tractive-effort basis was designed by Arthur H. Peppercorn. (John Marshall.)

The most powerful British 4–4–0 was the Southern Railway three-cylinder "Schools" Class designed by R. E. L. Maunsell. The first, the No. 900 *Eton*, was built in 1930.

The largest locomotives in Ireland were the Great Southern Railway three-cylinder 4–6–0s of which three were built at Inchicore, Dublin, in 1939–40 to a design prepared under E. C. Bredin, Chief Mechanical Engineer. The first, the No. 800 *Maeve* is shown in the illustration. They were built for the Dublin–Cork expresses.

The Great Southern Railway three-cylinder 4–6–0 No. 800 Maeve at Cork—the largest locomotive type in Ireland. (John Marshall.)

The largest driving-wheels used on any engine in Britain were 10 ft diameter on the freak Great Western 2–2–2 built by Mather, Dixon & Company of Liverpool to a specification by I. K. Brunel and delivered on 12th December 1838. It "worked" until June 1840.

The largest driving-wheels in regular use in Britain were 9 ft diameter on the eight magnificent 4–2–4 tank engines built for the Bristol & Exeter Railway by Rothwell & Company of Bolton, Lancashire, to a design by James Pearson in 1854. One of these, No. 41, achieved a record speed of 81·8 mile/h on Wellington Bank, Somerset, in June 1854, which remained the highest authenticated rail speed until 1890. They were replaced by new B. & E.R. engines of the same wheel arrangement in 1868–73.

The Bristol & Exeter Railway 4–2–4 tank engine with 9 ft diameter driving-wheels—the largest in Britain—built by Rothwell & Company of Bolton, Lancashire in 1854. (British Rail.)

The largest coupled wheels ever used in Britain were 7 ft 7·25 in diameter on Wilson Worsdell's "Q1" Class 4–4–0s Nos. 1869 and 1870 on the North Eastern Railway. Two were built in 1896 for taking part in the railway races to the north. (See *The Trains.*)

ARTICULATED STEAM LOCOMOTIVES

The articulated locomotive with one or two swivelling power bogies, was developed to provide great power on lines with severe curvature, or to spread the weight of a large locomotive over many axles to enable it to work on light track. The principal types have been the Fairlie, Meyer, Mallet and Garratt.

The world's first articulated locomotive was a 2–2–2–2 built at West Point Foundry in 1832 for the South Carolina Railroad, U.S.A. It had a central firebox and four boilers, two at each end. It was designed by Horatio Allen and formed the basis of the Fairlie type. Each engine had one central cylinder.

The next stage towards the Fairlie design was a 0–4–4–0 built by John Cockerill et Cie of Seraing, Belgium, for trials on the Semmering line in Austria.

Robert F. Fairlie (1831–1885) was a Scotsman. He patented his articulated locomotive design in 1863. The first, built in 1865, had two boilers, with back to back fireboxes and a power bogie under each. Later ones had a single common central firebox. Most Fairlies were 0–4–4–0 and 0–6–6–0, the largest being some 102 ton 0–6–6–0s for Mexico. The last was built in 1915 for the 60 cm (1 ft 11·5 in) gauge lines on the French war front. The only survivors are on the 1 ft 11·5 in gauge Festiniog Railway in Wales.

Jean-Jacques Meyer, of Mulhouse, France, and his son Adolphe patented his articulated locomotive in March 1861. It had a single boiler mounted on two power bogies. The design restricted the ashpan, but the Kitson-Meyer type, developed in Leeds, England, overcame this by lengthening the frame and placing the firebox between the power bogies. The first was a 0–6–6–0 built in 1894 for the Anglo-Chilian Nitrate & Railway Company of South America.

The first articulated locomotives in Africa were the 3 ft 6 in gauge Kitson-Meyer 0–6–6–0s built by Kitson for Rhodesia in 1903. At the time they were the largest and most powerful engines in southern Africa.

The largest articulated locomotives were the Mallets, patented by Anatole Mallet (see *The Pioneers*) in 1884. These were four-cylinder compounds with the high-pressure engine in the fixed rear frame and the low-pressure engine in the pivoted front frame. The first Mallet was a 60 cm (2 ft) gauge 0–4–4–0 tank built in 1887 by Ateliers Métallurgiques at Tubize, Belgium.

The largest Mallet tanks were the 0–8–8–0s built by Maffei in Germany for the Bavarian State Railways in 1913–14 and 1922–23. The first batch weighed 271,500 lb or 121 tons.

The first Mallet in North America was a 0–6–6–0 built by the American Locomotive Company (ALCO) in 1903 for the Baltimore & Ohio Railroad. It was followed by five 2–6–6–2s built by Baldwin in 1906 for the Great Northern Railway.

The greatest of all, the Union Pacific Railroad "Big Boy" 4–8–8–4s first built by ALCO in 1941, were not strictly Mallets because they were not compounds. The engine weighed 344·6 tons without tender.

The largest Russian locomotives, the "P38" 2–8–8–4s of 1954–55, were likewise not true Mallets. They weighed 214·9 tons without tenders.

GARRATT LOCOMOTIVES

Herbert William Garratt (1864–1914) invented the type of articulated engine named after him which was developed by the firm of Beyer Peacock & Company of Manchester, England.

The first Garratts were two tiny 0–4–0 + 0–4–0s built in 1909 for the 2 ft gauge North East Dundas Tramway, Tasmania. They were compounds with the cylinders at the inner ends of the engine units. They ran until 1930. In 1947 No. K1 was shipped back to England and after being stored at Beyer Peacock's in Manchester it is now on the Festiniog Railway in Wales where, however, it will have to undergo drastic alterations before it can run within the small F.R. loading gauge.

The first Garratt 0–4–0 + 0–4–0 compound engine was built in 1909 by Beyer Peacock & Company of Manchester (No. 5292) for the 2 ft gauge North East Dundas Tramway of Tasmania. (Manchester Museum of Science and Technology.)

The Tasmanian Government Railway "M" Class Garratt was a 3 ft 6 in gauge 4–4–2 + 2–4–4 remarkable for having eight cylinders and for running at speeds up to 55 mile/h. The coupled wheels were 5 ft diameter.

The most powerful locomotives in South Africa are the South African Railways "GL" Class 3 ft 6 in gauge 4–8–2 + 2–8–4 Garratt, first built in 1929 by Beyer Peacock & Company. They weigh 211·1 tons and have a tractive effort of 78,650 lb.

The first Garratt passenger locomotive was built by Beyer Peacock & Company in 1915 for the 5 ft 3 in gauge São Paulo Railway, Brazil. It was a 2–4–0 + 0–4–2 and ran until 1950.

The world's first express passenger Garratts were also built for the São Paulo Railway, as 2–6–2 + 2–6–2s in 1927. In 1931–32 they were rebuilt as 4–6–2 + 2–6–4s. They regularly ran trains at 60 mile/h.

The largest and most powerful metre-gauge steam locomotives are the 4–8–2 + 2–8–4 "59" Class Garratts built for the East African Railways. Thirty-four were

The East African Railways metre-gauge "EC3" Class 4–8–2 + 2–8–4 No. 5903, a Garratt built in 1955 by Beyer Peacock & Company of Manchester (No. 7634). Today the E.A.R. "EC3s" are the largest steam locomotives in the world. (Manchester Museum of Science and Technology.)

British Railways "Britannia" No. 70013
Oliver Cromwell *on a special train*
at Carnforth in 1968. (B. D. Walker.)

Two "5" Class 4–6–0s—Nos. 44871
and 44781 head a special in the last weeks
of steam on British Railways.
(B. D. Walker.)

London & South Western Railway 4–4–0
No. 120—the Drummond "T9"—now
preserved at Beaulieu Road, Hampshire.
(N. Fields.)

built by Beyer Peacock & Company and were delivered in 1955. The boiler is 7 ft 6 in diameter, the total weight is 251·68 tons and they produce a tractive effort of 73,500 lb. At the time of writing (1972) they are the world's largest and most powerful steam locomotives.

The largest and most powerful locomotive in Great Britain was the 2–8–0 + 0–8–2 Garratt built by Beyer Peacock & Company in 1925 for the London & North Eastern Railway, for banking coal trains from Wath up to Penistone in Yorkshire. It was numbered 2395 and classed "U1". Its two engine units were standard with H. N. Gresley's three-cylinder 2–8–0s.

The London & North Eastern Railway "U1" Class No. 2395, a Garratt built in 1925 by Beyer Peacock & Company of Manchester (No. 6209), was the largest and most powerful steam locomotive ever to work in Britain. (Manchester Museum of Science and Technology.)

Britain's last Garratt was a 0–4–0 + 0–4–0 built in 1937 for the Baddesley Colliery near Atherstone, Warwickshire, where it worked until 1965. It has a 5 ft diameter boiler and weighs 61·5 tons, and is now preserved at Bressingham, Norfolk.

The National Coal Board Baddesley Colliery Railway 0–4–0 + 0–4–0 William Francis, *Britain's last Garratt, was built in 1937 by Beyer Peacock & Company of Manchester (No. 6841). It is now preserved at Bressingham in Norfolk. (John Marshall.)*

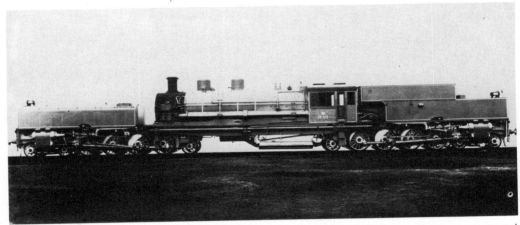

The largest Garratt locomotive ever built, the single 4–8–2 + 2–8–4 for the Soviet Railways, Russia, was constructed in 1932 by Beyer Peacock & Company of Manchester (No. 6737). It stood 17 ft high with 4 ft 11 in coupled wheels. (Manchester Museum of Science and Technology.)

The largest Garratt locomotive ever built was by Beyer Peacock & Company in 1932 for the Soviet Railways, Russia—their "R-01" Class. It was a 4–8–2 + 2–8–4 with 17 ft high bar-frames and a 7 ft 6 in diameter boiler. It weighed 262·5 tons and had a tractive effort of 78,700 lb.

The smallest Garratts ever built were two 0–6–0 + 0–6–0s built in 1913 for the Arakan Flotilla Company of Burma, of 2 ft 6 in gauge with a wheelbase of 24 ft 2 in. They weighed 23·55 tons.

The Buthidaung–Maungdon Tramway 2 ft 6 in gauge 0–6–0 + 0–6–0 No. 1 Buthidaung, the smallest Garratt ever built, was built in 1913 by Beyer Peacock & Company of Manchester (No. 5702) for the Arakan Flotilla Company of Burma. (Manchester Museum of Science and Technology.)

GEARED STEAM LOCOMOTIVES

Geared logging locomotives were produced to three basic designs, to negotiate light temporary tracks over rough ground with steep gradients.

The Shay geared locomotive was invented by Ephraim Shay and was produced by the Lima Machine Works, Ohio, U.S.A. (from 1901 the Lima Locomotive & Machine Company). The first appeared in 1880. It had a high-speed vertical engine on one side and the two bogies were driven by a system of shafts, universal couplings and spur-gears.

The Meadow River Lumber Railroad Shay geared locomotive No. 1 built at Lima, Ohio, U.S.A., in 1910. (John Marshall.)

The Climax locomotive was built by the Climax Manufacturing Company of Corry, Pennsylvania. It had two sloping cylinders, one on each side, connected by gearing and shafts to the two bogies. The company operated from 1884 to 1930.

The Heisler Locomotive Works, Erie, Pennsylvania, began producing a geared locomotive in 1898. This had two cylinders arranged like a V beneath the boiler, driving a longitudinal shaft geared to the bogies. This was the neatest and soundest of the three designs.

The Mason Lumber Company Climax-type geared locomotive No. 4. (John Marshall.)

The former International Shoe Company Heisler geared locomotive No. 4 built 1926. (John Marshall.)

OIL FUEL FOR STEAM LOCOMOTIVES

Some of the earliest experiments with oil fuel were made in the 1870s by a British engineer Thomas Urquhart. Similar experiments began in France in 1869.

In the U.S.A. early experiments with oil fuel were abandoned because of the cost and they were not taken up again until the 1890s.

The first regular use of oil fuel was on the Russian South Eastern Railway in 1883–84, using the Urquhart system.

Oil fuel was first used in Britain by the Great Eastern Railway. In 1887 James Holden, Locomotive Superintendent, invented an arrangement for burning the waste product from the plant producing oil-gas for carriage lighting. It was tried on the Johnson 0–4–4 tank No. 193 and was first regularly used on a 4–2–2 which was named *Petrolea*. About sixty engines were so fitted but the apparatus was removed when the price of oil rose to an uneconomic level.

The first oil-burning locomotive in Canada was introduced about 1910, converted from a coal-burner for work in the Rocky Mountains. The first complete class of oil-burners was built by the Canadian Pacific Railway in 1917–19.

In 1947 many British locomotives, on the Great Western, Southern and London & North Eastern railways, and on the Irish railways, were fitted up to burn oil fuel during the acute coal shortage in Britain. However, the increasing cost of oil led to its removal after very little use.

STEAM-TURBINE LOCOMOTIVES

The first steam-turbine locomotive was designed by Professor Belluzzo and was built in Milan, Italy, in 1908 by S.A. Officine Mechaniche. It was a 0–4–0 side-tank engine. The four turbines were of single-wheel velocity compound type with the lower part of the blades for forward drive and the upper part for backward.

A steam-turbine-electric locomotive was designed by Sir Hugh Reid and W. M. Ramsey and was built in Glasgow in 1910 by the North British Locomotive Company. An impulse-type turbine with condenser was coupled to a variable voltage dynamo which supplied the four d.c. traction motors at 200–600 V.

A second Ramsey-type locomotive, a 0–6–6–2 type, was built in 1920 and was tested by George Hughes at Horwich on the Lancashire & Yorkshire Railway and on the North Eastern Railway in 1921. Turbines and electrical equipment were by Oerlikon, Switzerland. It was built by Armstrong Whitworth & Company, Newcastle upon Tyne.

The Zoelly turbine locomotive was converted from a Swiss Federal Railways 4–6–0 in 1921 by the Swiss Locomotive & Machine Works, Winterthur. It had a 1,200 hp impulse turbine across the front of the machine, driving the wheels by gearing and a jack-shaft and side-rods. A surface condenser was positioned beneath the boiler. A similar engine built by Krupp of Essen, Germany, in 1922 ran on the German State Railways.

The Ljungstrom-type turbine condensing locomotive was first built in 1921 at the Ljungstrom Locomotive Works near Stockholm, Sweden. It was rebuilt in 1922 but withdrawn in 1924.

The third Ljungstrom steam-turbine condensing locomotive, built by Beyer Peacock & Company of Manchester in 1926. (Manchester Museum of Science and Technology.)

The second, built at Trollhattan in 1924–25 to the metre gauge for the Argentine State Railway, was capable of travelling 500 miles without rewatering.

The third, built by Beyer Peacock & Company of Manchester, England in 1926, was given extensive trials on the Midland Section of the London, Midland & Scottish Railway. It suffered from the tunnels where soot entered the condenser and caused blockages.

A fourth and last, built in 1927, was similar in design and gave good service in Sweden for many years.

The Reid-Macleod turbine locomotive was built by the North British Locomotive Company of Glasgow in 1923–24. It was of the 4–4–4–4 type with high- and low-pressure turbines and an air-cooled condenser with a bhp of 1,000.

The London, Midland & Scottish Railway turbine "Pacific" No. 6202 was a non-condensing machine with one turbine for forward running and a smaller one for reverse. It was built at Crewe in 1935 to the design of William Stanier and ran successfully on the London–Liverpool expresses. In 1952 it was rebuilt into a conventional engine and named *Princess Anne*, but after only a few months' service it was involved in the collision at Harrow and Wealdstone Station in October 1952 and was subsequently scrapped.

The Union Pacific Railroad, U.S.A. had a pair of turbine-electric locomotives built by the General Electric Company in 1937–39. They were of the 2 Co Co 2 type and could work either singly or together under the control of one man. Their maximum speed was 125 mile/h. They each had high- and low-pressure turbines and condensers, and together had an output of 5,000 hp. The semi-flash-type boiler worked at a pressure of 1,500 lb/in².

The first direct-drive turbine locomotive in the U.S.A. was the Pennsylvania Railroad No. 6200, a 6–8–6-type non-condensing machine built by Baldwin in 1944 in co-operation with the Westinghouse Company. Like the London, Midland & Scottish Railway machine of 1935 it had two turbines, one forward of 6,500 hp at 70 mile/h and a reverse of 1,500 hp at 22 mile/h.

The Chesapeake & Ohio Railroad obtained a giant steam-turbine-electric locomotive built by Baldwin and the Westinghouse Company in 1947–49. It was a 154 ft long 2 D + 2 D 2 type with a starting tractive effort of 98,000 lb and a continuous of 48,000 lb.

The Norfolk & Western Railroad obtained a 4,500 hp turbine-electric non-condensing locomotive in 1954, built by the Baldwin-Lima-Hamilton Corporation with the

Westinghouse Company, and a boiler by Babcock & Wilcox. It measured 161 ft 1·5 in long and weighed 525 tons in working order. It could run up to 60 mile/h.

LARGE CLASSES OF LOCOMOTIVES

The first very large class of locomotives to be built in Britain was the Ramsbottom "DX" Class 0–6–0 of the London & North Western Railway, of which 943 were built between 1858 and 1874, including some for the Lancashire & Yorkshire Railway.

The largest class of modern locomotives in Britain was the London, Midland & Scottish Railway Class "5" 4–6–0 designed by William Stanier and first built in 1934. Including several variations in the design, the class eventually numbered 842 engines.

The first locomotive type to be adopted by the British Government for war service was the Great Central Railway "8K" Class 2–8–0 designed by J. G. Robinson (1856–1943) and first built at Manchester in 1911. During the First World War many were built by the G.C.R. and by various contractors making a grand total of 647 engines. After the war they were dispersed, most going to the London & North Eastern Railway (as successor to the G.C.R.) and others to the Great Western Railway and to China, Australia and elsewhere. Many of them put in over fifty years' hard service. They were among the finest British freight engines.

A Great Central Railway 2–8–0 at Daybrook, Nottingham. (John Marshall.)

The German "Austerity" 2–10–0 introduced in 1941 numbered more than 8,000 when the last was built in 1947.

The world's largest class of locomotives was the Russian "E" Class 0–10–0 introduced in 1912 and at length numbering about 14,000 engines.

Between 1891 and 1923 9,500 "O" Class 0–8–0s were built in Russia.

LOCOMOTIVE-BUILDING RECORDS

In February 1888 F. W. Webb (1835–1904), Locomotive Superintendent of the London & North Western Railway, had a six-coupled goods engine constructed in Crewe Works in twenty-five and a half hours.

The following June this record was reduced to sixteen and a quarter hours by the Pennsylvania Railroad at the Altoona Works, U.S.A.

The all-time record was achieved by the Great Eastern Railway under James Holden at Stratford, London. On 10th December 1891 the 0–6–0 No. 930 was completely assembled and given one coat of paint in nine hours and fifty-seven minutes. It was steamed and tested on the line immediately afterwards. As the London & North Eastern Railway "J15" Class No. 7930 this engine ran until January 1935.

THE LAST STEAM LOCOMOTIVES

The last steam locomotives in France were the American "141R" Class 2–8–2s, a fine rugged modern design by Baldwin imported after the Second World War to help in the rehabilitation of the French railways. They were equally at home on freight and passenger trains.

The construction of steam locomotives for the U.S.A. railroads ended in 1949 in which year thirteen were built for home use.

The last steam locomotives built in Russia were completed in 1956. They were the "L" Class 2–10–0s, making a class totalling about 4,700; the "LV" Class 2–10–2s and the "P36" Class 4–8–4s.

The last express passenger engine built in Britain was the three-cylinder Caprotti valve-gear 4–6–2 No. 71000 *Duke of Gloucester*, completed at Crewe in 1954.

The last steam locomotive built for British Railways was the standard 2–10–0 No. 92220 *Evening Star* completed at Swindon in March 1960.

British Railways standard "9" Class 2–10–0 No. 92220 Evening Star, *the last steam locomotive built for British Railways and completed at Swindon in March 1960. (British Rail.)*

DIESEL RAIL TRACTION

The "compression ignition" system was invented by Ackroyd Stuart who developed the idea between 1886 and 1890.

Dr. Rudolf Diesel (1858–1913) was born in Paris and became a Professor at Munich. He invented his internal-combustion engine in 1892, to use a fairly crude oil so as to be less costly to run than a petrol engine. It was first demonstrated in 1898. Dr. Diesel disappeared from a steamer to Harwich in 1913 during a journey to London.

The first diesel locomotive was a direct-drive 1,000 hp Diesel-Klose-Sulzer unit built in Germany in 1912–13. It ran experimentally, for a few months only.

The first diesel-railway vehicle in revenue service was an Atlas-Deva 75 bhp diesel-electric railcar built in 1913 for the Mellersta & Södermanlands Railway, Sweden. It ran until 1939.

The first "production" diesels were five 200 hp diesel-electric railcars built by Sulzer in Switzerland in 1914 for the Prussian & Saxon State Railways.

The first diesel-electric switchers (or "shunters" in English) were built in the U.S.A. by the General Electric Company in 1918; three 200 hp units.

The first "commercially successful" diesel-electric locomotive in America was a 300 hp unit built in 1923 by the American Locomotive Company (ALCO) with an Ingersoll-Rand engine and General Electric Company controls and transmission. Four more were made in 1925. The first was sold to the Jersey Central Railroad, becoming No. 1000, and worked until 1957 when it was presented to the Baltimore and Ohio Transportation Museum.

One of the most curious locomotives was the Kitson-Still steam-diesel locomotive built by Kitson & Company of Leeds, England, and tested on the London & North Eastern Railway in April 1927. It was a 2–6–2 tank engine with eight cylinders operating with internal combustion on one side of the piston and with steam on the other side. The internal-combustion engine helped in raising steam. It attempted to combine the power at slow speed of the steam-engine with the fuel economy of the internal-combustion engine. It gave a good performance on freight trains between York and Hull, but was excessively noisy, and the design was not repeated.

The first experiment with diesel-traction on British railways was in 1924 when the London & North Eastern Railway tried an Austrian-built diesel locomotive for a short period.

The first main-line use of diesel-electric-traction was on the Canadian National Railways in 1925 when eight railcars were put into service. They had eight-cylinder engines made by Beardmore of Scotland. One of these covered the 2,930 miles from Montreal to Vancouver in sixty-seven hours.

The first main-line diesel locomotive was the Lomonossoff 1,200 bhp diesel-electric built in 1925 to a design by George V. Lomonossoff (1876–1952).

The first road or "main-line" diesel-electric locomotive in North America was introduced by the Canadian National Railways in 1928. It was a twin unit of 2,660 hp.

The first British diesel-electric train was adapted by the London, Midland & Scottish Railway in 1928 from an ex-Lancashire & Yorkshire Railway Manchester–Bury electric train, by fitting it with a 500 hp Beardmore engine and English Electric traction equipment. It ran for a time on the Preston–Blackpool service and was later reconverted to an electric train.

The first use of diesel-traction in Ireland was in 1929 when Kerr Stuart & Company of Stoke-on-Trent tried out a 0–6–0 diesel-mechanical locomotive on the Castlederg & Victoria Bridge Tramway in County Tyrone. It ran for about six months.

The first regular use of diesel-traction in the British Isles was on the 3 ft gauge County Donegal Railway in Ireland, in September 1931. The diesel railcar No. 7 was powered by a 74 hp Gardner engine. With a second, No. 8, built in November 1931, it was scrapped in 1939.

Diesel-traction made its first appearance in Great Britain on the London & North Eastern Railway in December 1931 when three diesel-electric cars were used in north-east England. They had General Electric Company traction equipment, and could haul a coach.

The first diesel locomotive in regular service in Britain was rebuilt from a Midland Railway 0–6–0 tank engine by the London, Midland & Scottish Railway in 1931. A Paxman engine was used with Haslem & Newton hydrostatic transmission.

The first British diesel railbus was produced by Hardy Motors Limited who converted an A.E.C. "Regal" road coach to run on rails in 1933, so beginning the long association of A.E.C. with railcars.

The first Great Western Railway diesel railcar was by Hardy Motors Limited in 1933, built by A.E.C. with coachwork by Park Royal. It was fully streamlined, was 63 ft 7 in long and weighed 20 tons. It seated seventy Third Class passengers and had a top speed of 75 mile/h. After achieving considerable attention at the International Commercial Motor Exhibition in London it was sold to the G.W.R., becoming their diesel car No. 1 and entering service in 1934.

The first Great Western Railway diesel railcar began service in 1934. (British Rail.)

The first high-speed diesel streamlined train, the "Flying Hamburger", ran between Berlin and Hamburg and was introduced in the spring of 1932. It was scheduled to run at speeds of over 100 mile/h. On tests it reached over 124 mile/h.

The "Burlington Zephyr" of the Chicago, Burlington & Quincy Railroad entered service in 1934 as the world's first diesel-electric streamliner. On 26th May 1934 it travelled the 1,015 miles from Denver to Chicago non-stop at an average speed of 77·6 mile/h. The train is preserved at the Museum of Science and Industry, Chicago, alongside a captured German submarine.

The "Burlington Zephyr" of the Chicago, Burlington & Quincy Railroad—now preserved, alongside a captured German submarine, at the Museum of Science and Industry, Chicago. (Museum of Science and Industry, Chicago.)

The first British streamlined diesel train was built by the London, Midland & Scottish Railway in 1938. It consisted of three articulated coaches powered by Leyland diesel engines and hydro-mechanical transmission. After successful service between Oxford and Cambridge, and Nottingham and London, it was stored throughout the war and afterwards dismembered.

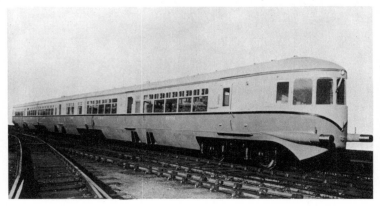

The London, Midland & Scottish Railway three-car articulated diesel unit Nos. 80000–80002. This first British streamlined diesel train was built in February 1938 and operated over various sections of the L.M.S.—mainly over the Midland Division. Withdrawn from stock in 1945, it did not operate during the war. (British Rail.)

The greatest landmark in the progress of the diesel locomotive was the "Electro-Motive" No. 103 produced in the U.S.A. in 1939, a four-unit freight diesel rated at 5,400 hp. In a year's trials it covered 83,000 miles on twenty-one roads in thirty-seven States in temperatures from 40 degrees below zero to 110 above at altitudes from sea-level to 10,200 ft. Up the 25 miles of 1 in 40 on the Southern Pacific/Santa Fé climb to Tehachapi Pass from the west it hauled 1,800 tons in one and a half hours, completely outclassing the biggest steam locomotives. From then on the fate of the steam locomotive in America and round the world was sealed.

The diesel revolution in the U.S.A. In 1945 there were 38,853 steam locomotives, 842 electric locomotives and 3,835 "other types". In 1961 there were 110 steam, 480 electric and 28,150 diesel units.

The London, Midland & Scottish Railway diesel-electric locomotive No. 10000—the first British mainline diesel-electric locomotive—approaching London. (British Rail.)

The first British main-line diesel-electric locomotives were built by the London, Midland & Scottish Railway in 1947—Nos. 10000 and 10001. They were Co Co type with English Electric Company 1,600 hp engines and six nose-suspended traction motors, and weighed 128 tons each, very heavy for their power.

Diesel multiple-unit trains first appeared in Britain in 1954, and were first put to work between Leeds and Bradford.

A multiple-unit diesel-electric train for Darlington at Middleton-in-Teesdale, County Durham, England. (John Marshall.)

Four-wheeled diesel railbuses of various designs were tried on lightly used lines in Britain for several years from 1958. Two of these railbuses are preserved for use on the Keighley & Worth Valley Railway, Yorkshire, and two more are at Sheringham, Norfolk.

Multiple-unit diesel-electric trains on the Southern Region of British Railways were first used on the London to Hastings via Tunbridge Wells service on 6th May 1957. They are in six-car sets with a 500 bhp English Electric Company supercharged diesel engine and generator in each end car. The centre cars are identical with the "Southern Electric" suburban sets.

The first of the "Deltics" was introduced by the English Electric Company at their Vulcan Works, Lancashire, in 1955. It was then **the most powerful single-unit diesel-electric locomotive in the world**, rated at 3,300 bhp, with a weight of 106 tons. After extensive trials on the London Midland Region an order was placed for twenty-two units for the East Coast main line between London and Edinburgh on which they are timed at speeds of 100 mile/h.

The first of the British Railways Western Region diesel-hydraulic locomotives was completed at Swindon in 1958. It was a B B type (based on the successful German "V200" Class) weighing only 78 tons and producing 2,100 bhp. The first of the five A1A A1A type appeared from the North British Locomotive Company in the same year.

The first main-line diesel-hydraulic locomotive for British Railways Western Region. (British Rail.)

The world's most powerful single-unit diesel locomotive is at present the Union Pacific Railroad "Centennial Locomotive" No. 6900, built in 1969 (a hundred years after the completion of the first transcontinental railroad). It is 96 ft long and is rated at 6,600 hp.

GAS-TURBINE LOCOMOTIVES

The gas-turbine was first applied to rail-traction in 1941 when a 2,140 hp gas-turbine-electric locomotive was built for the Swiss Federal Railways by Brown Boveri. It was a 53 ft 9 in long 1 Bo Bo 1 type and weighed 92 tons.

The Great Western Railway in England ordered a Brown Boveri gas-turbine-electric locomotive with an output of 2,500 hp which was delivered in 1949 and first used in February 1950. It was numbered 18000 by the British Railways Western Region.

The first British-built gas-turbine-electric locomotive was a 3,000 hp unit built by the Metropolitan-Vickers Electrical Company Limited for the Western Region of British Railways in January 1952 and numbered 18100. It was 66 ft 8 in long and weighed 130 tons. It was withdrawn in January 1958 and was rebuilt into an electric locomotive for the 25 kV electrification to be used for training drivers and numbered E1000.

British Railways Western Region gas-turbine-electric locomotive No. 18100—the first built in Britain. (British Rail.)

The largest gas-turbine-electric locomotives are the two-unit 8,500 hp machines built by General Electric of Schenectady, U.S.A., for the Union Pacific Railroad. Forty-five were built, from 1957, following the success of the twenty-five U.P.R. 4,500 hp gas-turbine-electrics built from 1950 which showed economies over diesels. The 1957 machines are 165 ft long and weigh 408 tons.

Direct-drive gas-turbine locomotives were built by Renault in France (1,000 hp) and at Gotaverken in Sweden (1,300 hp).

Union Pacific Railroad 8,500 hp gas-turbine-electric locomotive and freight on No. 3 line at Dale, Wyoming. (Union Pacific Railroad.)

LOCOMOTIVE-TESTING

The first recorded use of a stationary plant for testing locomotive performance was a small one built at Kiev in Russia in 1886 to designs by an engineer named Borodin.

The first modern testing plant was built at Perdue University, U.S.A., in 1891 to designs by Professor W. F. M. Goss. Others in the U.S.A. were built by the North Western Railway at Chicago in 1895 and by Columbia University in 1899.

The Pennsylvania Railroad Altoona plant was originally built for the St. Louis Exposition in 1904.

The first European testing plant was designed by G. J. Churchward and built at Swindon, England, by the Great Western Railway in 1904.

In France the testing plant at Vitry near Paris was completed in 1934. One of the first locomotives to be tested on it was the London & North Eastern Railway 2–8–2 *Cock o' the North*, Britain's first eight-coupled express passenger engine.

The largest testing plant for steam locomotives was built at Rugby, England. It was begun jointly by the London, Midland & Scottish and the London & North Eastern railways in 1936, but work was suspended during the war, and it was completed by British Railways in 1948. It had only a brief period of use.

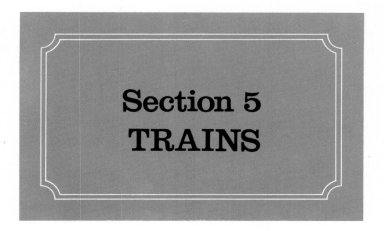

Section 5
TRAINS

PASSENGER CARRIAGES

The first railway passenger carriage was a mere "garden shed on wheels" which was pulled by a horse on the Stockton & Darlington Railway in 1825.

The first scheduled passenger service on a railway began on the Stockton & Darlington Railway on 16th October 1826. The first coach, pulled by a horse, was named "The Union". It was simply an ordinary horse carriage mounted on railway wheels.

In America the first passenger car to make a regular scheduled run was another "shed on wheels" pulled by a horse, on the Baltimore & Ohio Railway in 1829.

On the Liverpool & Manchester Railway in 1830 passenger carriages were similar to horse road carriages mounted on a railway-wagon chassis, on four wheels.

Bogie carriages were introduced in America as early as 1831. The reason was primarily the very light track.

The first compartment coach was built by Nathaniel Worsdell (see *The Pioneers*) for the Liverpool & Manchester Railway in 1834. It was named "Experiment", and consisted of three horse-carriage bodies on a four-wheeled truck. From this developed the standard compartment carriage used in Britain and throughout most of Europe.

The compartment carriage was never adopted in America where different traditions prevailed and the "open" type of car was adopted. Through the influence of the Pullman Car Company this reached Europe in the 1870s and now, a century later, it is being adopted as the standard type in Britain.

Above left: Landwasser Viaduct on the Albula line of the metre-gauge Rhaetian Railway, Switzerland. Top right: The 3 ft gauge Denver & Rio Grande Western Railroad with trains at Silverton, Colorado, U.S.A., on 2nd July 1970. (John Marshall.) Above right: The Penn Central Railroad turbo train crossing City Island Bridge, Manhattan, New York. (A. Barlow.)

The Durango to Silverton train in the Animas Canyon, Colorado, U.S.A., on the Denver & Rio Grande Western Railroad. (John Marshall.)

Steam-heating was introduced in America in 1881. In Britain hot-water cans continued in use until the end of the nineteenth century. Steam-heating was introduced only gradually after about 1890.

Electric lighting was introduced in British trains in 1881 (see "Pullman Trains", page 171) and in America in 1887.

Vestibule trains were introduced in the U.S.A. in 1887.

Corridor trains were introduced in Britain on the Great Western Railway on 7th March 1892. The connections between the coaches were at first locked and used only by the guards. Corridor trains next appeared on the northern lines out of London and then, in 1900, on the London & South Western Railway.

The first corridor train introduced by the Great Western Railway on 7th March 1892. (British Rail.)

Articulated coaches were introduced in Britain by H. N. Gresley in 1907. He mounted the bodies of two old Great Northern Railway six-wheelers on three bogies, thus improving the riding and reducing the weight and length. The idea was developed into the "quad-arts", four coaches on five bogies, so familiar to a generation of long-suffering north London commuters.

Air-conditioned cars first appeared in the U.S.A. as an experiment in 1927. They were first put into regular service in 1930.

"Vista-Dome cars" were introduced in the U.S.A. in 1945.

The first double-decked train in Britain, designed by O. V. Bulleid (see *The Pioneers*), went into service on the Southern Region of British Railways on 2nd November 1949. Its higher capacity made longer station stops necessary, so its advantage was lost and it was withdrawn in 1970.

The first train of the new British Railways coaches, featuring wide doors, forced air heating and ventilation, double-glazed windows, sound-proofing and specially designed seats, began a twelve-month trial on 15th June 1964.

BRAKES

Early trains had no continuous brakes. The only brake power was on the engine tender and the guard's van. From 30 mile/h a train might take up to half a mile to stop. Hence the great height of early signals, to be seen from a distance.

The earliest practical continuous brakes were mechanical systems such as those patented by George Newall of the East Lancashire Railway in 1852 and by Charles Fay (1812–1900) of the Lancashire & Yorkshire Railway in 1856.

The Westinghouse automatic continuous air-brake was introduced in 1872–73. (See Westinghouse in *The Pioneers*.)

The Gresham automatic vacuum-brake was introduced in Britain in 1878 but it was about 1890 before all passenger trains were equipped.

Most of the world's railway systems use the air-brake. Countries using the vacuum-brake are mainly:

Europe—British Isles (except new British Rail stock); Austrian minor railways; Denmark; Norway; Spain; Portugal.

Australasia—Western Australia; Tasmania.

Africa—South Africa; Rhodesia; United Arab Republic.

Asia—most railways in India and Pakistan; Malaysia; Thailand (Siam); Burma.

South America—most railways except the Transandine; Antofagasta & Bolivia; Central of Brazil; high-altitude lines in the Andes.

PASSENGER CLASSES

Third Class passengers were first carried in Britain in 1838, in open wagons without seats.

Gladstone's Railway Act of 1844 ruled that railways must carry Third Class passengers in closed carriages with seats at one (old) penny a mile on at least one train a day. "Parliamentary" trains as they were known were often run at the most inconvenient times and at the slowest speeds.

The first British railway to carry Third Class passengers on all trains was the Midland Railway, on 1st April 1872. The Great Eastern Railway followed the same year.

Second Class was abolished on the Midland Railway and also on the joint services with the Glasgow & South Western Railway on 1st January 1875.

Bogie carriages for First and Third Class were introduced in Britain by the Midland Railway in 1875.

The use of Third Class carriages by "wearers of kid gloves and kid shoes" was strongly condemned by the Chairman of the Lancashire & Yorkshire Railway in 1880, because of the danger of "Americanising our institutions"!

Third Class passengers were carried on all trains of the Great Western Railway from 1st October 1890.

First Class was abolished on the Metropolitan and District railways, London, from 1st February 1940. From that date only one class operated on all London Transport services.

Third Class was redesignated Second Class on British Railways on 3rd June 1956 and by the Ulster Transport Authority (which had retained three classes) on 1st October 1956.

Greece and Turkey adopted two classes only from 1st January 1957, leaving only Spain and Portugal in Europe with three classes.

SLEEPING AND DINING CARS

The world's first sleeping-car service began in the U.S.A. in 1837, but the sleeping arrangements were simply adapted from the seating.

The world's first proper sleeping cars were designed by Samuel Sharp and built at Hamilton, Ontario, by the Great Western Railway of Canada, in 1857. The design was adopted by the Wagner and Pullman companies. The first Pullman sleeping car appeared in 1859.

"Parlour cars" first appeared in Canada in 1860 on the Grand Trunk, Great Western, and Buffalo & Huron railways. They were fitted out with every possible luxury; the Grand Trunk car even had a form of air-conditioning.

Canada's first dining cars, or "hotel cars", appeared in regular service on the Great Western Railway in 1876.

First Class sleeping cars were introduced on Scottish expresses to and from London in 1873, on the East Coast route on 31st July and on the West Coast route on 1st October. On the Great Western Railway they first appeared in December 1877.

Dining cars were introduced on the London–Leeds trains by the Great Northern Railway on 1st November 1879.

The "Flying Scotsman" was first provided with corridor stock throughout and with dining cars on 1st August 1900. The twenty-minute lunch stop at York was ended.

Third Class sleeping cars were introduced in Britain by the London, Midland & Scottish, the London & North Eastern and the Great Western railways on 24th September 1928.

Air-conditioning was first brought into regular use in Canada in 1935 when the sleeping car "Sturgeon Falls" was so equipped.

A weekly through sleeping-car service between Togliattigrad in Russia and Turin in Italy was introduced on 1st June 1969. The 2,486 miles are covered in eighty-eight hours.

PULLMAN CARS AND TRAINS

George Mortimer Pullman (1831–1897) introduced his first car in the U.S.A. on 1st September 1859, which ran between Bloomington and Chicago. It was a sleeping car rebuilt from a Chicago & Alton Railroad coach. The first car to bear his name was the "Pioneer", introduced in 1863.

Pullman sleeping cars were introduced on Canadian railways in 1870. The Grand Trunk Railway cars were among the best appointed of their time. The convenience could be enjoyed for an extra payment of $1.

Pullman cars were introduced in Britain on 1st June 1874 on the Midland Railway between London and Bradford. They were so popular that by the end of 1874 the M.R. had thirty-six in operation, including eleven sleeping cars. In 1876 the services were extended to Edinburgh and Glasgow over the new Settle & Carlisle line.

The Midland Railway Pullman parlour-car No. 8, built in the U.S.A. in 1876 for the London to Edinburgh and Glasgow services. (The Science Museum, London.)

The first "restaurant car" in Britain was a Pullman named "Prince of Wales", introduced on the Great Northern Railway between London (King's Cross) and Leeds on 1st November 1879.

The first all-Pullman train in Britain was on the London, Brighton & South Coast Railway in December 1881. It was also the first train in Britain to be electrically lit throughout. The London–Brighton sixty-minute Limited Pullmans (Sundays only) began on 2nd October 1898.

The Pullman Company Limited was registered in England from 1882 to 1907. It was then owned by Mr. Daviason Dalziel until 1915 when the Pullman Car Company Limited was formed to acquire the interests.

Pullman introduced the first vestibule train, in America, in 1887.

The Pullman Car Company Limited introduced the first two all-steel trains in England in May 1928. They formed the "Queen of Scots" train on the London & North Eastern Railway and ran between London, Leeds, Harrogate and Edinburgh.

The all-Pullman "Southern Belle" was introduced by the London, Brighton & South Coast Railway on 1st November 1908. At the same time Buckeye couplings and drawgear were introduced into Great Britain by the Pullman Company. The "Southern Belle" was renamed the "Brighton Belle" in 1934, and it made its last run on 30th April 1972.

The Pullman observation car was introduced into Britain on 3rd August 1914 when the Caledonian Railway "Maid of Morven" began running between Glasgow and Oban. It was a wooden vehicle with rear windows extending down to the floor. It was withdrawn from 28th February 1915 to 1st March 1919, and was finally withdrawn by the London, Midland & Scottish Railway after a few years when its patrons deserted to the motor car.

The Pullman observation car "Maid of Morven", on the Caledonian Railway, Scotland.

The most famous of all-Pullman trains, the "Golden Arrow" service between London and Paris was introduced on 12th September 1926 with Pullman cars between Calais and Paris. From 15th May 1929 it became all-Pullman throughout the journey.

The first diesel multiple-unit Pullman train was the six-car First Class only "Midland Pullman" inaugurated on 4th July 1960. It ran between London (St. Pancras) and Manchester (Central) and between London and Leicester. The latter service was withdrawn on 31st December 1960. The "Midland Pullman" was withdrawn in 1966 with the introduction, on 18th April, of the electrically hauled London to Manchester and Liverpool Pullman trains.

SLIP CARRIAGES

The earliest "slip" carriages were on the London & Blackwall Railway during cable operation from 1840 to 1849 when coaches were detached from the moving ropes at all intermediate stations between Minories and Blackwall.

The first carriages to be slipped from moving trains were on the London, Brighton & South Coast Railway in February 1858 when a portion for Eastbourne was slipped at Hayward's Heath from the 16.00 express from London Bridge to Brighton.
Three months later the South Eastern Railway slipped a portion for Canterbury off the 12.30 express from London Bridge to Ramsgate and Margate.

The first Great Western Railway slip carriages were introduced in December 1858 at Slough and Banbury.

In 1914 there were 200 slip-carriage services, operated by most of the main-line companies in Great Britain and Ireland, of which the Great Western Railway operated seventy-two. By 1918 the G.W.R. total was down to seventeen.

Slip carriages on the Great Western Railway, England. (British Rail.)

The last slip carriage on the London, Brighton & South Coast Railway was the East Grinstead and Forest Row portion off the Southern Railway 17.20 London (Victoria) to Eastbourne at Three Bridges on 30th April 1932.

The last slip working in Britain was at Bicester off the 17.10 Paddington–Wolverhampton train on 9th September 1960, at the end of the summer service.

SPECIAL TRAINS

The first excursion train was organised by the Nottingham Mechanics Institute, England, and was run to Leicester on 20th July 1840. The second, from Leicester to Nottingham on 24th August 1840, carried 2,400 passengers.

In the 1860s the Lancashire & Yorkshire Railway carried excursion passengers in open cattle trucks. Only after numerous complaints in the Press were temporary roofs fitted.

Queen Victoria's first railway journey, from Slough near Windsor to London (Paddington), on the Great Western Railway, was on 13th June 1842.

The first royal railway carriage was built by the London & Birmingham Railway in 1842 for Queen Adelaide.

The first "club trains" were run by the South Eastern and London, Chatham & Dover railways between London and Dover in 1889.

The first "railway enthusiasts' rail tour" in Britain was organised by the Railway Correspondence and Travel Society in September 1938 when the Great Northern Railway Stirling 8 ft single-wheeler No. 1 took a train of old six-wheeled carriages from London (King's Cross) to Peterborough and back. The fare was five shillings (25p).

MAIL TRAINS

Mail was first carried by train on the Liverpool & Manchester Railway on 11th November 1830.

The carriage of mail by rail was authorised by Act of Parliament in 1838.

The first travelling post office was an adapted horse-box run between Birmingham and Liverpool by the Grand Junction Railway on 6th January 1838.

The first sorting carriage to be specially constructed was designed by Nathaniel Worsdell (see *The Pioneers*) and included the first apparatus for picking up and dropping mail-bags while in motion. It was built by the Grand Junction Railway at Liverpool in 1838.

Mail was first carried by rail in Canada on the Great Western Railway between Niagara and London in 1854, letters being sorted on the train under the supervision of P. Pardon, pioneer mail clerk of North America.

The first North American railway to employ regular mail cars was the Grand Trunk Railway of Canada. In 1854 the baggage cars were replaced by specially fitted-up mail cars, at least ten years before such cars appeared elsewhere in North America.

The first special postal train in the world was inaugurated by the Great Western Railway between London and Bristol on 1st February 1855. Passengers were carried from June 1869 when one First Class carriage was attached.

The first mail train between London and Aberdeen was inaugurated by the London & North Western and Caledonian railways on 1st July 1885. It did not carry passengers.

Travelling sorting offices and exchange apparatus were discontinued in Britain from 22nd September 1940 until 1st October 1945.

Apparatus for exchanging mail-bags on British railways was last used on 4th October 1971, just north of Penrith.

Mail-bag exchanging apparatus in operation. (British Rail.)

FREIGHT SERVICES

Containers were introduced in Britain and Europe during the early 1920s. These large boxes could be transferred bodily from train to truck or ship, so avoiding much loading and unloading.

Automatic couplers were adopted on the Imperial Japanese Government Railway on 17th July 1925, after eight years of preparation. The conversion was completed in twenty-four hours.

Freight-liner services on British Railways were introduced between London and Glasgow on 15th November 1965; London and Manchester on 28th February 1966; London and Liverpool on 13th June 1966; Liverpool and Glasgow on 5th September 1966; Manchester and Glasgow on 12th September 1966; London and Aberdeen on 31st October 1966. By the end of 1966 some 27,000 loaded freight-liner containers had been carried.

The British Railways service for carrying new cars between Dagenham, Essex, and Halewood near Liverpool using two-tier "Cartic" units began on 13th July 1966.

The first British 100 ton bogie tank wagon for Shell oil products was completed on 21st February 1967.

The Harwich–Zeebrugge container service between England and Belgium was introduced on 18th March 1968, using special cellular container ships and wide-span transporter cranes.

The first container shipped from Japan over the Trans-Siberian Railway arrived at Harwich, England, in May 1969 after a journey of 7,600 miles.

The longest and heaviest freight train on record was run on 15th November 1967 over the 157 miles between Iaeger, West Virginia, and Portsmouth, Ohio, U.S.A. The 500 coal cars weighed 42,000 tons and stretched about 4 miles. The load was shifted by three 3,600 hp diesels in front and three behind.

The heaviest single piece of freight ever carried by rail was a 106 ft tall hydrocracker reactor weighing 549·2 tons, from Birmingham, Alabama, to Toledo, Ohio, U.S.A., on 12th November 1965.

The heaviest load carried by British Railways was a 122 ft long boiler drum weighing 275 tons from Immingham Dock to Killinghome, Lincolnshire, in September 1968.

The railways of Russia form one of the largest and most advanced systems in the world, with 80,927 miles of 5 ft gauge route. By 1939 the entire wagon stock was fitted with continuous brakes and hundreds of thousands of wagons had automatic couplings. Today about 94 per cent of the Russian goods stock consists of high-capacity vehicles on four or six axles.

The record run by a "Super C" freight in the U.S.A. was made in January 1968 on the Atchison, Topeka & Santa Fé Railroad between Corwith and Hobart yards. The 2,202·1 miles were covered in 34 hours 35 minutes 40 seconds at an average speed of 63·6 mile/h.

RAILCARS

The first railcar was a four-wheeled vehicle designed by James Samuel, Engineer of the Eastern Counties Railway. It was built by W. Bridges Adams (see *The Pioneers*) at Fairfields Works, Bow, London, and was named *Express*. It first ran on

23rd October 1847. It had a vertical boiler. Although it could run at 47 mile/h, and burned only 3·02 lb of coke a mile, it carried only four passengers and was hardly an economic proposition!

The first large railcar was again by J. Samuel and W. B. Adams. Built in 1848 for the 7 ft gauge Bristol & Exeter Railway it was named *Fairfield* and put to work on the Tiverton Branch. It also had a vertical boiler.

Their next, *Enfield*, built in 1849 for the Eastern Counties Railway was the first with a horizontal boiler.

After a quarter of a century the railcar idea was again taken up and in 1873 McDonnell of the Great Southern & Western Railway in Ireland produced a 0–4–4 tank type with a staff saloon on the rear.

Other staff railcars were built by the Great Eastern Railway in 1874; by Stroudley on the London, Brighton & South Coast Railway in 1885; and the famous Dougald Drummond "Cab" incorporating a single driver engine, on the London & South Western Railway in 1899.

In Belgium the railcar was introduced in 1877 by M. A. Cabany of Malines. A total of fifteen were built some with six and some with eight wheels.

The next railcar phase came in 1903–11 when many railways were trying to economise on working branch lines. Most of these cars had a small 0–4–0 locomotive forming one bogie. About twenty-five companies in England, Scotland, Wales and Ireland produced about as many different designs. Among the best, and the longest lived, were the Lancashire & Yorkshire Railway cars of George Hughes.

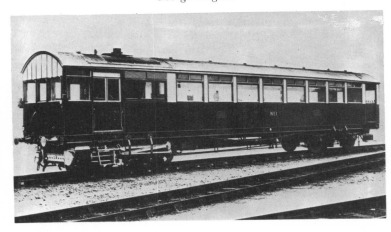

The Great Western Railway steam railcar No. 1 built at Swindon in 1903. (British Rail.)

The Lancashire & Yorkshire Railway Hughes railcar No. 8, built in June 1906 at Horwich, Lancashire. (British Rail.)

Geared steam railcars were first produced in Britain in 1905 and later were developed by the Sentinel Wagon Works at Shrewsbury and by Cammel-Laird Limited in 1923. They had a vertical high-pressure water-tube boiler, and were in use all over the world. The biggest user of these cars in Britain was the London & North Eastern Railway.

The first British internal-combustion-engined railcar was the "Petrol-Electric Autocar" built by the North Eastern Railway in 1903.

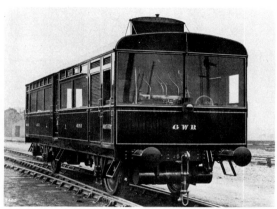

The Great Western Railway petrol-electric railcar No. 100, designed by British Thomson-Houston Company, who supplied all the electrical equipment. It entered service in 1911 and was sold in 1919 to Lever Brothers Limited at Port Sunlight, Cheshire, who used it until 1923. (British Rail.)

Direct-drive petrol (gas) engined vehicles were being tried at the same time in America. In 1904 a Napier car fitted with flanged wheels was tested over 1,000 miles of railway in the U.S.A. and Canada.

The "gas-electric" car was introduced in the U.S.A. by the General Electric Company in 1906 when a combined passenger and baggage car was built for the Delaware & Hudson Railroad. It was 68 ft 7 in long and weighed 43·8 tons.

Many railcars for light railways, particularly in Ireland, were adapted from old buses, the first being run on the 3 ft gauge County Donegal Railway in Ireland in 1928.

The first "road-railer" was placed in service by the London, Midland & Scottish Railway in 1931. Designed by J. Shearman of the L.M.S., it was a Karrier chassis with a Craven body and could be quickly adapted for rail or road use. It was used between Blisworth and Stratford on Avon, being used on the road in Stratford. It could run at 70 mile/h on rails and 60 mile/h on the road. It was scrapped after only a few years.

Pneumatic-tyred railcars were introduced in France in 1931 by the Michelin Tyre Company. A similar car was tried on the London, Midland & Scottish and Southern railways in England in 1932. In 1935 the L.M.S. tested the "Coventry Pneumatic Railcar", a sixteen-wheeled vehicle by Armstrong Siddeley with Michelin tyres. Pneumatic-tyred cars, though much used in France, never went into public service in Britain.

Petrol (or gas) vehicles never found much favour on railways, largely because of the danger of fire.

For developments in diesel railcars see "Diesel Rail Traction", page 157.

The record for being the world's most extraordinary railcar must surely be held for all time by the Brighton & Rottingdean Seashore Electric Tramroad, Sussex, England. The line was about 2·75 miles long and was built by Magnus Volk (see *The Pioneers*) on the seashore, with a total gauge of 18 ft. At high water the four rails were covered by about 15 ft of water. The car stood on legs about 23 ft high and had a cabin like a ship. It was the only railcar to carry a lifeboat and lifebelts as normal equipment. The railway opened on 28th November 1896 and ran until January 1901.

The Brighton & Rottingdean Seashore Electric Tramroad built by Magnus Volk, ran from 1896 to 1901.

RAILWAY RACES

In the Great Locomotive Chase on 12th April 1862, during the American Civil War, Captain James J. Andrews and his Yankee raiders seized the Confederate Rogers 4–4–0 *General* at Kennesaw, about 30 miles north of Atlanta, Georgia. They drove it 87 miles to within 20 miles of Chatanooga where it ran out of fuel and was caught by the Confederates in another 4–4–0, *Texas*. The chase was over light unballasted track at speeds of over 60 mile/h. For 50 miles the *Texas* was running tender first.

Both engines are preserved; the *General* at Chatanooga Union Station and the *Texas* at Grant Park, Atlanta.

In the race from London to Edinburgh in 1888 the West Coast companies (London & North Western and Caledonian) on 13th August covered the 399·7 miles in 7 hours 6 minutes at an average speed of 56·2 mile/h.

On 31st August 1888 the East Coast companies (Great Northern, North Eastern and North British) set up a record over their 393·2 mile route, taking 6 hours 48 minutes at an average speed of 57·7 mile/h.

In the race from London to Aberdeen, the West Coast companies set up a world speed record on 22nd August 1895 by covering the 541 miles in 512 minutes at an average speed of 63·3 mile/h including three stops and the climbs over Shap and Beattock, but with only a 70 ton train.

The best East Coast time was 518 minutes for 523·5 miles on 21st August 1895, but they had reached Edinburgh in 6 hours 18 minutes, averaging 62·3 mile/h with three stops and with a 120 ton train, thereby beating their record of 1888.

When the Atlantic liners called at Plymouth there was great rivalry between the Great Western and London & South Western railways in getting passengers and mail to London.

On 9th May 1904 the G.W.R. "Ocean Mail" ran the 128·5 miles from Plymouth to Bristol in 128 minutes, with the 4–4–0 locomotive No. 3440 *City of Truro*. Down Wellington Bank it reached a very high speed, but the reputed maximum of 102 mile/h has since been seriously questioned and is no longer accepted.

With the 4–2–2 *Duke of Connaught* the 118·5 miles from Bristol to London were covered in 106 minutes.

The Great Western Railway 4–4–0 No. 3440 City of Truro *back in service on a Didcot–Southampton train at Winchester Chesil. (John Marshall.)*

The disastrous derailment at Salisbury at 13.57 hours on 1st July 1906 brought the racing to an end. The London & South Western Railway boat express was wrecked taking a sharp curve at excessive speed. Twenty-four passengers and four railwaymen were killed.

The world's longest non-stop run was established by the London & North Eastern Railway in the summer timetable of 1927 with the 268·3 miles between London and Newcastle.

Not to be outdone the London, Midland & Scottish Railway immediately cut out the Carnforth stop in the run of the 10.00 train out of London (Euston), which had just been named the "Royal Scot", and ran the 301 miles non-stop to Carlisle.

On 1st May 1928 the London & North Eastern Railway decided to run the 10.00 train from London (King's Cross), the "Flying Scotsman",

The London & North Eastern Railway "Flying Scotsman" hauled by a "Pacific" locomotive. (British Rail.)

non-stop between London and Edinburgh, 392·75 miles, thereby establishing another world record. For this purpose H. N. Gresley designed his famous corridor tender enabling the engine crew to be changed during the journey.

On the Friday before this, however, the London, Midland & Scottish Railway stole the glory by dividing the "Royal Scot" and running the two halves non-stop from London to Edinburgh and Glasgow.

The Edinburgh portion of six coaches was taken by the 4–4–0 compound No. 1054 whose run of 399·7 miles was certainly a British record for a 4–4–0 and probably a world record.

"Royal Scot"-type 4–6–0 No. 6113 *Cameronian* with the Glasgow portion achieved a world record with any locomotive by running the 401·4 miles non-stop.

The London, Midland & Scottish Railway crowned this achievement on 16th November 1936 by running a special 230 ton train non-stop from London to Glasgow in 5 hours 53 minutes 38 seconds at an average speed of 68·1 mile/h behind the Stanier "Pacific" No. 6201 *Princess Elizabeth*.

The following day it returned with 260 tons in 5 hours 44 minutes 15 seconds at an average speed of 70 mile/h.

The London, Midland & Scottish Railway "Pacific" No. 6201 Princess Elizabeth. *(British Rail.)*

The result of this exercise was the inauguration of the London, Midland & Scottish Railway "Coronation Scot" streamlined train which ran between London and Glasgow in six and a half hours on 5th July 1937, stopping, however, at Carlisle for change of crew. On the same day the London & North Eastern Railway introduced the "Coronation" between London and Edinburgh, streamlined from the front of the "A4" Class "Pacific" to the tail of the rear observation car. It called at York and Newcastle upon Tyne going north and at Newcastle upon Tyne going south. The journey time was six hours.

RAILWAY SPEED RECORDS

America claimed the earliest rail speed records but most of these are unauthenticated and are not internationally accepted.

The first mile-a-minute run was claimed in 1848 when the locomotive *Antelope* ran from Boston to Lawrence, Massachusetts—26 miles in twenty-six minutes.

The first hundred-mile-an-hour run was claimed on 9th May 1893 when the "Empire State Express" of the New York Central & Hudson River Railroad (introduced on 26th October 1891) running between Syracuse and Buffalo, New York, reached 102·8 mile/h at Grimesville. On 11th May it was said to have reached 112·5 mile/h at Crittenden West, New York State. The engine was the 4–4–0 No. 999, and the Engineer was Charles Hogan. This engine, rebuilt with 5 ft 8 in driving-wheels in place of its original 7 ft 2 in, is now displayed at the Museum of Science and Industry, Chicago.

The first run at 120 mile/h was claimed by the Plant System, Florida, on 1st March 1901 when the "Florida Mail" was said to have covered the 5 miles between Fleming and Jacksonville in two and a half minutes. This is mentioned as a matter of interest, but it is no longer accepted as authentic.

On 15th June 1902 the New York Central & Hudson River Railroad inaugurated the "Twentieth Century Limited" between New York and Chicago, covering the 961 mile route in twenty hours. On the same day the Pennsylvania Railroad introduced the "Pennsylvania Special" taking twenty hours over its 897 mile route.

The New York Central & Hudson River Railroad route included a 15 mile/h journey of a mile through the main street of Syracuse. This stretch was replaced by a viaduct on 24th September 1936.

The Pennsylvania Railroad route included 400 miles through the Allegheny Mountains, round the famous horseshoe curve, and over a summit of 2,194 ft.

The fastest long-distance train in the world was the claim made by the Pennsylvania Railroad on 11th June 1905 when the "Pennsylvania Special" began running between New York and Chicago in eighteen hours. The following day it was claimed that the train had run 3 miles at 127·2 mile/h at Elida, Ohio, with the "Atlantic"-type engine No. 7002 and had covered the whole journey in 16 hours 3 minutes at an average speed of 56·07 mile/h.

In May 1905 the Atlantic City Railroad ran a train from Camden to Atlantic City covering the 55·5 miles in 42 minutes 32 seconds at an average speed of 78·3 mile/h.

In July 1905 the Atchison, Topeka & Santa Fé Railroad achieved a record with a run from Los Angeles to Chicago covering the 2,244·5 miles in 44 hours 54 minutes at an average speed of 50 mile/h.

The same railroad, over a shortened route of 2,228·6 miles, achieved a time of 36 hours 49 minutes at an average speed of 60·5 mile/h in May 1937.

The "Twentieth Century Limited" of the New York Central & Hudson River Railroad had its time cut to eighteen hours in 1908 but was later restored to twenty hours until reduced to eighteen again in April 1932. On 15th June 1938 the new streamlined trains reduced the time to sixteen hours. In 1929 the route was shortened to 958·7 miles by the Cleveland By-pass. Steam-traction with the famous N.Y.C. "Hudson"-type 4–6–4s ended in March 1945. The "Twentieth Century Limited" made its last run on 13th March 1967.

The earliest speed record with electric-traction was 101 mile/h attained by a German double-bogie locomotive of 1901 built by Siemens & Halske, operating on 15,000 V d.c., but it caused severe damage to the track.

On 6th October 1903 a twelve-wheeled electric railcar with motors by Siemens & Halske reached a speed of 126 mile/h on the military railway between Marienfeld and Berlin. A similar car with Allgemeine Elektricitäts Gesellschaft (A.E.G.) equipment reached 130·5 mile/h on 23rd October 1903.

A new world rail speed record was established in Germany on 21st June 1931 when a petrol railcar driven by an air-screw maintained 143 mile/h for 6·25 miles between Karstadt and Dergenthin.

The world's fastest train was the claim made by the Great Western Railway, England, on 6th June 1932 when the "Cheltenham Spa Express" behind the "Castle" Class 4–6–0 *Tregenna Castle* ran the 77·3 miles from Swindon to London (Paddington) in 56 minutes 47 seconds, at an average speed of 81·6 mile/h. The maximum speed was 92·3 mile/h. The train became known as "The Cheltenham Flyer", but the record was held only until 1935.

"The Cheltenham Flyer" with a "Castle" Class 4–6–0 engine. (British Rail.)

In Germany a speed record for steam was established in May 1935 when the streamlined 4–6–4 No. 05.001 reached 124·5 mile/h on a test run between Berlin and Hamburg. The engine was built by the Borsig Locomotive Works, Berlin in 1935.

The second engine, No. 05.002, achieved 120 mile/h with a 200 ton train in June 1935.

The fastest recorded speed with a steam locomotive in Canada was on a test run in 1936 when a Canadian Pacific Railway "Jubilee" Class 4–4–4 reached 112 mile/h.

The Canadian Pacific Railway "Jubilee" Class 4–4–4 engine. One of this type reached 112 mile/h in 1936, the fastest speed with steam in Canada.

The record speed for diesel-electric traction was achieved in Germany on 23rd June 1939 when a high-speed diesel train reached 133·5 mile/h.

The diesel-electric "Zephyr" of the Chicago, Burlington & Quincy Railroad, U.S.A., on 26th May 1934, ran the 1,017 miles from Denver to Chicago at an average speed of 77·6 mile/h throughout.

On 23rd October 1936 it ran from Chicago to Denver in 12 hours 12 minutes at an average speed of 91·6 mile/h; 750 miles were covered at 90 mile/h, 26·6 miles at 105 mile/h, and a maximum speed of 116 mile/h was reached.

The Union Pacific Railroad achieved a record for diesel-traction with the first American diesel-electric streamlined express. In October 1934 during tests it covered 60 miles at 102·8 mile/h, and reached 120 mile/h. It crossed the continent from Los Angeles to New York—3,259 miles—in 56 hours 56 minutes at an average speed of 62 mile/h. In service it ran the 2,272 miles between Chicago and Portland in 39·25 hours.

In the mid 1930s the steam-hauled streamlined "Hiawatha" express of the Chicago, Milwaukee, St. Paul & Pacific Railroad regularly covered the 410 miles from Chicago to St. Paul in six and a half hours with a 4–4–4 locomotive, reaching speeds of 100–105 mile/h. One of the Milwaukee semi-streamlined 4–6–4s on the "Hiawatha" covered 19 miles at over 100 mile/h, reaching a maximum of 120 mile/h.

The first authentic 100 mile/h run in Britain was made by the London & North Eastern Railway "Pacific" No. 4472 *Flying Scotsman* on 30th November 1934 on a test train from London to Leeds and back. Outward with 145 tons it covered the 185·8 miles in 151 minutes 56 seconds, and on the return trip with 208 tons in 157 minutes 17 seconds, reaching 100 mile/h down Stoke Bank between Grantham and Peterborough.

Bugatti railcars in France achieved some high speeds in 1935, one of them reaching 115·5 mile/h near Le Mans.

A world speed record for steam was achieved by the London & North Eastern Railway on 5th March 1935 when the "Pacific" No. 2750 *Papyrus*, during a round trip of 536 miles from London to Newcastle and back at an over-all average speed of 70 mile/h, reached 108 mile/h down Stoke Bank. The outcome of this test was a new four-hour service between London and Newcastle in October 1935.

The first of the famous Gresley "A4" Class "Pacifics", the No. 2509 *Silver Link*, broke the record the same year, on 27th September 1935, when it twice reached 112·5 mile/h, and averaged 107·5 mile/h for 25 miles, 100 mile/h for 43 miles and 91·8 mile/h for 70 miles continuously, with a 230 ton train.

The highest speed in ordinary service reached by steam in Britain was with the London & North Eastern Railway "A4" Class No. 2512 *Silver Fox* which reached a speed of 113 mile/h when working the "Silver Jubilee" streamlined train of 270 tons.

The London & North Eastern Railway "Silver Jubilee' streamlined train. (British Rail.)

The record was next stolen by the London, Midland & Scottish Railway on 29th June 1937 during a trial of the streamlined "Coronation Scot" express with the "Pacific" No. 6220 *Coronation*. At a point only 2 miles south of Crewe a speed of 114 mile/h was registered, followed by a hazardous entry into Crewe Station.

The all-time record for steam-traction was recaptured by the London & North Eastern Railway on 3rd July 1938 when the "A4" Class 4–6–2 No. 4468 *Mallard* with a seven-coach train weighing 240 tons reached 126 mile/h on Stoke Bank. Five miles (mileposts 94–89) were covered at an average speed of 120·4 mile/h. It was not achieved without risk and the engine suffered severe damage. The driver, Joseph Duddington, retired in 1944. *Mallard* is preserved in the Museum of British Transport, Clapham, London.

The London & North Eastern Railway "A4" Class 4–6–2 "Pacific" streamlined locomotive No. 4468 Mallard *was designed by Sir Nigel Gresley, Chief Mechanical Engineer of the L.N.E.R. The* Mallard *achieved fame on 3rd July 1938 when, hauling a seven-coach train weighing 240 tons, it set a world record for steam-traction of 126 mile/h. (The Museum of British Transport.)*

In Italy new records were achieved by three-car electric units. On 27th July 1938 the 132·9 miles from Rome to Naples were covered in eighty-three minutes at an average speed of 96·1 mile/h and with a maximum of 125 mile/h.

On 20 July 1939 the 195·8 miles from Florence to Milan were covered in 115·2 minutes at an average speed, start to stop, of 102 mile/h with a maximum of 126 mile/h.

In Germany a record for a diesel train was made on 23rd June 1939 with a speed of 133·5 mile/h.

The highest speeds achieved on rails at the time of writing (1972) have been made in France. On 21st February 1953 the Co Co electric locomotive No. 7121 with three coaches averaged 149 mile/h for 3 miles between Dijon and Beaune, reaching a maximum speed of 150·9 mile/h.

On 28th March 1955 No. 7107 reached 205·6 mile/h with a three-coach train of 100 tons between Facture and Morcenx on the Bordeaux–Hendaye line. The following day this speed was equalled by Bo Bo locomotive No. 9004.

The world's present rail speed record of 235 mile/h was achieved in France on 4th December 1967 between Gometz-le-Châtel and Limours by "L'Aerotrain" powered by jet aero-engines.

The highest recorded speed on rails achieved in the U.S.A. was 183·85 mile/h in July 1966 by a Budd diesel car fitted with two turbo-jet "J-47" aircraft engines mounted on the forward end. The run was made on the New York Central Railroad near Bryan, Ohio, between mileposts 350 and 345. The 5 miles were covered in 1 minute 39·75 seconds at an average speed of 181 mile/h. The record was achieved near milepost 347 over a length of 300 ft.

The first regular scheduled service at over 100 mile/h was introduced in Japan on 1st November 1965 on the new 4 ft 8·5 in gauge Tokaido line when trains began running between Tokyo and Osaka—321 miles—in 3 hours 10 minutes at an average speed of 101·3 mile/h, with a maximum of over 130 mile/h, covering the 212·4 miles between Tokyo and Nagoya in 120 minutes at an average speed of 106·2 mile/h. The twelve-car trains weigh 72 tons and run on single-phase a.c. at 25 kV. In 1969 Japan ran thirty-two daily trains at an average speed of over 100 mile/h.

The Tokaido line was opened on 1st October 1964. The new Sanyo line, now under construction to extend the Tokaido line from Osaka to Hakata in northern Kyushu, is planned to be completed in 1975. Trains

A super-express train crossing the Fuji River in view of Mount Fuji on the New Tokaido line. (Ministry of Foreign Affairs, Japan.)

Construction of the Sanyo Extension, west of Osaka.

will travel the 664 miles between Tokyo and Hakata in 6 hours 40 minutes at maximum speeds of 155·25 mile/h.

The fastest booked time in Britain is between Crewe and Watford Junction where trains cover the 140·5 miles in 101·5 minutes at an average speed of 83·1 mile/h.

FASTEST SCHEDULED TRAINS IN THE U.S.A. AND CANADA IN 1971

The Penn Central Railroad electric "Metroliners" were introduced between New York and Washington on 10th January 1969, covering the 224·6 miles with five stops in 2 hours 59 minutes at an average speed of 75·3 mile/h. On 2nd April 1969 a non-stop schedule of two and a half hours was established at an average speed of 89·8 mile/h, but this was discontinued.

Eight Penn Central Railroad "Metroliners" are booked over the 68·4 miles from Baltimore to Wilmington in forty-three minutes at an average speed of 95·4 mile/h. In the reverse direction nine "Metroliners" take forty-four minutes at an average speed of 93·3 mile/h.

With diesel-traction two Canadian National Railways "Rapidos" cover the 115·3 miles between Dorval and Brockville in eighty-seven minutes at an average speed of 79·5 mile/h. Two other C.N.R. "Rapidos" cover the 100·5 miles between Guildwood and Belleville in seventy-six minutes also at an average speed of 79·5 mile/h.

Diesel-traction freight. On the Santa Fé Railroad a "Super C" freight is booked over the 127·2 miles between Winslow and Gallup in 105 minutes at an average speed of 72·7 mile/h. Another S.F.R. "Super C" takes 175 minutes over the 205·2 miles between Waynoka and Amarillo at an average speed of 70·3 mile/h.

ACCIDENTS

The first recorded fatal railway accident occurred on the opening day of the Liverpool & Manchester Railway, 15th September 1830, when William Huskisson, Member of Parliament for Liverpool, was run over by Stephenson's *Rocket* at Parkside near Newton le Willows. His thigh was fractured and he died later at Eccles.

The first notable railway accident was in France on 8th May 1842. A fifteen-coach express from Versailles to Paris crashed when an axle of one of the two engines broke and several coaches piled on top of it. Locked compartment doors prevented people from escaping, and forty-eight were burned to death. This ended the locking of train doors in France.

Charles Dickens escaped with a shaking when he was involved in the derailment at Staplehurst, Kent, on the South Eastern Railway, on 9th June 1865, in which ten people were killed when the train ran on to a viaduct where repairs were being carried out. He never fully recovered and he died on 9th June 1870, exactly five years later.

The only major British railway disaster in which there were no survivors was on 28th December 1879 when the Tay Bridge collapsed in a gale while a train was crossing. All seventy-three passengers and crew of three were drowned. Some bodies were never recovered. (See Bouch in *The Pioneers*.)

The first serious accident to an electric train in Britain was at Hall Road on the Liverpool–Southport line of the Lancashire & Yorkshire Railway. A signalman's error led to a collision in which twenty-one people were killed.

The worst accident on a London "tube" railway was at Stratford on 8th April 1953 when twelve people were killed.

One of Britain's most curious railway disasters was at Swinton near Manchester on 28th April 1953 when the roof of the Clifton Hall (Black Harry) Tunnel collapsed under a filled-in shaft. A pair of semi-detached houses above collapsed into the crater causing five deaths.

The tunnel was on the Patricroft–Clifton Branch of the London & North Western Railway and was opened on 2nd February 1850.

No passengers were killed on British Railways in 1949, 1954, 1956 and 1966 in more than 15,000,000,000 journeys each year. In 1959 and 1963 only one passenger was killed in each year.

Worst Railway Disasters in various countries

Country	Date	Place	No. killed	Cause
France	12.12.1917	Modane	543	Derailment
Italy	2.3.1944	Salerno	526	Stalled in tunnel
Spain	16.1.1944	Leon Province	500–800	Wreck in tunnel
Pakistan (West)	29.9.1957	Montgomery	250	Collision
Mexico	3.4.1955	Near Guadalajara	c. 300	Derailed into canyon
Argentina	4.2.1970	Near Buenos Aires	236	Collision
Scotland	22.5.1915	Near Gretna	c. 227	Double collision
Poland	22.10.1949	Nowy Dwor	c. 200	Derailment
Japan	29.1.1940	Osaka	200	Collision
Brazil	20.3.1946	Near Aracaju	185	Wreck
Jamaica	1.9.1957	Kendal	178	Derailed into ravine
New Zealand	24.12.1953	Near Waiouru	155	Bridge collapse
U.S.S.R.	13.7.1882	Near Tchery	c. 150	Derailment
Nigeria	16.2.1970	Northern Nigeria	c. 150*	
India	23.11.1956	Marudaiyar River	143	Derailment
Germany	22.12.1939	Near Magdeburg	132	Collision
England	8.10.1952	Harrow & Wealdstone	112	Double collision
Czechoslovakia	14.11.1960	Pardubice	110	Collision
U.S.A.	9.7.1918	Nashville, Tennessee	c. 101	Head-on collision
Rumania	25.12.1938	Near Kishinev	c. 100	Collision
Switzerland	14.6.1891	Near Basle	c. 100	Collision
Portugal	26.7.1964	Custoias near Oporto	94	Wreck
Indonesia	28.5.1959	Java	92	Derailed into ravine
Netherlands	8.1.1962	Woerden	91	Collision
Canada	29.6.1864	Beleil near St. Hilaire	c. 90	Points wrongly set
South Africa	4.10.1965	Near Durban	81	Derailment
Northern Ireland	12.6.1889	Armagh	c. 80	Runaway collision
Burma	9.12.1965	Near Toungoo	76	Collision
South Korea	31.1.1954	Near Seoul	56	
Philippines	2.9.1954	Negros Island	56	
Hungary	22.12.1968	Budapest	c. 43	Collision
Yugoslavia	14.2.1971	Belgrade	34	Fire

* A further 52 (survivors) were killed in a lorry on their way to hospital.

TRAIN FERRIES

The first wagon ferry was operated by the Monkland & Kirkintilloch Railway, Scotland, on the Forth & Clyde Canal in 1833. It was simply a barge fitted with rails and a turnplate.

The world's first "train ferry" was designed by Thomas Grainger and was built in 1849 by Robert Napier & Sons on the Clyde. Named *Leviathan*, it ferried goods wagons across the Firth of Forth, Scotland, between Granton and Burntisland.

    In 1858 a similar vessel named *Carries* was put on the Tayport–Broughty Ferry crossing near Dundee.

    Thomas Bouch (see *The Pioneers*) is sometimes credited with the design of these; actually he designed only the loading mechanism.

The Harwich–Zeebrugge train ferry between England and Belgium began operating under Great Eastern Train Ferries Limited on 24th April 1924.

The Dover–Dunkerque train ferry was inaugurated on 14th October 1936. Through trains between London and Paris were operated by the Southern Railway of England, the Northern Railway of France, the Société Anonyme de Navigation Angleterre-Lorraine-Alsace, and the International Sleeping Car Company.

One of the most famous train ferries was the *Baikal* which operated across Lake Baikal in Siberia as a link in the Trans-Siberian Railway. It was launched on 29th July 1899 and entered service in April 1900, combining the duties of train ferry and ice-breaker. It remained in use as a ferry until the Circum-Baikal Railway was completed in 1904 round the south of the lake, and it was destroyed in the civil war of 1918–20.

THE LAST STEAM TRAINS

The last steam-worked transcontinental trains on the Canadian Pacific Railway after sixty-seven years, ran in October 1954.

Steam locomotives were finally withdrawn on the Canadian National Railways on 25th April 1960.

The last steam-hauled trains on the Metropolitan Line, London, ran on 9th September 1961.

The last regular steam trains at London (Paddington)—formerly the Great Western Railway, opened in 1839—ran on 11th June 1965. The last steam special was run on 27th November 1965.

Steam-traction was eliminated from British Railways on 8th August 1968, except for the summer only service on the Vale of Rheidol narrow-gauge line in Wales.

A commemorative "Farewell to Steam" tour was operated by British Railways on 11th August 1968 from Liverpool to Carlisle and back. The fare was £15·75.

The last expresses worked by the famous French compound "Pacifics" ran between Calais and Amiens on 26th May 1971.

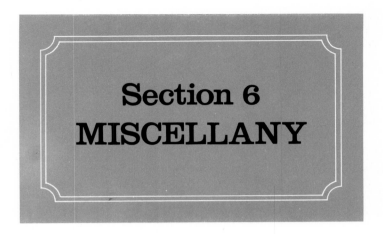

Section 6
MISCELLANY

BRITISH AND IRISH RAILWAYS

Under the Railways Act of 19th August 1921, a total of 123 separate British railway companies were amalgamated into four groups: the London, Midland & Scottish, the London & North Eastern, the Great Western and the Southern. Certain inter-group joint companies continued to operate separately. The grouping came into effect on 1st January 1923.

All-Irish railways wholly in the "Free State" (Eire), both 5 ft 3 in and 3 ft gauge, were grouped into the Great Southern Railways on 1st January 1925.

The London Passenger Transport Board was incorporated by Act of Parliament on 13th April 1933 and began to operate from 1st July. It took over the Metropolitan Railway, the Metropolitan District Railway, the London Electric Railway, the City & South London Railway, the Central London Railway, all London street tramways (now abandoned) and nearly all bus and coach undertakings in its area. It became part of the British Transport Commission on 1st January 1948. Under the Transport Act of 1962 it was renamed London Transport Board on 1st January 1963.

The London Electric Railway was an amalgamation of the original City & South London Railway and its extension which became the Northern Line, the Bakerloo Line, and the Piccadilly Line.

The London Transport Board owns 224·5 miles of railway, all but 2 miles electrified, and runs its trains over a total of 252 miles of route.

The Irish Transport Company (Coras Iompair Eireann) formed under the Eire Transport Act of 19th November 1944 began operation on 1st January 1945. Under it the Great Southern Railways and the Dublin United Transport Company Limited were merged.

The proposal to nationalise British railways was first announced by the Government on 19th November 1945. Canals and long-distance haulage were included.

The Transport Act received Royal Assent on 6th August 1947, nationalising British railways and canals from 1st January 1948.

The Transport Act (Northern Ireland) received Royal Assent on 10th August 1948, incorporating the Ulster Transport Authority. The Northern Ireland Road Transport Board, the Belfast & County Down and the Northern Counties railways and other transport services were acquired by 1st April 1949.

The last "early-morning" (workmen's) tickets on British Railways were issued at the end of 1961.

The last main line into London, the Great Central Railway (formerly the Manchester, Sheffield & Lincolnshire Railway) was opened to passengers on 15th March 1899. Coal traffic had begun on 25th July 1898 and general freight began on 11th April 1899. The railway was pioneered by Edward Watkin when he was Chairman of the Manchester, Sheffield & Lincolnshire, the Metropolitan and the South Eastern railways and of the Channel Tunnel Company. He saw the London Extension as part of a main line linking Manchester, London and Paris. The name "Great Central" was adopted on 1st August 1897.

The G.C.R. became part of the London & North Eastern Railway on 1st January 1923 and was run down and finally closed by British Rail in the late 1960s.

AMERICAN RAILWAYS

The U.S.A. Transportation Act was passed on 12th August 1958. The Department of Transportation was established by Public Law 89–670 on 15th October 1966 and began operation on 1st April 1967 to co-ordinate national transport policies. It also administers the Uniform Time Act.

The Penn Central Company was formed on 1st February 1968 by the merging of the Pennsylvania and the New York Central railroads. On 31st December 1968 the New York, New Haven & Hartford Railroad became part of the Penn Central Company, which now owns 20,500 miles and operates nearly 22,000 miles of railroad of which 720 miles are electrified in sixteen States, two Canadian provinces and the District of Columbia. It carries nearly 300,000 passengers a day and operates nearly 3,000 freight trains every twenty-four hours with 4,400 locomotives (200 electric and 4,200 diesel-electric), 5,000 passenger cars (including 900 multiple-unit electric cars) and 205,300 freight cars and other vehicles.

The Burlington Northern Railroad was formed on 2nd March 1970 by the merging of the Chicago, Burlington & Quincy, the Great Northern, the Northern Pacific and the Spokane, Portland & Seattle railroads. It operates 24,519 miles of route with 1,987 diesel-electric units including railcars, 115,730 freight cars, 1,285 passenger cars, and extends from Chicago to Vancouver and Seattle.

LARGE NATIONALISED RAILWAYS

South African Railways was formed in 1910 on the unification of the Cape, Orange River, Transvaal and Natal Colonies. The Administration runs 13,267 miles of 3 ft 6 in gauge lines of which 2,334 miles are electrified and 439 miles of 2 ft gauge.

Chinese People's Republic Railways. The Chinese Government took over control of railways from 1908. The mileage open in 1969 was about 21,750, mostly 4 ft 8·5 in gauge.

The Indian Railway Board was constituted in its present form in 1951. It owns 17,768 miles of 5 ft 6 in gauge, 15,867 miles of metre gauge, 2,310 miles of 2 ft 6 in gauge and 383 miles of 2 ft gauge.

Japanese National Railways was formed under the Railway Nationalisation Law of 1906. In 1970 12,945 miles of 3 ft 6 in gauge and 230 miles of 4 ft 8·5 in gauge were open. Railways are still under construction. The electrified mileage in 1970 was 3,605 of 3 ft 6 in gauge.

The U.S.S.R. Railways. By 1913 the Russian railway network comprised twenty-five State and thirteen private lines. The entire system was nationalised after the Revolution of 1917. The total mileage on 1 January 1968 was 81,927 miles of 5 ft gauge of which 18,075 were electrified; 1,108 miles of 1 ft 11 in of metre-gauge lines; 473 miles of 3 ft 6 in gauge in South Sakhalin formerly controlled by Japan, and 54 miles of 4 ft 8·5 in gauge.

National Railways of Mexico was formed by mergers and acquisitions beginning in 1908. The last was the Interoceanic Railway in June 1947. It operates 8,329 miles of 4 ft 8·5 in gauge of which 64 miles were electrified and 249 miles of 3 ft gauge including 29 miles of mixed gauge. Standard-gauge stock consists of 816 diesel-electric locomotives and 46 diesel-electric railcars, 1,575 carriages and 19,360 wagons. Narrow-gauge stock consists of 16 diesel-electric locomotives, 49 carriages and 343 wagons.

EUROPE

Belgian National Railways is the world's oldest nationalised system. The present administration, formed on 23rd July 1926 took over the system operated by the Belgian State Railways. The system is one of the densest in the world for railway mileage per square mile of country. Mileage at the end of 1968 was 2,661 of which 699 miles were electrified, all 4 ft 8·5 in gauge.

In addition Belgian National Light Railways operates 229 miles of narrow-gauge and other light railways and 6,615 miles of bus route.

Czechoslovak State Railways was first established in 1919 and was re-established in May 1945. It operates 8,102 miles of 4 ft 8·5 in gauge, 110 miles of metre and 1 ft 11·625 in gauge and 63 miles of the Russian 5 ft gauge (1,484 miles are electrified).

French National Railways (Société Nationale des Chemins de fer Français; S.N.C.F.) was formed on 31st August 1937 and operated 23,238 miles of 4 ft 8·5 in gauge of which 5,474 miles were electrified, in December 1968.

The German Federal Railway (Deutsche Bundesbahn; D.B.) was established on 1st April 1920, but on 11th October 1924 by the Railway Act of 30th August, amended by the Act of 13th March 1930, the system was made independent of the

Government. It was placed once more under State control on 30th January 1937. The D.B. was reorganised by the State Railways Act of 13th December 1951. Mileage on 31st December 1968 was 18,546 of which 5,028 miles were electrified.

The German State Railway (Deutsche Reichsbahn; D.R.) in East Germany operates 9,143 miles of 4 ft 8·5 in gauge of which 680 miles are electrified, and 629 miles of narrow gauge.

Italian State Railways was formed in 1905–07. It operates 10,078 miles of 4 ft 8·5 in gauge of which 4,917 miles are electrified.

Spanish National Railways (Red Nacional de los Ferrocarriles Españoles; R.E.N.F.E.) was formed under the Law of 27th February 1943. It operates 8,508 miles of 5 ft 6 in gauge of which 1,939 miles are electrified.

Switzerland has 3,210 miles of railways of which 1,810 miles form the Swiss Federal system. A total of 877 miles are narrower gauge, mainly metre. There are fourteen rack and pinion railways (excluding mixed rack and adhesion lines) totalling 59 miles, and fifty funicular or rope-worked railways totalling 31 miles.

Switzerland leads the whole of Europe in the frequency of its trains in relation to its area and in the world is second only to Japan. Of the private railways, the largest is the metre-gauge Rhaetian system in Graubünden, with 244 miles of route, which with the Furka–Oberalp and the Brig–Visp–Zermatt railways form the largest metre-gauge network in Europe. Second in size is the standard-gauge Bern–Lötschberg–Simplon Railway with 155 miles.

The standard-gauge South-Eastern Railway, between Pfäffikon and Arth-Goldau, includes gradients of 1 in 20 (5 per cent). Bridges on the Swiss Federal Railways number 5,455 of a total length of 53 miles. The 670 tunnels include three of the world's longest, the Simplon (12 miles 537 yd), the St. Gotthard (9 miles 562 yd) and the Lötschberg (9 miles 140 yd). The St. Gotthard Tunnel handles 244 trains daily including freight trains carrying some 100,000 tons every day.

Eleven, or nearly a third, of the fast and luxurious "Trans-Europe-Express" or T.E.E. trains serving all the principal cities in western Europe begin or end their journeys in Switzerland, or pass through it.

There are about 1,800 electric locomotives and motor coaches, and a few diesels for special duties. The most powerful electric locomotive is 11,000 hp. The average annual electricity consumption on Swiss Railways is 2,000,000,000,000 kWh.

LOADING GAUGES

Britain pays the penalty for being first with railways by suffering a restricted loading gauge of only 12 ft 8 in high by 8 ft 10 in wide, though some sections such as the Great Northern, the Lancashire & Yorkshire and the Great Western considerably exceeded this.

The world's largest loading for standard-gauge lines is the American, 15 ft 6 in high by 10 ft 9 in wide.

The standard for European lines is 14 ft 0·5 in high by 10 ft 4 in wide. Australian standard-gauge lines are about the same—14 ft by 10 ft 6 in.

Steam locomotive No. 1210 of the New South Wales Government Railways, which in 1914 pulled the first train to the construction site of Canberra, the Federal Capital of Australia, is now a national monument in that city. No. 1210 was built in 1878 by Beyer Peacock & Company of Manchester to a design based on the "Metropolitan" type of tank engine. (Australian News & Information Bureau.)

A giant 2–10–2 of the Spanish National Railways.

The world's biggest loading gauge is the Russian standard for 5 ft gauge—17 ft 4·75 in high by 11 ft 2 in wide.

The South African loading gauge for its 3 ft 6 in gauge lines is larger than the British Standard—13 ft high by 10 ft wide.

The widest rolling stock ever used in Britain was the 10 ft wide Liverpool–Southport electric stock of the Lancashire & Yorkshire Railway, introduced in 1904.

The biggest loading gauge on metre-gauge lines is on the East African Railways—13 ft 6 in high by 10 ft 6 in wide.

DIRECTION OF RUNNING ON DOUBLE LINES

The first railway to be planned and built as a double line was the Liverpool & Manchester Railway, opened on 15th September 1830. Left-hand running was adopted from the start.

Sections of the Stockton & Darlington Railway had been doubled previously, but in the form of extended passing loops. Doubling between Brussleton Incline and Darlington was not undertaken until 1831–32.

The following British railways adopted right-hand running at the beginning:

The Clarence Railway in County Durham of which the first portion opened in 1833. It became part of the Stockton & Hartlepool Railway on 1st January 1851 and of the West Hartlepool Railway on 1st January 1851 and of the West Hartlepool Harbour & Railway Company on 17th May 1853. The right-hand running continued until its absorption by the North Eastern Railway on 1st July 1865.

The London & Greenwich Railway, the first railway in London, opened in 1836–38. Right-hand running was adopted very early in the line's history but the date when it changed to left-hand running cannot be found.

The Manchester & Bolton Railway, opened on 29th May 1838, changed from right- to left-hand running when it was joined at Clifton by the East Lancashire Railway in September 1846.

The Newcastle & Carlisle Railway, opened on 18th June 1838, changed from right- to left-hand running on 7th March 1864, after its absorption by the North Eastern Railway in 1862.

Right-hand running operates on the following railways:

Europe—Austria (some sections), Bulgaria, Czechoslovakia, Denmark, Finland, Germany, Hungary, the Netherlands, Norway, Poland, Spain (the former Madrid, Zaragoza & Alicante Railway only), Turkey, the U.S.S.R. and Yugoslavia.

Asia—China (some sections) and the U.S.S.R.

North America—Canada and the U.S.A. (except the Chicago & North Western Railroad).

Other countries use left-hand running or have no double-line sections.

Using modern signalling methods, several railroads in the U.S.A. are now equipped for either-direction running on both lines, with complete safety, so allowing one train to overtake another and thus increasing line capacity.

WATER-TROUGHS

Water-troughs ("track-pans" in the U.S.A.) were invented by John Ramsbottom (1814–1892) while Locomotive Superintendent at Crewe on the London & North Western Railway, England, in 1859, and were patented in 1860.

The first-water troughs were installed in 1860 at Mochdre on the Chester–Holyhead section of the London & North Western Railway and were transferred to Aber on the same line in 1871.

The highest water-troughs in the world were at Garsdale on the Midland Railway Settle–Carlisle line at 1,169 ft above sea-level.
  Only 27 miles away, on the London & North Western Railway at Hest Bank near Lancaster, the water-troughs were almost at sea-level.

Water-trough in the south end of the up-line Standedge Tunnel between Manchester and Huddersfield on the London & North Western Railway. Overflow water drained into the canal tunnel alongside. (John Clarke.)

The only water-troughs inside a tunnel were in the Diggle end of the three 3 mile bores of the Standedge Tunnels on the London & North Western Railway between Manchester and Huddersfield. The Tunnels were the only level stretch on the whole route.

The total number of water-troughs in Britain was 141. Some, for example on the Lancashire & Yorkshire Railway, were steam-heated in frosty weather.

Track-pans were used in the U.S.A. from 1870 to 1956. Britain and the U.S.A. were the only countries to make extensive use of water-troughs.

The first mechanical locomotive coaling plants in Britain were at Crewe (North) in 1913 and Hull (Dairycoates) shortly afterwards.

SNOW-PLOUGHS

The rotary snow-plough was invented by J. W. Elliott, a dentist of Toronto, Canada, who patented a "compound revolving snow shovel" in 1867. The idea was not taken up, however.

The first rotary snow-plough was built by Leslie Brothers of Orangeville, Ontario, in 1883–84 and was tested by the Canadian Pacific Railway.

Its success led to an improved design constructed in 1887 by the Dunforth Cooke Company (which became part of the American Locomotive Company (ALCO) in 1901) and which was put into operation on the Union Pacific Railroad.

Rotary snow-plough on the Bernina Section of the Rhaetian Railway, Switzerland. (John Marshall.)

RAILWAY AIR SERVICES

The first air service operated by a British railway was by the Great Western Railway linking Cardiff, Torquay and Plymouth on 12th April 1933, in conjunction with Imperial Airways, using a three-engined Westland "Wessex" plane.

*Railway Air Services
Limited with four De
Havilland planes operating
in conjunction with the
Great Western Railway,
England. (British Rail.)*

Railway Air Services Limited was incorporated on 21st March 1934, in Great Britain. De Havilland "Dragon"-type eight-seater two-engined planes were used. In 1939 it became known as the "Great Western & Southern Air Lines". It was suspended at the outbreak of war in September 1939 and was resumed afterwards by Imperial Airways, later British European Airways.

The railway with the most extensive air services is the Canadian Pacific.

DOCKS AND SHIPS

The Lancashire & Yorkshire Railway operated more ships than any other British railway. Twenty-nine (including some owned jointly with the London & North Western Railway) were handed over to the London, Midland & Scottish Railway at the Grouping in 1923.

British Rail are the world's largest dock-owners, with docks, harbours and wharves in seventy-six places, with a total quay length of 501,402 ft, or about 95 miles. At the end of 1969 B.R. used 36,330 ft of quays in its own harbours.

The world's largest graving dock, at Southampton, is owned by British Rail.

The British Rail "Seaspeed" Hovercraft service between Southampton and Cowes, Isle of Wight, began operation on 5th July 1966. British Rail operated six Hovercraft at the end of 1969.

British Rail owned sixty-five ships at the end of 1969.

The world's highest railway-owned ships are operated by the Southern Railway of Peru on Lake Titicaca in the Andes at a height of 12,500 ft. The first ship, *Yavari*, was built in 1861 and was carried up from the coastal port of Mollendo in sections on the backs of mules and Indians to Puno on the lake. The illustration dates from 1890. More recently the steam-engine was replaced by a diesel. She was still at work in the 1960s.

Another ship, the 700 ton *Inca*—228 ft long and 50 ft beam—was built at Hull, England, in 1905, sailed out round Cape Horn to Mollendo, was dismantled and transported up the Southern Railway (completed to Puno in 1876) and reassembled on the lake. There are several ships at work on an itinerary of 1,350 miles. The longest voyage, Puno to Guaqui, takes twelve hours for the 120 miles.

RAILWAY ROAD SERVICES

The first railway-operated buses in Britain began on Monday, 17th August 1903 when the Great Western Railway inaugurated a service between Helston and the Lizard, Cornwall.

Another service began on 31st October between Penzance and Marazion; the North Eastern Railway meanwhile introduced buses on 7th September 1903.

The London & South Western Railway began operating buses on 1st June 1904.

The steamship Yavari *on Lake Titicaca, 12,500 ft above sea-level, operated by the Southern Railway of Peru. Built in 1861 and carried up from the coastal port of Mollendo in sections on the backs of mules and Indians to the slip at Puno, it was still in use as a tanker in the 1960s between Puno in Peru and the Bolivian lakeport of Guaqui. The steam-engine has been replaced by a diesel. (Southern Railway of Peru.)*

In Scotland the first railway buses were operated by the Great North of Scotland Railway between Ballater and Braemar on 2nd May 1904. By 1911 the company operated six services.

A Milnes-Daimler bus at Helston on the Great Western Railway in 1903. (British Rail.)

By 1928 the Great Western Railway operated 330 buses on 154 routes. In the early 1930s, however, along with other railway companies, the road interests were sold to other bus companies operating in the area and a great opportunity for developing a unified transport system was lost.

SIGNALLING

The first use of the electric telegraph on a railway was on the Great Western Railway in England, in 1839. Cooke and Wheatstone who had been experimenting on the London & Birmingham Railway installed it between London (Paddington) and West Drayton. It was extended to Slough in 1843.

In 1845 it was instrumental in the arrest at Paddington Station of a murderer, named Tawell, who had boarded a train at Slough. From that moment the telegraph was established.

The block system with Cooke and Wheatstone's electric telegraph was first used at Clay Cross Tunnel on the North Midland Railway near Chesterfield in Derbyshire in 1841.

Semaphore signals were first used for railways, also in 1841, at New Cross, Kent, on the South Eastern Railway.

The first railway to use the block system from opening was the Norwich & Yarmouth Railway, opened on 1st May 1844.

Staff working on single lines was introduced by the London & North Western Railway in 1853.

Interlocking of signals and points was patented by John Saxby in England in 1856.

Somersault signals, pivoted in the centre, were adopted by the Great Northern Railway, England, following the double collision at Abbott's Ripton caused by a signal being put out of order by snow. They were also used on the Barry, Brecon & Merthyr and Ryhmney railways in Wales and on the Northern Counties Railway in Ireland.

Somersault signal on the Great Northern Railway, England. (John Marshall.)

The Regulation of Railways Act enforcing the block system, interlocking of signals and points and the provision of continuous automatic brakes on passenger trains on British railways, came into operation on 30th August 1889.

Automatic signalling was installed on the London & South Western Railway between Andover and Grately, Hampshire, and was brought into use on 20th April 1902.

Audible cab signalling was introduced by the Great Western Railway, England, on the double-track Henley Branch on 1st January 1906 and on the single-line Fairford Branch on 1st December when the ordinary distant signals were removed.

The Great Western Railway audible cab signalling was first installed on a main line in 1908, on the four-track section between Slough and Reading, Berkshire, and was extended to London (Paddington) in 1912. About this time the automatic brake application was added, becoming known then as the "Automatic Train Control" (A.T.C.).

*Automatic train-control
apparatus on the Great
Western Railway, England.
(British Rail.)*

The first electro-pneumatic signalling installation in Britain was on the Lancashire & Yorkshire Railway at Bolton in 1904.

The Great Western Railway began installing A.T.C. on all main routes in 1931 completing much of it in that year. More was done in 1937 making a total of 2,850 route miles equipped.

The Hudd Intermittent Inductive A.T.C. apparatus was installed at 112 distant signal locations on the London, Midland & Scottish Railway London–Southend line in 1938. This system was first used on the London & North Eastern Railway on 13th August 1939 on the Edinburgh–Glasgow line.

The first push-button route-selecting signalling control system in Britain was brought into operation by London Transport at Ealing Broadway on 29th November 1952.

London Transport's last electro-pneumatic semaphore signal was removed from service on 21st November 1953.

British Railways system of A.T.C. for use with non-electric traction was approved by the Minister of Transport on 30th November 1956.

STATIONS

The world's oldest railway station, still with its original buildings, is at Liverpool Road, Manchester, England, the original terminus of the Liverpool & Manchester Railway, opened on 15th September 1830. Its passenger service ended, however, when Manchester (Victoria) was connected to the L. & M. on 5th May 1844, and since then it has been a goods station.

Top left : Prague Main Station, Czechoslovakia. (K. B. Smith.)

Top right : Milan Station on the Italian State Railways. (K. B. Smith.)

Middle : Seville Station, Spain. (K. B. Smith.)

Bottom : Interior of Kent Station, Cork, Ireland showing the tiled platform typical of Irish stations. (K. B. Smith.)

*Liverpool Road Station,
Manchester, is the world's
oldest railway station.
(John Marshall.)*

The world's oldest passenger station still in use on the original site is the Mount Clare Station of the Baltimore & Ohio Railroad in Baltimore. It was completed on 24 May 1830.

The highest station and junction in the world, at 15,610 ft, is Ticlio, on the Central Railway of Peru, opened in 1904. From here the Morococha Branch leaves the main line and climbs to 15,848 ft, the world's highest railway summit.

*Ticlio Station and Junction
on the Central Railway of
Peru at 15,610 ft are the
world's highest. The
illustration shows the west
end of the Galera Tunnel
with Mount Meiggs.
(Brian Fawcett, M.I.L.E.)*

The world's largest station is the Grand Central Terminal, New York, U.S.A. It has forty-four platforms, all below ground, on two levels, with forty-one tracks on the upper and twenty-six on the lower, and covers 48 acres. It was built in 1903–13. It is used by 550 trains and 180,000 people daily.

Other large stations are:

Pennsylvania Terminal, New York	32 platforms
Union Station, Washington	32 platforms
Saint-Lazare, Paris	27 platforms

Largest British Stations

	Platforms	Total length (ft)	Area (acres)
Clapham Junction	17	11,165	27·75
Waterloo, London	23*	15,352	24·5
Victoria, London	17	18,412	21·75
Crewe	16	11,394	23
Waverley, Edinburgh, Scotland	19	14,305	18
London Bridge	21	13,574	
Liverpool Street, London	18	11,410	16
Paddington, London	16	15,025	14·75

* Including two Waterloo & City Railway platforms below ground.

Longest Railway Station Platforms

	(ft)
Chicago, Illinois (State Street Center subway platform staging)	3,500
Kharagpur, Bihar, India (formerly Bengal & Nagpur Railway)	2,733
Sonepur, India (formerly Bengal & North Western Railway)	2,415
Bulawayo, Rhodesia	2,302
New Lucknow, India (formerly East India Railway)	2,250
Manchester (Victoria No. 11 + Exchange No. 3), England (Exchange closed on 5th May 1969)	2,194
Bezwada, India (formerly Madras & Southern Mahratta Railway)	2,100
Jhansi, India (formerly Great Indian Peninsula Railway)	2,025
Colchester, England	1,975
Kotri, India (formerly North Western Railway)	1,896
Mandalay, Burma	1,788
Bournemouth, England	1,748
Perth, Scotland	1,714
York, England	1,692 and 1,575
Edinburgh (Waverley), Scotland	1,596
Trichinopoly, India (formerly South India Railway)	1,546
Ranaghat, India (formerly Eastern Bengal Railway)	1,522
Crewe, England	1,509
London (Victoria), England	1,500
Dakor, India (formerly Bombay, Baroda & Central India Railway)	1,470
Newcastle (Central), England	1,389
Cambridge, England	1,254

The largest span station roof ever built was the 300 ft of the second Broad Street Station, Philadelphia, U.S.A., built in 1892.

The Pennsylvania Railroad at Jersey City, U.S.A., built in 1888 had a roof span of 252 ft.

The largest station roof span in Britain is in London (St. Pancras), built by the Midland Railway. It has a span of 240 ft, and is 100 ft high above rail-level. It was designed by W. H. Barlow and was completed in 1868.

St. Pancras Station in London built by the Midland Railway has the largest span roof in Britain. (British Rail.)

Manchester (Central) owned originally by the Cheshire Lines Railway, had a roof span of 210 ft and was 90 ft high. It was opened in 1880 and closed on 5th May 1969. It formed the terminus of Midland Railway trains from London (St. Pancras) and C.L.R. trains from Liverpool (Central) and Chester.

Milan (Central), Italy, designed by Ulisse Stacchini and completed in 1930, has a central roof span of 236 ft. The main building is one of the most grandiose in existence.

The largest station waiting-room in the British Isles, and the most elegant was the Great Hall at Euston, London. It was designed by P. C. Hardwick and opened to the public on 27th May 1849. It measured 126 ft long, 61 ft wide and 64 ft high. The flat panelled ceiling was the largest of its kind in the world. One of London's architectural treasures, it was demolished along with the Doric Arch in the rebuilding of Euston Station in 1962.

Built in 1860, St. Pancras Station, London, is a superb example of Victorian Gothic architecture. The architect was Sir George Gilbert Scott. (British Rail')

*The Great Hall of Euston
Station in London was
designed by P. C. Hardwick
and opened on 27th May
1849. It was demolished in
1962. (British Rail.)*

The world's largest waiting-rooms are those in Peking Station, China, opened in September 1959, with a total capacity of 14,000 persons.

At Dartmouth, Devon, is the only station in use on British Rail which has never had any trains. It is connected by ferry with Kingswear Station across the Dart Estuary.

*A platform ticket of
Llanfairpwllgwyngyllgogery-
chwyrndrobwllllantysiliogo-
gogoch in Anglesey, North
Wales. (British Rail.)*

The station with the longest name was Llanfairpwllgwyngyllgogerychwyrndrobwllllantysilio-gogogoch in Anglesey, North Wales. Translated this means "Mary's church by the white hazel pool near the fierce whirlpool with the church of Tysilio by the red cave." It was closed on 14th February 1966 but brought back into use after the Britannia Bridge was damaged by fire on 23rd May 1970 until the bridge was partly reopened on 31st January 1972.

The highest station in Great Britain is Corrour, Inverness-shire—1,347 ft—between Crianlarich and Fort William on the West Highland Section of British Rail.

A British Railways Type "4" diesel D18 on down Waverley line at Dent Station, Yorkshire at 1,150 ft above sea-level, the highest main-line station in Britain. (John Marshall.)

The highest main-line station in Great Britain was Dent on the Midland Railway Settle–Carlisle line, opened on 6th August 1877. It was 1,150 ft above sea-level, and 5 miles from the village after which it was named. It became an unstaffed halt on 2nd January 1967 and was closed on 4th May 1970.

At Trent Station, between Nottingham and Derby, the 10.00 train from London (St. Pancras) to Glasgow via Nottingham and Derby stopped at the same platform, in the same direction, as the 10.00 from Glasgow to London (St. Pancras) via the Erewash Valley line. Trent Station was purely a junction in the midst of fields; it closed on 1st January 1968 and is now demolished.

At Nottingham Midland trains to London via Leicester and via Melton Mowbray used to leave in opposite directions.

At Plymouth (North Road) and at Exeter (St. David's) one could see trains from London to Plymouth via the Great Western Railway and London & South Western Railway routes on opposite platforms facing in opposite directions, and vice versa.

At Chester (General) trains to London via the former London & North Western Railway and Great Western Railway routes left in opposite directions.

The London, Tilbury & Southend Railway was the only main-line system operating into London which did not have its own terminus. It worked its trains into the Fenchurch Street terminus of the Great Eastern Railway and St. Pancras Station of the Midland Railway.

ELECTRIC RAILWAYS

The first electric railway in the world was made by Thomas Davenport, a blacksmith in Vermont, U.S.A. in 1835. It was a small railway powered by a miniature electric motor.

The first serious attempt at electric power on a railway was made by Robert Davidson in 1842 when he tried out a battery locomotive weighing 5 tons on the Edinburgh & Glasgow Railway where it ran at 4 mile/h.

The electric dynamo was perfected between 1860 and 1870 but its use as a motor came some years later.

The first practical electric railway was built by the German engineer Werner von Siemens for the Berlin Trades Exhibition—31st May to 30th September 1879. It was a 600 yd long narrow-gauge line. The electric locomotive had a 3 hp motor, picking up current at 150 V from a centre third rail and returning it via the wheels and running rails. It could pull about thirty passengers on three cars at 4 mile/h.

The first public electric railway in the world was opened on 12th May 1881 at Lichterfelde near Berlin. It was 1·5 miles long. The car ran on a 100 V supply and carried twenty-six passengers at 30 mile/h.

The first public electric railway in Britain was Magnus Volk's Electric Railway, Brighton, first opened on 4th August 1883 with 2 ft gauge. It was rebuilt to 2 ft 9 in gauge and extended and reopened on 4th April 1884. It was taken over by Brighton Corporation on 1st April 1940.

The first electric railway to run on hydroelectric power was the 6 mile long 3 ft gauge Portrush–Giant's Causeway Tramway, Ireland, formally opened on 28th September 1883. It was engineered by W. A. Traill. Cars could run at 12 mile/h on the level. At first an outside conductor rail was used, but the Town Section was worked by two steam-tram engines from W. Wilkinson & Company of Wigan. In 1899 the entire system was converted to overhead wire collection. It was closed in 1950.

Portrush–Giant's Causeway Tramway in Ireland, showing the original third-rail pick-up. The cars are passing Dunluce Castle. (National Library of Ireland.)

Port Rush–Giant's Causeway Tramway in Ireland, before the overhead trolley wire was erected in 1899, showing the steam-tram engine made by W. Wilkinson & Company of Wigan on the Town Section in Main Street, Port Rush. (National Library of Ireland.)

The first electric underground railway in the world was the City & South London, England, opened on 18th December 1890. At first it used fourteen four-wheeled electric locomotives built by Mather & Platt of Salford. By 1907 there were fifty-two locomotives. They ran until the line was reconstructed in 1924. One is preserved in the Science Museum, London, and a coach is in the York Railway Museum.

The first electric locomotive in the U.S.A. for use on standard gauge was designed by L. Daft for the Mount Macgregor & Lake George Railroad in 1883.

Electric locomotives were introduced on the Baltimore & Ohio Railroad on 4th August 1895, on the Belt line from Henrietta Street, Baltimore (just south of Camden Station) to Waverley Tower—3·75 miles through ten tunnels amounting to 48 per cent of the distance. Passenger traffic began on 1st May 1895, with coke-burning locomotives, and goods traffic began with the electrification. The first trials with electric-traction were on 27th June 1895, originally with an overhead electric slot pick-up, replaced in March 1902 by a third rail.

The world's first electric elevated city railway was the Liverpool Overhead Railway, England. The first section opened on 6th March 1893. The line was closed, to avoid massive renewals, on 30th December 1956.

The New York Elevated Railway (the "El"), established with steam-traction in 1878, was completely electrified by the early years of this century.

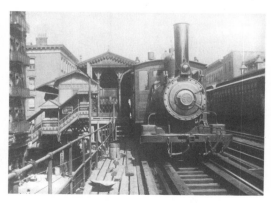

*The New York Elevated
Railway at Third Avenue
and 89th Street on 11th
March 1902 in the last
years of steam.*

*The Chicago Elevated
Railway looking south along
Wabash Street. (John
Marshall.)*

The Chicago Elevated Railway saw its first electric cars in 1895, after the system had been operated for a few years by the Forney-type 0–4–4 tanks.

The Berlin Elevated Railway began as an electric line in 1902.

The New York City suburban railways of the Pennsylvania, New York Central and others were electrified between 1905 and 1907.

The first railway in Britain to be electrified at 1,500 V d.c. with overhead catenary was the Shildon–Newport (Tees-side) Section of the North Eastern Railway. Electrically hauled coal trains with Bo Bo locomotives designed by Vincent Raven, the Chief Mechanical Engineer, began running on 1st July 1915. It was proposed to adopt this system on the main line between York and Newcastle and a prototype 2 Co 2 express locomotive, No. 13, was built in 1922, but the grouping into the London & North Eastern Railway and severe shortage of money following the First World War prevented further progress.

With the decline of coal traffic, the Shildon–Newport Section reverted to steam-haulage early in 1935. The locomotives were stored and subsequently scrapped. No. 13 survived the Second World War but was never used.

*The North Eastern Railway
2 CO 2 electric passenger
locomotive No. 13 of 1922.
(British Rail.)*

The 1,500 V d.c. overhead system was recommended for adoption as a British standard by the 1921 "Electrification Committee" Report and by the subsequent Pringle (1928) and Weir (1931) Reports.

The first passenger railway in Britain to be electrified at 1,500 V d.c. was the Manchester–Altrincham Section of the London, Midland & Scottish Railway/London & North Eastern Railway Joint, where the electric multiple-unit trains began running on 8th May 1931. The line was changed to 25,000 V a.c. on 3rd May 1971.

The first mercury-arc rectifier to be installed on a British railway was at Hendon on the Morden–Edgware line of the London Underground, in 1930. It marked one of the most important technical improvements in d.c. electric-traction and made unmanned substations possible. Previously permanently manned rotary converters had to be used.

The first British suburban railway electrification was inaugurated by the North Eastern Railway between Newcastle (New Bridge Street) and Benton on 29th March 1904.

The Lancashire & Yorkshire Railway was a close runner-up when it introduced electric trains between Liverpool and Southport on 5th April 1904. In a desperate bid to beat the North Eastern Railway some trains were introduced before this but the haste resulted in a partial breakdown and steam trains were not completely withdrawn until 13th May.

The first portion of the "Southern Electric" was the South London line of the London, Brighton & South Coast Railway. Electric trains began on 1st December 1909 using a.c. at 6,000 V with overhead collectors. It was later converted to 600 V d.c. third rail to conform to the other electrified lines south of London.

The first British main-line electrification was the Southern Railway London to Brighton and Worthing, brought into use on 1st January 1933. The system is 600 V d.c. third rail.

Electrification of the London (Liverpool Street)–Shenfield line at 1,500 V d.c. overhead (20 miles) came into operation on 26th September 1949. It was extended to Chelmsford (9·5 miles) on 11th June 1956 and to Southend (Victoria) (15·5 miles) on 31st December 1956. It was converted to 25 kV a.c. in 1960.

Britain's first "all-electric" main line (passenger and freight traffic) was the Manchester–Sheffield line of the former Great Central Railway. Through passenger services began on 14th September 1954, following the opening, on 3rd June, of the new Woodhead Tunnel. The "standard" 1,500 V d.c. system was used. The passenger service was withdrawn from 5th January 1970.

The decision to adopt 25,000 V (25 kV) 50 c/s electrification as the future British standard was made on 6th March 1956.

The first British railway to operate on 25 kV was the 24·5 mile Colchester–Clacton–Walton line, on 16th March 1959.

The first British main line to operate on 25 kV was the Crewe–Manchester, on 12th September 1960. The Crewe–Liverpool line followed on 1st January 1962.

The first electric trains in Scotland (excluding the Glasgow District Subway) were the Glasgow suburban services—31 miles of line at 25 kV. They began on 7th November 1960 but were withdrawn for alteration from 17th December 1960 to 1st October 1961.

The second stage—27 miles of line south of the Clyde—was inaugurated on 27th May 1962.

The London–Manchester–Liverpool full electric service began on 18th April 1966. Some trains had run through from 22nd November 1965. It was extended to the Birmingham area on 6th March 1967.

A British Railways 25 Kv "86" Class locomotive on an express leaving the north end of Shugborough Tunnel, Staffordshire on 9th August 1967. (T. A. Fletcher, Manchester.)

British Railway Southern Region main-line electrification to Southampton and Bournemouth was completed on 10th July 1967, enabling through trains to run from London, using 600 V d.c. third rail. On the same day 90 mile/h push-and-pull services were introduced, following successful tests at 100 mile/h. **The occasion marked the end of steam on B.R. Southern Region.**

The extension of the electrification from London to Glasgow, covering the lines from Weaver Junction, Cheshire, to Motherwell in Lanarkshire, Scotland, was approved by the Minister of Transport in March 1970. Its cost was estimated at £25,000,000.

The world's most powerful electric locomotives were built at the Novocherkassk Works, North Caucasus, Russia. They are Bo Bo-type "VL80K" (1963) and "VL80T" (1966) weighing 184 tons, and are based on semi-conductor rectifiers of 6,320 kW to run on routes electrified on the 25 kV 50 c/s system. They have a tractive effort on an hourly rating of 99,400 lb.

The world's most advanced electric locomotives are the French quadri-current C C type built in 1965–66. They can run equally well on 25 kV 50 c/s single-phase a.c. and 1,500 V d.c. (France); 3,000 V d.c. (Belgium); or 15 kV 16·66 c/s

The French National Railways quadri-current 4,500 hp "40101" Class No. 40104.

single-phase a.c. (Germany and Switzerland). They have an output of 4,500 hp and a top speed of 150 mile/h. They are used on the Trans-Europe Express (T.E.E.) services between Paris and Brussels—195 miles non-stop in 2 hours 20 minutes.

The longest electrified railway in the world is from Moscow to Irkutsk—3,240 miles—on the Trans-Siberian Railway, Russia.

UNDERGROUND RAILWAYS

The earliest recorded "underground railway" and probably the first in the world was a 3 mile line from East Kenton Colliery near Newcastle upon Tyne to the River Tyne in Northumberland. It was begun about 1770 by Christopher Bedlington. Wooden rails were used, until the line was closed when the colliery ceased work in 1810. This could also be claimed as the **world's first railway tunnel**.

The first underground passenger railway in the world was the Metropolitan Railway, London. It was opened, with mixed 7 ft and 4 ft 8·5 in gauge, from Bishop's Road to Farringdon Street on 10th January 1863 and extended to Moorgate on 23rd December 1865. Its trains were lit by gas. The broad-gauge outer rails were removed on 1st March 1869.

The Metropolitan Railway, London—an early 7 ft gauge train at Bellmouth, Praed Street in 1863. (London Transport Executive.)

Baker Street Station on the Metropolitan Railway, London in 1886. (From a chromolithograph by Samuel J. Hodson; London Transport Executive.)

The District Railway, London 4–4–0 tank No. 4 of about 1905. (London Transport Executive.)

The first section of the District Railway, London, from Kensington to Westminster, was opened on 24th December 1868. This and the Metropolitan Railway used Beyer Peacock & Company 4–4–0 tank engines with condensers, first built in 1864.

The world's first "tube" railway was the Tower Subway beneath the River Thames in London. It was opened, using cable-traction, on 2nd August 1870, though it had worked experimentally since April. From 24th December 1870 it closed as a railway and was used as a footway until March 1896. It now carries a water-pipe.

The Inner Circle of the Metropolitan and District railways, London, was completed, and the connection with the East London Railway through Marc Brunel's Thames Tunnel was opened, on 6th October 1884.

The Mersey Railway between Liverpool and Birkenhead was opened on 1st February 1886. It includes 1 in 27 gradients under the River Mersey and at its lowest point it is 128·6 ft below Ordnance Datum. It was worked at first by steam locomotives, one of which, the Beyer Peacock 0–6–4 tank No. 5 *Cecil Raikes* (1885) is preserved at Liverpool, awaiting restoration. The illustration shows it at work at Shipley Colliery near Nottingham on 20th April 1940. On 3rd May 1903 the Mersey Railway became the first steam underground railway to be electrified.

The ex-Mersey Railway 0–6–4 tank No. 5 Cecil Raikes, *built in 1885 by Beyer Peacock & Company of Manchester at Shipley Colliery, Derbyshire. (John Marshall.)*

The first electric underground railway in the world was the City & South London, England, opened on 18th December 1890. (See "Electric Railways", page 209.)

The Glasgow District Subway was opened on 14th December 1896. It was 4 ft gauge, cable-operated and consisted of two parallel tunnels, for either direction, forming a loop round the city centre, twice crossing beneath the River Clyde. It was electrified at 600 V d.c. in 1935, the "inner circle" coming into operation on 28th March and the "outer circle" on 5th December. It was the first electric passenger railway in Scotland.

The Waterloo & City Railway, London, was opened on 8th August 1898 by the London & South Western Railway. It has always been separate from the other city underground lines. Cars are raised and lowered in a hoist near Waterloo Station.

The Central London Railway was opened on 30th July 1900, followed by the Great Northern & City Railway on 14th February 1904.

The Central London Railway—an electric locomotive and train of 1900. (London Transport Executive.)

The first section of the Paris Underground (the Métro) from Port-Vincennes to Porte-Maillot was opened in 1900.

The Inner Circle of the Metropolitan and District railways, London, was electrified from 12th September 1905. The last steam trains ran on 22nd September.

The District Railway, London—a seven-car train of "B" stock in 1905. (London Transport Executive.)

The District Railway, London—Beyer Peacock & Company of Manchester 4–4–0 tank engines awaiting scrapping at Ealing Common following electrification. (London Transport Executive.)

The Bakerloo (Baker Street–Waterloo Station) Railway, London, first section, opened on 10th March 1906.

The first driverless underground railway was the Post Office Subway in London. It was begun in 1914 and fully opened in December 1927. It is 2 ft gauge and 6·5 miles long, from Paddington Station to the Eastern District Post Office. The main double-track tunnels are 9 ft diameter. It carries about 30,000 mail-bags a day.

Underground railways were first opened in other towns as follows:

Boston, U.S.A., 1898; Berlin, 1902; New York, 1900; Philadelphia, 1908; Hamburg, 1912; Buenos Aires, 1913; Madrid, 1919; Barcelona, 1924; Sydney, 1926; Tokyo, 1927; Moscow, 1933; Osaka, 1933; Chicago, 1943; Stockholm, 1950; Toronto, 1954; Rome, 1954; Leningrad, 1955; Cleveland, Ohio, 1956; Nagoya, 1957; Lisbon, 1959; Haifa, 1959; Kiev, 1960; Milan, 1964; Montreal, 1966; Munich, 1971.

Pneumatic-tyred trains were introduced on the Paris Métro on 8th November 1956.

The Victoria Line, London, was begun on 20th September 1962. Powers to extend it to Brixton were obtained on 9th August 1966 and work on the extension began on 4th August 1967. The first section, Walthamstow Central to Highbury and

The first train on the Victoria Line, London, at Seven Sisters on 3rd January 1969. (London Transport Executive.)

Islington (5·5 miles) was opened on 1st September 1968; to Warren Street on 1st December 1968 and through to Victoria on 7th March 1969. The Brixton Extension was opened on 23rd July 1971.

The first London Transport train with automatic driving equipment entered experimental service on the District Line on 8th April 1963. Full-scale trials, on the 4 mile Woodford–Hainault shuttle service of the Central Line, began on 5th April 1964.

The longest station escalator is on the Leningrad Underground where one has a vertical rise of 195 ft. On the Moscow Underground is one with a rise of 164 ft.

The longest escalator on the London Underground is that serving the Piccadilly Line at Leicester Square Station. The shaft is 161 ft 6 in long with a vertical rise of 80 ft 9 in.

Leicester Square escalator on the Piccadilly Line, London. (London Transport Executive.)

MOUNTAIN AND RACK RAILWAYS

The world's first rack railway was the Middleton Railway near Leeds, England. John Blenkinsop (see *The Pioneers*) took out a patent in 1811 for a rack-rail system, for which the first engine was built by Matthew Murray in 1812. The "rack" teeth were cast in the outside of one rail. The engine was propelled entirely by the rack mechanism; the carrying-wheels were idle. (See *The Beginnings*, page 11.)

The first railway with a central rack was the Jefferson Incline on the north bank of the Ohio River near Madison, Indiana, U.S.A., built in 1847. The eight-coupled engines had a separate vertical-cylindered engine for driving the rack mechanism.

The first mountain rack railway was opened on 3rd July 1869. It was built by Sylvester Marsh (1804–1885) to carry passengers to the 6,293 ft summit of Mount Washington in New Hampshire, U.S.A. The railway is standard gauge, 3 miles long, and has a maximum gradient of 1 in 3·1 (32·26 per cent). A wrought-iron ladder-type rack was used.

Old Peppersass, the first locomotive on the Mount Washington Cog Railway, New Hampshire, U.S.A. (John Marshall.)

Nicholas Riggenbach (1817–1899) designed a similar type of rack which he patented in 1863. The first railway to use his system was the 4·5 mile standard-gauge line from Vitznau to the summit of the Rigi, Switzerland, opened on 21st May 1871. The last 2 miles were opened on 27th June 1873 to a summit-level of 5,741 ft.

The Riggenbach rack is used also on the metre-gauge Brünig and Bernese Oberland railways in Switzerland.

The Vitznau–Rigi Railway in Switzerland, opened in 1871 was the first mountain railway in Europe. (Swiss National Tourist Office, London.)

Roman Abt (1850–1933) invented his rack system in 1882. It was first used in 1884 on a railway at Blankenberg in the Harz Mountains.

Three-quarters of the world's rack railways use the Abt system in which two or sometimes three flat steel bars having teeth in their upper edge are fixed side by side so that the gap in one comes opposite the tooth of the next or, in the triple rack, a third of the space of one tooth.

The steepest rack railway in the world is the Mount Pilatus Railway in Switzerland, with a gradient of 1 in 2·1. A special rack was devised by Edward Locher. It has horizontal teeth on each side which prevent any possibility of slipping or derailment. The railway was opened on 4th June 1889 with steam and was electrified on 15th May 1937.

For this railway a gauge of 800 mm, or 2 ft 7·5 in was chosen, which Roman Abt adopted as his standard. It was used for eleven mountain railways in Switzerland, and others elsewhere.

The 2 ft 7·5 in gauge Snowdon Mountain Railway in Wales uses the Abt double rack, and steam locomotives built in Switzerland. It was opened on 6th April 1896. In its 4·5 miles it climbs from Llanberis to the summit at 3,493 ft on gradients of 1 in 5·5.

The Abt system rack is used on "main lines" on the Furka–Oberalp and the Brig–Visp–Zermatt railways in Switzerland and on the Trans-andine Railway in Chile.

The world's first electric mountain rack railway was the Gornergrat Railway at Zermatt, Switzerland, opened on 20th August 1898. It is metre gauge with Abt rack and operates on three-phase a.c. at 540 V.

*Train approaching Tua,
Portugal in the Tua Gorge
on the metre-gauge Tua
Railway. (N. Fields.)*

*Metre-gauge train leaving
Conde for Porto, Portugal
behind engine E141.
(N. Fields.)*

*The 2 ft 7·5 in gauge
Brienzer–Rothorn
Railway is the only steam
mountain railway in
Switzerland. The
illustration shows three
trains climbing towards the
summit with Brienzersee
far below. (N. Fields.)*

The Gornergrat Railway at Zermatt, Switzerland—the first electric mountain rack railway. (Swiss National Tourist Office, London.)

The highest railway in North America is the Manitou & Pike's Peak Railway in Colorado. This standard-gauge line is 8·9 miles long with an average gradient of 1 in 6 (16·66 per cent). The lower terminus is at 7,538 ft and the summit is 14,110 ft. On Windy Point Hill it climbs for 2 miles at 1 in 4. It was opened on 1st June 1891 with steam-power. Diesel-electric cars, built in Switzerland, were introduced in 1963. One of the compound steam locomotives is preserved at Manitou and another at the Colorado Railroad Museum, Golden, near Denver.

The highest railway in Europe is the metre-gauge Jungfrau Railway, Switzerland, opened on 1st August 1912. At Jungfraujoch it is 11,332 ft high and 4 miles 750 yd long. The upper section is entirely in tunnel. The Abt rack is used.

The Jungfrau Railway, Switzerland, is the highest in Europe. (Swiss National Tourist Office, London.)

The second highest railway in Europe is the metre-gauge Bavarian Zugspitz Railway in Germany which reaches an altitude of 8,692 ft at Schneefernerhaus. This electric line, opened in 1928, uses the Riggenbach rack.

Switzerland's only steam mountain railway is now the Brienzer & Rothorn Railway—2 ft 7·5 in gauge with the Abt rack. It was opened on 17th June 1892. The summit is at 7,707 ft.

John Barraclough Fell (1815–1902) invented the centre-rail friction-drive system named after him in 1863–69. It was devised for the railway over the Mont Cenis Pass, opened in 1868 and used until the Mont Cenis Tunnel was completed in 1871.

The most famous Fell centre-rail railway was the Rimutaka Incline in New Zealand on the line from Wellington to Masterton, opened on 12th October 1878. Gradients were 1 in 14–16 for 3 miles. It was closed when the Rimutaka Tunnel was opened in 1955.

Hauled by four "H" Class 0–4–2 Fell tank locomotives, a Masterton–Upperhut excursion train passes the windbreaks on "Siberia" Curve while ascending the centre-railed 1 in 15 Rimutaka Incline (1878–1955) between Cross Creek and Summit Stations. (New Zealand Railways Publicity.)

The Fell centre rail is used on the 3 ft 6 in gauge Snaefell Mountain Railway in the Isel of Man, but for braking purposes only. The electric cars climb the 2,034 ft to the top by adhesion.

The first and only railway to the top of a volcano was built by Thomas Cook & Son, the travel agents, to the top of Vesuvius in Italy. The funicular railway, with gradients as steep as 1 in 1·9, was opened in 1880 to the summit station at 4,012 ft, just below the crater.

The composer Luigi Denza (1846–1922) wrote a popular song "Funiculi—Funicular" to celebrate the occasion. Richard Strauss thought this was a Neapolitan folk-song and incorporated it in the Finale of his symphonic fantasy *Aus Italien* (1886).

MONO RAILWAYS OR MONORAILS

The first recorded mono railway was built by Henry Palmer in 1821 for transporting foodstuffs from warehouses to wharves at London Docks. It consisted of boards supported on posts straddled by the cars which were pulled by horses.

The first passenger-carrying monorail was built in 1876 by General Roy Stone in Fairmont Park, Philadelphia, as part of the city's centenary exhibition.

The first commercial monorail was also American, built in 1880 to connect Brooklyn and Coney Island, New York. It ran for a few months but failed through lack of revenue.

The Listowel & Ballybunion Railway, County Kerry, Ireland which was opened on 1st March 1888. The railway closed in October 1924. (National Library of Ireland.)

Only two types of monorail have achieved success. The type invented by Charles Lartigue in 1883 was used for the Listowel & Ballybunion Railway in County Kerry, Ireland. This 9 mile line opened on 1st March 1888. The twin-boilered locomotives and the cars straddled the rail which was supported on trestles, as shown in the illustration. The most comical pieces of the equipment were the mobile steps which were marshalled into the train to enable passengers to cross the line. Loads had to be balanced. Once when a piano had to be transported it was balanced by a cow. The cow had to be returned by balancing it with two calves which were then sent back one on each side. The railway closed in October 1924.

Lartigue-type monorails were also built in North Africa, central France, Russia, Guatemala and Peru.

The Tokyo–Haneda Monorail in Japan is a modern version of the Lartigue system. It was opened in October 1964 to connect Tokyo with the international airport at Haneda. Trains cover the 8 miles in fifteen minutes.

The other type of monorail, still in operation, is the 9·3 mile long Wuppertalbahn from Elberfeld to Barmen in Germany. This is the Langen suspended type, much of it straddling the Wupper River. It was opened on 1st March 1901. By 1960 it had carried 1,000,000,000 passengers. It was this system which inspired Feldmann to build the first mountain aerial ropeway, up the Wetterhorn in Switzerland, which opened in July 1908 and closed in 1914.

The Tokyo–Haneda Monorail, opened in October 1964. (Ministry of Foreign Affairs, Japan.)

NARROW GAUGE
(less than 1 m gauge)

The current fascination with narrow-gauge railways is largely because, while other railways have progressed continuously, narrow-gauge railways stopped progressing about 1900–10 and so represent steam railways of that period or earlier. Many people find in them a relief from the streamlined rush of modern travel, *provided the journeys are not too long.*

Many such lines were built to open up backward areas and their ultimate closure in the face of road competition can be seen more as a measure of their success than of their failure.

GAUGES

3 ft 0 in (0·914 m). Formerly extensively used in Colorado, U.S.A. and in Ireland. Still used in the Isle of Man and secondary lines in Central America, Colombia, Peru and Mexico.

2 ft 11 in (0·891 m). Some tracks in Sweden.

2 ft 7·5 in (0·8 m). Mountain rack railways.

2 ft 6 in (0·762 m). Welshpool & Llanfair Railway, Wales; formerly the Leek & Manifold Valley Railway, England; the Zillertalbahn, Austria and secondary lines in India (including the Kalka–Simla line) and Ceylon.

2 ft 0 in (0·610 m) or 1 ft 11·5 in (0·6 m). Sierra Leone and secondary lines in Wales, South Africa, India, Pakistan, South America. Formerly the Lynton & Barnstaple Railway, England.

The world's first public narrow-gauge railway was the 1 ft 11·5 in (0·6 m) gauge Festiniog Railway in Wales, engineered by James Spooner and opened for slate traffic on 20th April 1836. Trains ran by gravity from Blaenau Ffestiniog to Portmadoc and empties were pulled back by horses which rode down on the trains. Steam locomotives were introduced in 1863. Passenger traffic officially began on 6th January 1865, but passengers had been carried unofficially for years before that. (See Spooner in *The Pioneers*.)

James Spooner was also Engineer to the 2 ft 3 in gauge Corris and Talyllyn railways in Wales.

The railway from Corris to Machynlleth was opened for horse-drawn slate trains in 1859. Steam-traction began in February 1879. Passengers were carried from 4th July 1883 to 1st January 1931 and the line closed on 23rd August 1948.

The Talyllyn Railway from Towyn to Abergynolwyn—6·75 miles—was opened in December 1865. Passengers were carried from October 1866.

The Talyllyn Railway was the world's first privately preserved railway. The Preservation Society was formed in 1950.

The first narrow-gauge railroad in America was the 3 ft gauge Denver & Rio Grande Western Railroad from Denver to Colorado Springs opened on 26th October 1871.

The Denver & Rio Grande Western Railroad 3 ft gauge 2–8–0 No. 346 is the oldest narrow-gauge locomotive in Colorado, U.S.A. (John Marshall.)

Australia's smallest regular service train affectionately known as "Puffing Billy". Originally used to bring timber from the forests in the hills near Melbourne, the locomotive now hauls holiday-makers along part of the same 2 ft 6 in gauge line at week-ends. (Australian News & Information Bureau.)

Small locomotives pull trucks with cane from the fields to the mills for crushing in Queensland. (Australian News & Information Bureau.)

After attaining a maximum of about 3,000 miles the 3 ft gauge in Colorado was finally abandoned in the late 1960s except for the 45 mile long Durango–Silverton Branch and part of the Alamosa–Durango line over the 10,015 ft Cumbres Pass, both preserved as tourist attractions.

Typical of the Colorado 3 ft lines was the Unitah Railroad which in 13 miles had 233 curves from 1,425 ft to 72 ft radius, including 27 sharper than 114 ft radius.

In contrast, the D. & R.G.W.R. between Villa Grove and Alamosa was dead straight for 53 miles, falling from 7,900 ft above sea-level to 7,550 ft at Alamosa.

The first 2 ft gauge line in America was the Bedford & Billerica Railroad which opened on 28th November 1877. There were fourteen systems operating 2 ft gauge in the U.S.A., ten of which were in Maine. The last to close was the Monson Railroad in December 1944.

In the U.S.A. 2 ft gauge steam may still be enjoyed on the 5·5 mile Edaville Railroad at South Carver, Massachusetts; Silver Dollar City, Missouri; Cripple Creek, Colorado and a few short lines elsewhere.

The Monson Railroad 2 ft gauge 0–4–4 tank No. 3 Edaville. (John Marshall.)

The total mileage of narrow-gauge railroad in the U.S.A. in 1890 was about 10,000, operated by about 500 independent companies.

In the Isle of Man the first of its 3 ft gauge railways, from Douglas to Peel, opened on 1st May 1873. The system grew to 46·75 miles.

Combined Peel and Ramsey trains at Douglas, Isle of Man, with 3 ft gauge railway engines No. 14 Thornhill *and No. 12* Hutchinson. *(John Marshall.)*

Ireland's first 3 ft gauge line opened in 1873. Over 500 miles were built mostly in isolated sections. The last, the West Clare, closed on 1st February 1961.

In north-west England the Ravenglass & Eskdale Railway was opened as a 3 ft gauge line on 24th May 1875 (taking passengers from November 1876) for 7·5 miles into the Cumbrian Fells. It was rebuilt as a 15 in gauge line in 1915–17. Today it is operated by a preservation company formed on 30th March 1961.

The Ravenglass & Eskdale Railway in its 3 ft gauge days with the 0–6–0 Devon, *built by Manning Wardle about 1875, at Boot. (Ravenglass & Eskdale Railway Company Limited.)*

The Ravenglass & Eskdale Railway—a 15 in gauge train entering Dalegarth Terminus on 5th April 1968. (John Marshall.)

Britain's longest narrow-gauge railway was the 1 ft 11·5 in gauge 21·25 mile long Welsh Highland Railway from Dinas—on the London & North Western Railway Caernarvon–Afon Wen Branch—to Portmadoc where it connected with the Festiniog Railway.

It was built in three portions, the oldest being the Croeser Tramway built in 1863 from Croeser Quarries to Portmadoc. On 14th May 1881 the North Wales Narrow Gauge Railway, engineered by C. E. Spooner, was opened from Dinas Junction to South Snowdon.

The final link from South Snowdon to Croeser Junction was opened on 1st June 1923 and the connection to the Festiniog Railway on 8th June.

The entire railway closed on 19th September 1936.

The longest narrow-gauge railway in England was the 1 ft 11·5 in gauge 19·75 mile long Lynton & Barnstaple Railway in Devon which opened on 11th May 1898 and closed on 29th September 1935.

Austria's most famous narrow-gauge railway, the 2 ft 6 in gauge 36 mile (61 km) long Salzkammergutlokalbahn from Salzburg to Bad Ischl was opened throughout on 3rd July 1893 and closed on 14th October 1957.

Austria is linked with Wales by the close relationship between the 2 ft 6 in gauge Zillertalbahn and the Welshpool & Llanfair Railway.

The Zillertalbahn, from Jenbach to Mayrhofen, is 21 miles long.

The Welshpool & Llanfair Railway opened on 4th April 1903. Passenger services ended on 7th February 1931 and the railway closed on 31st October 1956. A preservation company was formed on 4th January 1960 and part of the line was reopened on 6th April 1963. Some of its stock is from the Zillertalbahn.

British Rail's only steam railway is the 2 ft gauge Vale of Rheidol Railway, Wales, opened on 22nd December 1902.

The Vale of Rheidol Railway 2 ft gauge 2–6–2 tank No. 7 Owain Glyndwr *at Devil's Bridge in Wales. (John Marshall.)*

The oldest working narrow-gauge locomotive in Britain is the vertical-boilered 0–4–0 *Chaloner*, built by De Winton & Company of Caernarvon in 1877. It worked in Penybryn Quarry until 1897, then Pen-yr-Orsedd Quarry until 1952, both in the Nantlle Valley, Wales. It now runs on the Leighton Buzzard Narrow Gauge Railway, Bedfordshire.

Scotland's only narrow-gauge railway was the Campbeltown & Machrihanish Light Railway across the Mull of Kintyre. It was of 2 ft 3 in gauge and 6 miles long. It was opened on 17th August 1906 and closed in the autumn of 1932. There were four 0–6–2 tank engines and six carriages.

A narrow-gauge railway which carried standard-gauge wagons on transporter trucks was the 2 ft 6 in gauge 8·25 mile long Leek & Manifold Valley Light Railway in Staffordshire, England. It opened on 27th June 1904 and closed on 10th March 1934.

The Leak & Manifold Valley Light Railway 2 ft 6 in gauge locomotive E. R. Calthorp *at* Hulmen End. *The railway closed on 10th March 1934.*

England's smallest public railway is the 15 in gauge 14 mile long Romney, Hythe & Dymchurch Railway in Kent. The first section was opened on 16th July 1927.

One of the most interesting industrial narrow-gauge railways was the 1 ft 10 in gauge system operated by Arthur Guinness, Son & Company (Dublin) Limited, the famous brewers in Ireland. It was built in 1874–78 and was on two levels connected by an 864 ft long spiral tunnel with 2·65 turns on a radius of 61 ft 3 in and a gradient of 1 in 40. The first of the 0–4–0 steam locomotives

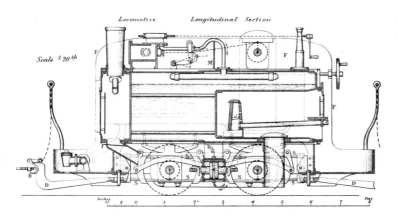

Section of Geoghegan Patent Locomotive.

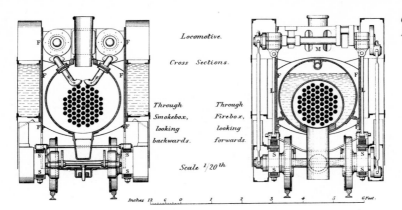

Locomotive.

Cross Sections.

Through Smokebox, looking backwards.

Through Firebox, looking forwards.

Scale ¹/20th

Cross-section of Geoghegan Patent Locomotive.

Inches 12 6 0   1   2   3   4   5   6 Feet.

Steam locomotive at work. (N. Fields.)

Diagram of haulage truck.

Transverse Section.

Longitudinal Section

Scale ¹/40th

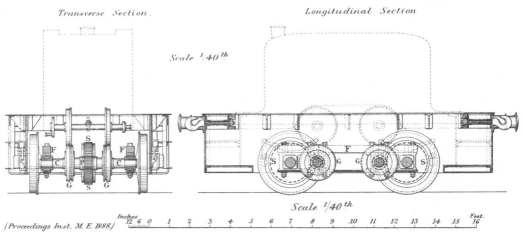

Scale ¹/40th

(Proceedings Inst. M. E. 1888.)

Inches 12 6 0 1 2 3 4 5 6 7 8 9 10 11 12 13 14 15 Feet. 16

was supplied by Sharp Stewart & Company of Manchester in 1875 and it ran until 1913. Various other locomotives were obtained but none was absolutely satisfactory until a special design was prepared by Samuel Geoghegan, the Brewery Engineer. The first of these "Geoghegan Patent" engines was built by the Avonside Engine Company of Bristol in 1882. As shown in the drawing, it had two cylinders mounted above the boiler to keep working parts as much as possible away from ground dirt. Eighteen more were built from 1887 to 1921 by William Spence of Dublin. Diesels were introduced in 1947 and the last steam-engines ran in 1957.

The company also had a 5 ft 3 in gauge connecting line. For working this Geoghegan designed a special "haulage truck" into which a narrow-gauge engine could be fitted, propelling it by a friction drive from its wheels. Two were built in 1888, another in 1893 and the fourth in 1903, as shown in the drawing. Broad-gauge working ended in 1965.

The 3 ft gauge West Clair Railway, Ireland, showing the Ennis train at Ennistymon. (N. Fields.)

Broad-gauge steam locomotive used by Guinness to transfer full and empty casks to the adjoining Kingsbridge (now Heuston) Station. Note on the right the unique adaptation of a narrow-gauge locomotive for use on a broad-gauge track. The rail link with Kingsbridge Station was discontinued in 1965. (Arthur Guinness Son & Company (Dublin) Limited, Ireland.)

Appendix

RAILWAY WORKERS

The youngest locomotive engineer ever appointed was probably Richard Peacock (1820–1899). He was appointed Locomotive Superintendent of the Leeds & Selby Railway in 1838 at the age of eighteen. In 1841 he became Locomotive Superintendent of the Manchester, Sheffield & Lincolnshire Railway and founded its works at Gorton, Manchester.

In 1854, when aged thirty-four, he joined Charles Beyer to found the famous works of Beyer Peacock, also at Gorton.

Daniel Gooch was just twenty-one when he was appointed first Locomotive Superintendent of the Great Western Railway, under I. K. Brunel in 1837. He founded the famous works at Swindon in 1841–43. (See *The Pioneers*.)

Bowman Malcolm was appointed Locomotive Engineer at the age of twenty-one on the Belfast & Northern Counties Railway in 1876. He remained in that position until his retirement forty-six years later in 1922 at the age of sixty-eight. He had served the railway for fifty-two years. He died on 3rd January 1933 aged seventy-nine.

In the workshops at Guadalupe on the Central Railway of Peru in 1926 were three workers whose combined ages were 298 years. The labourer in the Castings Store was a hundred and four, his foreman was his junior by six years, aged ninety-eight. The Pattern Store keeper was a mere youngster of ninety-six. The senior member of the trio exasperated his two junior colleagues by addressing them as "sonny". Two of them died shortly afterwards, still in harness.

RAILWAY SOCIETIES

The oldest British society for railway enthusiasts is the Railway Club, London (112 High Holborn, London WC1), founded in 1899.

The Stephenson Locomotive Society with members throughout Britain and all over the world (34 Darley Avenue, Pinner, Middlesex) was formed in 1909. It maintains a lively monthly journal catering for the serious enthusiast with an interest in technical matters and in railways generally.

The Newcomen Society for the Study of the History of Engineering and Technology, was founded on 4th June 1920 and incorporated on 3rd May 1961. The *Transactions* contain many articles of great interest to railway historians. (The Science Museum, London SW7).

The Railway Correspondence and Travel Society, like the Stephenson Locomotive Society with a widely dispersed membership, was founded in Cheltenham in 1928. It also circulates a monthly journal which is largely concerned with keeping its members up to date with changes in stocks of locomotives and their allocations and other developments (82 Natal Road, London N11).

All the above societies organise programmes of lectures, the Railway Club in London, and the others in centres throughout Britain. Other activities include rail tours and visits.

The Canadian Railroad Historical Association was founded on 15th March 1932 at the Château de Ramezay Museum, Montreal. The *Bulletin* was first published in 1938, but ceased in 1941. In August 1941 the Association obtained a Charter. The *News Report*, now *Canadian Rail* has been published monthly since October 1947 (Box 22, Station B, Montreal 2, Quebec).

The National Railway Historical Society, U.S.A., was incorporated in 1937 to further the preservation of historical railway material (1908 Quintana Street, Arlington, Virginia 22205).

The Railway and Canal Historical Society was founded on 4th September 1954. Besides an interesting journal members enjoy lectures in various centres and a comprehensive programme of outdoor visits to railways and canals. (38 Station Road, Wylde Green, Sutton Coldfield, Warwickshire, England).

RAILWAY PUBLICATIONS

The first periodical devoted to Railways was *The Railway Magazine* which first appeared in May 1835 in London and ran weekly until December 1840 when it became *Haerapath's Railway Magazine* (later *Journal*) until December 1903 when it merged with *The Railway Times*.

The longest run of a railway periodical to date was *The Railway Times*, first published in London on 29th October 1837 and issued weekly until 28th March 1914, 76 years 7 months.

The oldest American railroad periodical was *The Western Railroad Gazette*, first published in Chicago in April 1856. In March 1870 it became *The Railroad Gazette*; in May 1908 it merged with *The Railway Age* (1876) as the *Railroad Age Gazette*, becoming the *Railway Age Gazette* in June 1909 and *The Railway Age* in December 1917.

The oldest railway periodical still published under its original name is *The Railway Magazine* (London) first issued in July 1897 and published monthly ever since except from May 1942 to December 1949 when it was issued every other month.

The oldest railway society journal is the *Western Railway Club Official Proceedings* (Chicago) first published in 1888.
     The *Central Railway Chronicle* of the Central Railway Club of Buffalo, and the *Southern & South Western Railway Club Proceedings*, Jacksonville, Florida, both began publication in 1890.

The Railway Club Journal (London) has been issued since 1902.

The Journal of the Stephenson Locomotive Society (Great Britain) was first published in 1924.

The oldest American magazine for enthusiasts is the *Railroad Magazine*, founded in 1906 and published monthly in New York.

The popular American monthly magazine *Trains* was first published in 1940 in Milwaukee, Wisconsin.

The author of the record number of railway books is O. S. Nock. His first, *The Locomotives of Sir Nigel Gresley* was published in 1945. By the end of 1971 he had produced nearly seventy books, besides innumerable articles.

The record for longevity as a railway author must be held by Cecil J. Allen. His first article "Great Eastern Expresses" appeared in *The Railway Magazine* in 1906 when he was twenty. His most recent book *Salute to the Great Western*, appeared in November 1970, and he is still writing at the age of eighty-five.

RAILWAY ARCHITECTURE

In Victorian England the railway was almost alone in maintaining a high standard of architectural design. Some of the finest architects applied their skills to the railway. Famous examples were:

London, Euston Station, the Doric Arch and Great Hall designed by P. C. Hardwick (1752–1829) and built in 1847–49.

Newcastle upon Tyne Station built in 1846–55 in the Classical style, by John Dobson (1787–1865).

London, King's Cross Station, built in 1851–52 in a style of the utmost dignity and simplicity by Lewis Cubitt (1799–1883).

Huddersfield Station designed by J. P. Pritchett & Son, has a magnificent central edifice flanked by Corinthian colonnades. It was built in 1847–48.

London, St. Pancras Station, 1860, one of the greatest pieces of Victorian Gothic, by Sir George Gilbert Scott (1811–1878). To pass through this building and to emerge beneath Barlow's tremendous arched roof is a startling experience.

York Station on the North Eastern Railway is one of the finest examples in England. Constructed in 1871–77 with three great arched roofs laid out in a long curve. The architects were Thomas Prosser, Benjamin Burley and William Peachy.

The 2 ft 6 in gauge
Welshpool & Llanfair
Railway, Wales. The
0–8–0 tank No. 699.01
from the Styrian Provincial
Railways, Austria, with
coaches from the
Zillertalbahn crossing the
River Stylfaen on
5th August 1971.
(Simon Marshall.)

The 2 ft 3 in gauge
Talyllyn Railway, Wales
with the 0–4–0 tank No. 6
Douglas of 1918 crossing
the Dolgoch Viaduct.
(Simon Marshall.)

The 1 ft 11·5 in gauge
Festiniog Railway, Wales
with the 2–6–2 tank
Mountaineer at
Tan-y-bwlch. (Simon
Marshall.)

The 2 ft 6 in gauge
Zillertalbahn, Austria
showing a train at Jenbach.
(K. B. Smith.)

Outstanding examples in Europe and America are:

> **Paris, Gare du Nord**, 1861–65, by Jacques Ignace Hittorf (1793–1867), and the **Gare du l'Est**, 1847–52, by François Duquesney (1800–1849).

> **Boston, Massachusetts, Kneeland Street Station**, by Gridley J. F. Bryant (1816–1897) was the most completely equipped station in America when it was completed in 1847.

> **Philadelphia, Broad Street Station** of the Reading Railroad, designed by F. H. Kimball (1849–1919) and built in 1891–93, has a distinguished building displaying Renaissance features, and the greatest of all arched roofs, of 300 ft span, by Wilson Brothers & Company, Engineers.

> **Helsinki Station**, designed in 1905 by the Finnish architect Eliel Saarinen (1873–1950) was not completed until 1914. It is one of the finest in Europe.

> **Stuttgart Station**, the work of the German architect Paul Bonatz (1877–1951), is a leading example of modern station architecture. It was built in 1928.

Some of the finest examples of modern station design are to be found on the London Underground system, mostly built in the 1920s and 1930s, by Adams, Holden and Pearson, largely inspired by Frank Pick.

RAILWAYS AND ART

The earliest railway pictures of any value are those produced as series of prints made during the construction or soon after the opening of some of England's earliest main lines. Chief among these are:

> **The Liverpool & Manchester Railway**, a series of coloured aquatints by T. T. Bury published by Ackermann & Company in 1830. One of these, of Edge Hill, appears on page 14.

> **The Newcastle & Carlisle Railway**, a series of drawings by J. W. Carmichael, a marine artist (1800–1868). These were reprinted in 1970.

> **The London & Birmingham Railway and the Great Western Railway**, two series of hand-coloured lithographs by John C. Bourne produced in 1837–1839. The G.W.R. pictures were reprinted in 1969 and the L. & B. in 1970. Bourne's view of Euston Arch is shown on page 24.

> **The Manchester & Leeds Railway**, a series of lithographs by A. F. Tait, published in both black and white and colour in 1845. They were reprinted in 1972. Tait's view of Summit Tunnel is shown on page 25.

> All these pictures, besides being works of art in themselves, possessed the additional advantage of technical accuracy and are valuable historical documents.

The first great artist to be inspired by the railway was J. M. W. Turner (1775–1851) whose famous painting *Rain, Steam and Speed, The Great Western Railway* (1844) hangs in the National Gallery, London.

> The French artist Claude Monet (1840–1926) during a visit to London was greatly impressed by Turner's work. In 1875 he produced his *Le train dans la neige* and in 1877 a series of ten impressions of the Gare Saint-Lazare, Paris.

Perhaps the best loved of all railway pictures is *The Railway Station* (1862) by W. P. Frith (1819–1909), showing a bustling scene at Paddington Station, London, with one of Gooch's broad-gauge engines, the *Great Britain* of 1847, on the left, and on the right the arrest of a criminal. Above all are the leaping arches of Brunel's great station roof.

The railway-carriage compartment was a popular setting for some mid-Victorian paintings. Abraham Solomon (1824–1862) produced a pair of paintings in 1854 entitled *First Class — The Meeting* and *Second Class — The Parting*. In the first a girl is fascinated by a young officer while her father talks animatedly between them. (In the original version the father was asleep in the corner, but this did not accord with Victorian decorum!) The second shows the sad parting of a mother and her son who is emigrating.

August Leopold Egg (1816–1863) left us *The Travelling Companions* (1862), now in the Birmingham City Art Gallery, showing two extravagantly attired women, one asleep and the other reading, in a First Class compartment, totally oblivious of the beautiful coastal scenery near Menton on the French Riviera.

The best-known railway artists at work in Britain today are both ardent railway enthusiasts. **C. Hamilton Ellis** is mentioned in "Railways In Literature" on page 244. His numerous paintings are distinguished for their technical accuracy.

The paintings of **Terence Cuneo** are remarkable for their animated life and energy. An outstanding example is his reconstruction of the opening of the Stockton & Darlington Railway.

In America Nathaniel Currier and James Ives formed a partnership in 1857 and for over fifty years mass-produced about three lithographs every week, hand coloured by one girl per colour. They depicted accurately every aspect of American life, and a great many were pictures of railways.

One of the leading American artists is Howard Fogg of Boulder, Colorado, whose vivid portrayal of railway scenes in Colorado are among the most colourful of railway pictures. In Fogg's pictures the pioneering days of the 3 ft gauge are brought once more to life.

RAILWAYS IN LITERATURE

The earliest English poem about railways by an important writer is "Steamboats, Viaducts and Railways" by William Wordsworth (1770–1850), No. 42 of his *Itinerary Poems* (1833). Three of his poems are anti-railway: "On the Projected Kendal & Windermere Railway", and "Proud were ye, Mountains", Nos. 45 and 46 of his *Miscellaneous Sonnets* (1844); and "At Furness Abbey", No. 48 (1845).

Robert Louis Stevenson (1850–1894) wrote two railway poems, "From a Railway Carriage" from *A Child's Garden of Verses*, and "The Iron Steed". In conjunction with his stepson, **Lloyd Osbourne**, he wrote a novel *The Wrong Box* in which a railway accident and a joker changing the labels on packages in a guard's van result in some exquisite situations.

Thomas Hardy (1840–1928) left us two railway poems: "Midnight on the Great Western" and "Faintheart in a Railway Train", as also did **Siegfried Sassoon** (1886–

1967), "A Local Train of Thought", a homely picture of a branch-line train, and "Morning Express", a vivid account of a train's arrival and departure.

Other railway poems were written by **Edmund Blunden** (b. 1896) and **Rupert Brooke** (1867–1915). The most prolific writer of railway poems and essays is **John Betjeman** (b. 1906).

Railway fiction is mainly in the form of the short story. In 1845 "**Tilbury Tramp**" (C. J. Lever (1806–1872)) published *Tales of the Trains*, five short stories based on train journeys.

William Makepeace Thackeray (1811–1863) has left us *Jeames on the Gauge Question*, a short story of a journey from London to Cheltenham with changes of carriage at Swindon and Gloucester and the confusion arising from the transfer of ninety-three packages and a baby.

Mark Twain (Samuel Langhorne Clemens (1835–1910)) wrote a comic short story *Punch, Brothers, Punch* based on the noise of wheels on rails.

Another writer was **Arthur Quiller-Couch** (1863–1944) several of whose works contain references to railways: *Delectable Duchy* (1893) in his native Cornwall, *The Destruction of Didcot* (1908) and *Pipes in Arcady* on a Cornish branch line, reprinted in *Sixteen On* edited by Charles Irving (1957).

One of the "Reginald" stories, *The Mouse* (1930) by **"Saki"** (H. H. Munro (1870–1916)), takes place in a railway carriage. **D. H. Lawrence** (1885–1930) wrote a short story called *Tickets, Please*, based on a journey on the Nottingham–Ripley Street Tramway, and **L. A. G. Strong** (1896–1958) wrote two, *Departure* (1929) at a country station and *The Gates* (1931) about a crossing-keeper.

Railways and crime have often been linked in authors' minds. Although railway journeys are frequently mentioned in the "Sherlock Holmes" stories of **Arthur Conan Doyle** (1859–1930) in only one, *The Adventure of the Bruce Partington Plans*, (1924) do railway features, in this the Metropolitan Railway, form an important part of the story. "The Lost Special" from his *Round the Fire Stories* (1908) describes the events leading to the total disappearance of a train.

Three of the "Dr. Thorndike" stories by **R. Austin Freeman** (1862–1943) have railway settings, or railway incidents form an essential part of the plot: *The Moabite Cipher*, *The Blue Sequin* and *The Case of Oscar Brodski* (1928).

The *Mysterious Death on the Underground Railway* by **Baroness Orczy** (1865–1947) is another example of a crime story where the railway setting is an important ingredient. **F. W. Crofts** (1879–1957) wrote several crime stories with railway settings: *Crime of the Footplate*, *Death of a Train*, *Death on the Way*, *The Level Crossing*, *The Mystery of the Sleeping Car Express* and *Sir John Magill's Last Journey*.

Novels with a railway setting are less common. In his novel of the "Hungry Forties", *Sybil* (1845), **Benjamin Disraeli** (1804–1881) makes considerable references to railways.

The experimental advanced passenger train (A.P.T.-E.) standing at the Railway Technical Centre, Derby, during its commissioning programme. The A.P.T.-E. is the forerunner of two prototype trains (A.P.T.-P.)—one driven by electric motors, the other by gas-turbines—due to enter revenue-earning evaluation service in the mid 1970s. On specially designed new track the A.P.T. can reach 200 mile/h and 155 mile/h on existing tracks. (British Rail.)

Charles Dickens (1812–1870) was fascinated by railways and they figure prominently in many of his works. In *Dombey and Son* (1848) Chapters 6 and 15 contain accounts of the London & Birmingham Railway', *Our Mutual Friend* (1864–65) refers to the London & Greenwich and the Great Western railways and Paddington Station, not entirely accurately, and in a postscript Dickens describes his experiences in the Staplehurst accident in 1865 (see "Accidents", page 187). *The Uncommercial Traveller* refers to railways in Kent. *The Mystery of Edwin Drood* (unfinished at his death in 1870) makes reference to the South Eastern Railway. Of his other works, his story *A Flight* is based on a journey from London Bridge to Folkestone. Four of the "Mugby Junction" stories (1866) are by Dickens: *Barbox Brothers, Barbox Brothers & Co., Main Line: the Boy at Mugby* and *No. 1 Branch Line: the Signalman*. These stories came to be written as a result of an enforced stop at Rugby Junction on the London & North Western Railway, following a fire in the coach in which Dickens was travelling. Finally, *Lazy Tour of Two Idle Apprentices* contains references to the L.N.W.R. in the Chester district.

Besides his terrible experience in the Staplehurst disaster, Dickens had other railway adventures. During a journey to Holyhead, *en route* for Ireland, his train was snowed up near Bangor for four hours, with no train heating. On one of his American journeys, between Rochester and Albany, he was caught in one of the worst floods on record, when nearly 300 miles of line were inundated. After he had spent an enforced night at Utica, the railway company got him to Albany through floods and floating blocks of ice, taking ten hours, for a journey normally taking three.

The great American writer of Western thrillers, Zane Grey (1872–1939) gave a vivid picture of the construction of the Union Pacific Railroad in *The Roaring U P Trail* (1918), describing experiences of a young engineer and a girl.

E. Nesbit (1858–1924) produced one of the best loved of all railway stories, *The Railway Children* (1906) in which three children prevent a train from running into a landslip. A very successful film version was made on the Keighley & Worth Valley Railway in Yorkshire.

In *Hatter's Castle* (1931) by **A. J. Cronin** (b. 1896) the villain, Denis, perishes in the Tay Bridge disaster after the deceived heroine has left the train at a signal stop. This made a dramatic sequence in the film version.

C. Hamilton Ellis (b. 1909), the well-known railway writer and artist has produced two novels about railways: *The Grey Men* (1939), a mystery story on the West Highland Railway, and *Dandy Hart* (1947) set in southern England in the period 1830–60.

It is in the form of the essay that railway literature achieves its greatest profusion. Many, written as articles for periodicals, of an amusing, light-hearted or ephemeral nature, can hardly be classed as "literature", but there are some by **Paul Jennings** (b. 1918), **C. Hamilton Ellis** and others which can be read repeatedly with enjoyment. Among well-known writers who have given the railway consideration in essays are **Robert Lynd** (1879–1949) who wrote three: *In the Train, Railway Stations I Have Loved* and *Trains*; **A. A. Milne** (1882–1956) who gave us *A Train of Thought* (1921); and **J. B. Priestley** (b. 1894). *Man Underground* (1932), in which he philosophises on travelling beneath London.

Examples of factual writing on railways by great authors are *Across the Plains* (1892) by **Robert Louis Stevenson** and "The Great Locomotive Chase" from *A Book of Escapes and Hurried Journeys* (1925) by **John Buchan** (1875–1940).

The railway does not figure prominently in drama. John Galsworthy (1867–1933) wrote a one-act comedy in three scenes, *The Little Man* (1915) set on railway platforms and in a railway-carriage compartment. Perhaps the best-known play is *The Ghost Train* (1931) by **Arnold Ridley** (b. 1896) which was made into a film in the 1930s. In *Brief Encounter* by **Noel Coward** (b. 1899) part of the action is set in a railway station. The most completely railway play is probably *The Knotty*, first produced by the Victoria Theatre, Stoke-on-Trent, in 1966, a musical documentary outlining the history of the North Staffordshire Railway. Extracts are now available on a gramophone recording.

RAILWAYS AND MUSIC

One of the earliest composers to be influenced by the railway was the Dane, Hans Christian Lumbye (1810–1874), whose *Jolrndane* (Railway Galop) is an exhilarating orchestral item.

Johann Strauss junior (1825–1899) wrote a fast polka *Vergnügungszug* (Excursion Train), opus 281.

His brother Eduard Strauss (1835–1916) composed an immensely entertaining piece, *Bahn Frei*; a musical train ride complete with guard's whistle and engine hooter.

The Czech composer Antonin Dvořák (1841–1904) was a keen railway enthusiast and made daily visits to the main station in Prague where he was friendly with many engine crews. On one occasion he was too busy to go, so he sent his servant to note the number of the engine on a particular train. When the man returned he was severely reprimanded for having noted the tender number by mistake!

The French composer Arthur Honegger (1892–1955) was fascinated by the steam locomotive and in 1924 wrote his famous locomotive tone-poem for orchestra *Pacific 231*.

The Brazilian composer Heitor Villa-Lobos (1887–1959) gave us a delightful musical picture of a Brazilian narrow-gauge train in "The Little Train of the Caipira" which forms the final toccata section of his second *Bachianas Brasilieras* (Brazilian Bach pieces), composed in 1930.

The British composer and conductor Eugene Goossens (1893–1962) was a very knowledgeable railway enthusiast, as was **Constant Lambert (1905–1951).**

There are many other examples of organists, conductors, composers and instrumentalists with a keen interest in railways.

The most evocative of all "musical train rides" was written in 1826 or 1828 by a composer who had never heard of a railway—Franz Schubert (1797–1828). It is the fourth movement (Finale) of his Great C Major Symphony, No. 9, which has all the rhythm and energy of an express train behind a big steam-engine. It captures the atmosphere of a journey in a way that deliberate attempts have failed to achieve.

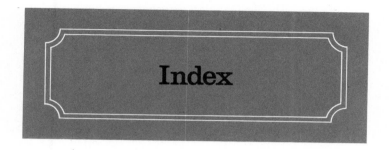

Index